THE TRAGIC STATE OF THE CONGO:

From Decolonization to Dictatorship

Jeanne M. Haskin

Algora Publishing
New York

Library of Congress Cataloging-in-Publication Data —

Haskin, Jeanne M., 1964-
The tragic state of the Congo: from decolonization to dictatorship / Jeanne
M. Haskin.
     p. cm.
Includes bibliographical references and index.
ISBN 0-87586-416-3 (trade paper: alk. paper) — ISBN 0-87586-417-1 (hard
cover: alk. paper) — ISBN 0-87586-418-X (ebook)
   1. Congo (Democratic Republic)—History--1960-1997. 2. Decolonization—
Congo (Democratic Republic) 3. Mobutu Sese Seko, 1930- 4. Congo
(Democratic Republic)—History—1997- I. Title.

DT658.H34 2005
967.5103—dc22
                                   2005015279

Front Cover:
Top: Village in Zaire Ruzizi Valley.
Image: © Paul Almasy/Corbis. 1970s
Bottom: Congolese Soldier Standing Guard
Image: © David Turnley/CORBIS
Photographer: David Turnley ca. 1994
Goma, Democratic Republic of Congo

TABLE OF CONTENTS

Introduction

Prior to the colonization of the Congo in 1876, the slave trade had wreaked havoc on the region for fully four centuries. The Portuguese alone claimed over 13.25 million lives during the space of this time. From the lively port of Lisbon, between ten and twenty thousand Africans per year were being shipped to the New World to serve as slave labor for the plantations. By the time of the seventeenth century, the Portuguese were trading in 15,000 slaves annually. In this, they competed with the Arabs, so that the total figures for the slave trade are much higher.

A "Civilizing" Mission

It was the under pretense of ending the slave trade and Christianizing the Congo that King Leopold II of Belgium finagled his way into the country. Claiming that he wanted to "pierce the darkness which envelops the entire population," Leopold called a conference in Brussels in 1876 to discuss colonization. Britain and France, which generally had strong interests in opposing the Portuguese (or any other rivals), decided to support King Leopold in this, provided that he would establish a free trade zone in the country. Support would also come from Berlin, where Bismarck held a conference in 1884, and the matter was decided. The Congo Free State, as it came to be called, was to be King Leopold's private possession.

In taking the Congo as his own, King Leopold invested his personal finances in the region and sought a system of development that would generate a strong return on that investment, in other words, the development of primarily extractive industries. Although it is true that missionaries, both Protestant and Catholic, were encouraged to abide in the country, they were largely used by the King in controlling the population and preparing them for their "duties." To that end, children were often seized by the missionaries and brought up apart from their parents, given a primary education, and trained for the Force Publique, which was King Leopold's army. The Force Publique was obliged to fight the Arab-dominated slave trade, which interfered with King Leopold's use of the population for a local system of forced labor. And it was also used to subdue the Congolese people in conjunction with the shareholders and overseers that Leopold had appointed.

COLONIAL GENOCIDE

The forced system of labor entailed a ruinous tax on every one of the Congolese, which had to be met out a mere pittance of wages. The shareholders and overseers focused mainly on the extraction of ivory, palm, and rubber, and no one was exempt from participation. Women and children were obliged to transport heavy loads on their heads and were also taken as hostages to guarantee the men's cooperation. Those who failed to meet their extraction quotas or to pay their assigned taxes were often brutally punished. The native Congolese who were assigned to oversight duties were forced to chop off hands and ears, and the practice of flogging violators of the system with the *chicotte* (a sharp, hard, spiraling strip of dried hippopotamus hide) left many permanently scarred and crippled. Some were shot, hanged, or beheaded. But the primary foe of the people was sheer exhaustion. Adam Hochschild estimates that between 5 and 10 million died during Leopold's tenure. Another author notes that the population was depleted from 30 to 8 million. This meant that two out of every three Congolese died, amounting to one of the worst genocides due to colonization.

By 1903, there was some effort to revise the system. The tax on the natives was fixed at forty hours of labor per worker each year. But the mandate was simply nullified by the shareholders and overseers whose only interest in the Congo was profit. Their abuse continued unabated until England mounted a campaign to oblige King Leopold to alter the system. He succumbed to foreign pressure in the year 1909, when he ceded the Congo Free State to the government of Belgium. Thereafter, the country was known as the Belgian Congo and limited steps were taken to improve conditions, though these would mainly center on education rather than working life. Within the Belgian Congo, hundreds of thousands more continued to die as a result of the repressive system.

THE FOCUS OF EDUCATION

Beginning in 1910, the Belgian Congo was ruled by the Church and the State in cooperation with private companies. The Catholic Church's concept of appropriate education for the natives was exemplified by the slogan, "no elite, no problem." In other words, education peaked at the secondary level so as to prevent the Congolese from aspiring to leadership roles. There was little effort to educate children over the age of fourteen and fewer than 25,000 Congolese received secondary education. This limitation applied most of all to the men in the Force Publique, who were commanded by Belgian officers.

Those who did receive secondary education were known as évolués or "evolved ones." After 1948, they formed the basis of the black bourgeoisie and were afforded special privileges and services. Although their rights were not consistent with those of the colonizers, even secondary education would prompt them to move in the directions that were most feared: they began organizing in groups to demand equal wages for equal work and, ultimately, Congolese independence. In this, they were aided by both Protestants and Catholics who formed social circles and encouraged the fledgling elites to engage in a free exchange of thought and to publicize their opinions.

THE ELITES AND THE FORCE PUBLIQUE

One of the most prominent study groups was the Union des Intérêts Sociaux, otherwise known as UNISCO. In 1946, the organization's treasurer, Joseph Kasavubu, gave a public speech urging "Congo for all of the Congolese." Kasavubu would later become president when the Belgian Congo gained independence, after more than ten years of struggle, in 1960. After de Gaulle had already offered independence to the French Congolese (in Brazzaville), there emerged another new leader within the Belgian Congo. This was Patrice Lumumba, who went on to become the prime minister of the Congo. Lumumba wrote a book (*Congo, My Country*, which was published posthumously), in which he expressed his political ideals as well as his socialist leanings. It is a concil-iatory work which forgives the Belgians for their abuses and excesses, claiming that these were simply "mistakes" which the Congolese should see fit to forget. This was in marked contrast to Lumumba's fiery speech at the time of indepen-dence.

By the time of the official ceremony launching the first Republic, Lumumba had evolved into a strident nationalist leader with fierce opposition to any continued engagement of the Belgians; and the Congolese soldiers, angry at the fact that there were no Congolese officers within the Force Publique, mutinied following independence. Nor were they inclined, under Lumumba, to permit the Belgians to stay during a period of transition. By then, the spirit of nationalism had been so roused against the Belgians that it emerged very soon that their safety could not be assured.

Yet the emergence of a new indigenous elite did not necessarily mean that the country was prepared for self-rule. Even the évolués had not previously been admitted to the country's ruling circles. Although they had plenty of ideas on how to re-order the country, they had had no experience in so doing. None of them had been schooled to qualify for higher positions; instead, they remained low-ranking and their pay rates were meager.

The revolt led to attacks upon Europeans, resulting in their flight from the country. Belgium responded quickly with troops to protect its people, thus setting off a lengthy crisis as the new Congolese leaders tried to evict them from the country with the help of the United Nations.

THE FIRST UN INTERVENTION

Actually, Lumumba sent his first plea for help to the United States. He was turned down by President Eisenhower and was urged to seek assistance within the United Nations. Although the West had a very great interest in ensuring that the newly independent Congo was not lured by the Communists, it was reluctant to engage directly for fear of a Soviet backlash. Thus, the United Nations became the forum for expelling the Belgians and pacifying the country. For, although Lumumba managed to quiet the Force Publique with a promise of advancement and higher wages, their mutiny was quickly followed by a movement of secession within the Katanga province. Katanga was supported with military and technical help by none other than the Belgians. And, following Katanga's example, the province of Kasai attempted to separate also.

Because both Katanga and Kasai are centers of great mineral wealth, their retention by the State was essential. Initially, the UN maintained a neutral position and sought to reconcile the provinces with the new central government through negotiation rather than force, as Lumumba himself desired. This attitude on the part of the UN made Lumumba turn to the Soviets, which ensured that he would be opposed by the West. While the Soviet intervention was limited and modest, it would result in orders from the CIA for the assassination of Lumumba.

First, an argument erupted between President Kasavubu and Prime Minister Lumumba. The former dismissed the latter for his engagement with the Soviet Union, and Lumumba likewise sought to dismiss the president. In an effort to resolve the situation, Colonel Mobutu, a twenty-eight-year-old army officer, proclaimed army rule. Although he accepted Kasavubu as head of state, he shut down the Parliament and formed a Government of university students from those who were fortunate enough to have been educated at home and abroad. He also ordered the immediate withdrawal of the Soviets and threatened to dismiss those peacekeeping contingents that were loyal to Lumumba, namely those from Ghana and Guinea.

When the assassination of Lumumba followed (allegedly at the hands of a Belgian mercenary, and with CIA involvement), the UN was in an uproar. The Soviets wanted to dismiss UN Secretary Dag Hammerskjold as a puppet of the West — they claimed he had been responsible for Lumumba's assassination; and there was full blown contention over whether Kasavubu's faction should be considered the legitimate government. The Soviet Union supported Gizenga, who had picked up Lumumba's banner. They continued to maintain that the breakaway provinces of Katanga and Kasai should be brought to heel by military means and reserved the right to intervene should the UN fail to do so.

The deadlock on leadership was broken when President Kasavubu selected Adoula as prime minister. And the UN went on to pacify Katanga, such that the ambitions of Moise Tshombe, the self-styled president of the province, were quashed by the end of the intervention. Tshombe was rewarded for conceding by eventually being appointed prime minister himself. But from the day that he first took office, he complained that he was surrounded by incompetents, so that little could be expected.

THE ISSUE OF PROTECTORATE OR TRUSTEESHIP

When the UN ended its operation in 1964, it exceeded its neutral mandate by reuniting the country. There was criticism of the use of force in achieving that goal and by no means did it occur with the full backing of the West. Belgium, Britain, and France had been consistently behind all efforts to keep the UN neutral toward Katanga as was, of course, desired by its internal mining interests. When unification came, it was with a commitment to a strong unitary system but there was little attention given to the necessary period of transition during which the UN could have prepared the Congo for effective self-administration. This failing on the part of the UN left the door wide open for the reestablishment of military rule in 1965 by the very same Mobutu who had dismissed Kasavubu and Lumumba. Under Mobutu, the Belgian Congo took the name of Zaire, as will be discussed below. And, as we shall see, Mobutu became a notoriously kleptocratic dictator who brought the country to ruin through three unbearable decades of leadership.

Thus, we will pause to ask why the UN was not empowered to make of the Congo a trusteeship or a protectorate until such time as it was properly prepared for native civilian control. We will cite three reasons for this failure. The first is that the sentiment of nationalism was so aroused within the country that none of its rising elites would have welcomed this path. The second is that the Soviet bloc opposed it. And the third is that the UN was itself bankrupted by the end of the operation in 1964. The West, and in particular the United States, was quite content with Mobutu as their regional strongman when he took power in 1965.

MOBUTU AND ZAIRE

Western support in the form of military and financial aid made its way to Mobutu until the early 1990s. He was particularly supported by the US under the administrations of Kennedy, Johnson, and Carter. The latter even supported military intervention to ensure the survival of Mobutu's regime against internal insurrection. But, in so doing, they committed the Zairian people to a life of misery. Their people were among the most impoverished in Africa and lacked the most fundamental rights, though the country possesses such mineral wealth that it could have been self-sufficient.

Mobutu ruled the country through a one-party state that offered fanciful slogans and empty promises as the means to co-opt the people. It was also a police state whose reach extended into every school and every village. Atrocities were committed as the means to strike fear into the people; it was a reign of terror. Furthermore, Mobutu's response to the genocide in Rwanda was to allow the Hutu genocidaires to take up residence in Zaire. This led to clashes with the Zairian Tutsis and with Rwanda and Burundi.

It was not until the United States began to withdraw its support in the mid-1990s that Mobutu was actually threatened. Then, the left-leaning Laurent Kabila was emboldened by the US withdrawal and the resentments of Rwanda and Burundi to launch a military take over with the help of Rwanda, Uganda, and Angola. Mobutu was quickly toppled and he died of cancer some months later.

FROM KABILA TO KABILA

Kabila came to power with promises of freedom, renaming the state the Democratic Republic of Congo. But he soon proceeded to absorb the centrist state and its nepotistic network of cronies. He demanded the departure of the soldiers from Uganda, Rwanda, and Angola, which had helped to bring him to power, even as opposition within the state was rising. His own movement rejected him, as did several new rebel networks. By 1998, they were all at war with Kabila. It was only the intervention of Angola, Zimbabwe, Chad, Namibia, and the Sudan which kept Kabila in power. Even so, he had lost parts of the eastern Congo, huge swaths of which were being held by the rebels.

Dubbed "Africa War I" for the number of states involved, the crisis promoted the second UN intervention. However, this was a slow-moving and almost reluctant enterprise. Although the UN, like the Organization of African Unity and several interested states, was partly responsible for the brokering of the Lusaka Accord that set terms for a country-wide cease fire and imposed a number of steps aimed at national reconciliation, the Accord went ignored by Kabila. He was assassinated, and was replaced by his son Joseph, who was no more inclined to hurry toward peace than his father. This was despite the fact that the war that his father started had thus far claimed over 3 million lives due to killing, disease, starvation, and other conditions of suffering.

THE CURRENT STATE OF AFFAIRS

Today, there remains a widespread problem regarding refugees. The lives of hundreds of thousands of people will continue to be at risk until the war is finally settled. For that to happen, Joseph Kabila must implement the Lusaka Accord right down to the letter. A nationwide dialogue must go on and the commitment that he has finally made toward holding free and fair elections must be kept, even if it has to be reinforced through guidance by the international community.

Chapter 1. The End of Belgian Rule

When King Leopold II of Belgium held his first conference on the Congo in 1876, he claimed that his purpose was to conduct a civilizing mission that would Christianize the Congolese and free them from a world of darkness.[1] Instead, he introduced a greater darkness than any that the Congolese could have ever imagined, with the establishment of the ironically-named Congo Free State in 1877. The Congolese, who had already lost thirteen and a quarter million people to the Portuguese slave-traders, found their ranks even further depleted by the system of forced labor that was adopted by King Leopold's administrators.[2] Through a tax and quota system, the Belgian administration set impossible standards for the extraction of rubber, palm, and ivory and the many Congolese who necessarily failed to meet them were either killed outright or were subjected to gruesome tortures.

Within this terrible system, the Congolese were also turned against each other. In many cases, children were taken at an early age and impressed into King Leopold's army, which was called the Force Publique. They were set above the common Congolese and given arms with which to kill their fellow men, with the added gruesome requirement that every expended bullet had to be accounted for with the severed hand of a victim delivered to their masters.

Through such practices, and also the spread of diseases such as smallpox (which the Europeans brought with them), early death was rampant. The Con-

---

1. M. N. Hennessy, *Congo: A Brief History and Appraisal* (London: Pall Mall Press, 1961) 13.
2. Ruth Slade, *King Leopold's Congo: Aspects of the Development of Race Relations in the Congo Independent State* (London: Oxford University Press, 1962) 11.

golese were further slain through starvation and outright exhaustion. In the end, the death toll was horrific.[3] In other words, the Belgians preyed on the very people that they needed for their workforce. This was noted by the British consul Roger Casement, who wrote the following in his diary:

> After a few hours we came to a State rubber post...At one place I saw lying about in the grass surrounding the post...human bones, skulls and in some cases complete skeletons. On enquiring the reason for this unusual sight: "Oh," said my informant, "when the *bambote* (soldiers) were sent to make us cut rubber there were so many killed we got tired of burying, and sometimes when we wanted to bury we were not allowed to." [I asked] "But why did they kill you so?" "Oh, sometimes we were ordered to go and the sentry would find us preparing food to eat while in the forest, and he would shoot two or three to hurry us along. Sometimes we would try and do a little work on our plantations, so that when the harvest time came we should have something to eat, and the sentry would shoot some of us to teach us that our business was not to plant but to get rubber. Sometimes we were driven off to live for a fortnight in the forest without any food and without anything to make a fire with, and many died of cold and hunger. Sometimes the quantity brought was not sufficient, and then several would be killed to frighten us to bring more. Some tried to run away, and died of hunger and privation in the forest in trying to avoid the State posts." "But," said I, "if the sentries killed you like that, what was the use? You could not bring more rubber when there were fewer people." "Oh, as to that, we do not understand it. These are the facts." And looking around on the scene of desolation, on the untended farms and neglected palms, one could not but believe that in the main the story was true. From State sentries came confirmation and particulars even more horrifying, and the evidence of a white man as to the state of the country — the unspeakable condition of the prisons at the State posts — all combined to convince me over and over again that, during the last seven years, this "Domaine Private" of King Leopold has been a veritable hell on earth.[4]

As was noted in this account, the Congolese were also prevented from providing for themselves. Their every waking, breathing moment was devoted to extraction. But Roger Casement was among those people who spoke out in Britain against the practices of the Belgians.

He was preceded in this matter by a man named Captain Burrows, who had tried to publish a book on the horrors of the Congo. Since Burrows was sued for libel by a well-known Belgian captain, his work was never made public. Yet, it did set off a tide of outrage in England. The publicity over the libel case resulted in the formation of the Congo Reform Association, which made appeals to Europe and the United States to press King Leopold to enact reform in the

---

3. Christian P. Scherrer, *Genocide and Crisis in Central Africa: Conflict Roots, Mass Violence, and Regional War* (Westport, CT: Praeger, 2002) 20.
4. Peter Singleton-Gates and Maurice Girodias, *The Black Diaries: An Account of Roger Casement's Life and Times with a Collection of His Diaries and Public Writings* (New York: Grove Press, 1959) 118.

Congo. Founded by Edmund Morel, the Congo Reform Association succeeded in garnering enough public support that it forced the British government to pressure King Leopold into giving up the Congo.[5] There were also many missionaries and nobles who joined to make this happen.

THE BELGIAN CONGO

Leopold transferred the Congo (as distinct from Congo Brazzaville – the French portion of the Congo) to the possession of the Belgian government in 1908.[6] Thereafter, it became the Belgian Congo, though little else changed for those who were employed in extraction. Even though efforts were made to reduce the heavy taxation that was imposed upon the natives, the shareholders and local overseers largely ignored them. Hundreds of thousands more continued to die.

Advances were made mainly in terms of education and in the development of housing, medical care, and social services for those who were employed in mining. There was also reform in education. Beginning in 1910, the country was ruled by the paternalistic Church and State in cooperation with private shareholders. The slogan "no elite, no problem" was indicative of the type of education that the Congolese received.[7] It was not in the interest of the Belgians to educate their subjects to the degree that they might begin to have higher aspirations. By 1958, there were 1,400,000 children enrolled in primary education at Roman Catholic schools. Fewer than 25,000 Congolese received secondary education, and at the time of independence there were only 30 university graduates throughout the entire country. The University of Lovanium had only been opened in Leopoldville in 1954, followed by the establishment of a university in Elizabethville in 1956.[8]

As Chester Bowles wrote in 1953:

---

5. Ruth Slade, 182.
6. Christian P. Scherrer, 332.
7. Tukumbi Lumumba-Kasongo, *The Dynamics of Economic and Political Relations Between Africa and Foreign Powers: A Study in International Relations* (Westport, CT: Praeger Publishers, 1999) 82.
8. Ernest W. Lefever, *Crisis in the Congo: A United Nations Force in Action* (Washington, DC: Brookings Institution, 1965) 9.

The weakness of the [Belgian] program appears to be their reluctance to allow the African to secure an advanced education...for fear that he will then demand a growing share of responsibility in the shaping of his future...The danger lies not so much in the possibility that the Belgians will not compromise eventually with the force of nationalism, but that when they do they will find the Africans almost totally inexperienced in handling the responsibilities which they are certain to demand and eventually to get.[9]

RELIEF FROM LEOPOLD'S DARKNESS

Although the situation remained largely unchanged with regard to the extraction of palm, rubber, and ivory, the case was vastly better for those people who were engaged in mining. The shareholders who owned the companies believed that their very viability depended on the health and well-being of the workforce, such that housing, medical care, and even social security were now afforded to their employees.[10] They set the standard for social services long before the Belgian government enacted specific reforms to make such services mandatory. At least, in 1922 the Belgians enacted a ration system, called the *posho*, which mandated employers to provide their workers with blankets, shorts, sweaters, and nutritious and adequate food. This decree was strengthened in the year 1940.[11]

Whereas Roger Casement had noted during the earlier years that the economy of the Congo was predominantly extractive — almost nothing was being imported, by comparison to the amounts that were being exported, on a massive scale — the focus of Belgium after World War II was to invest in the development of the colony. They therefore enacted a Ten-Year Plan in 1952.[12] Under this plan, it was estimated that government capital expenditures were approximately $500 million. As they proceeded with their works, however, the total estimated cost was nearer to $962,280,000.[13] Between 1952 and 1958 the Belgian government sponsored the building of more than 60,000 dwellings.[14] It also invested each of the 135 territories with a rural medico-surgical center, a

---

9. Alan P. Merriam, *Congo: Background of a Conflict* (Northwestern University Press, USA: 1961) 65.
10. Georges Brausch, *Belgian Administration in the Congo* (London: Oxford University Press, 1961) 13.
11. Alan P. Merriam, 40.
12. Ibid., 38.
13. Ibid., 39.
14. Georges Brausch, 7.

surgical section, and a prenatal and infant welfare advice center. By 1958, the Congo had the best-developed medical system in Africa.[15]

Most of this was done to westernize the country and to accommodate the rising black bourgeoisie that was the outgrowth of broader access to secondary education and, as noted before, to fend off the Communists. Those who were fortunate enough to have attended secondary education were employed as clerks, shopkeepers, nurses, building contractors, tradesmen, craftsmen, small manufacturers, market-gardeners, fishermen, transport contractors, bar-keepers and various kinds of middlemen. On July 4, 1954, this new bourgeoisie formed its first association, the ACMAF, or Association des Classes Moyennes Africaines.[16] In particular, the union was concerned that the pay rates for the Congolese were still 70 percent of European salaries, a factor which also concerned the many Congolese who aspired to political positions.

The bourgeoisie had started to organize politically by 1955. This began with the establishment of fraternal organizations known as *amicales*. Patrice Lumumba, who became the first prime minister of the Congo republic, was a member of one such organization in 1956.[17] Another was Joseph Kasavubu, the future president of the republic, who belonged to the organization known as UNISCO.[18] Within these *amicales*, the future leaders of the Congo were able to publicly express their feelings and desires — although they did so in respectful fashion, as the press was quite strictly censored by the Belgians. (This changed over time as the dynamics of politics and the demands of different organizations strongly came to the fore.)

At first, the Congolese were largely encouraged by the post-war reforms that the Belgians had enacted. Before 1947, native interests had been represented entirely by Belgians, but in 1947 two Africans were chosen to represent the Congolese within the government council. And, by 1951, the number of Africans serving in the council had advanced to a total of eight. Although the council was consultative, it nonetheless afforded the Congolese their first participation in matters of rural government. The attitude toward the Congolese also began to change. Rather than viewing them quite so paternalistically, the Minister of the Colonies, M. Buisseret, began to make statements regarding his desire to remove the color bar by removing discriminatory regulations between 1954 and 1955.[19]

---

15. Ibid., 8.
16. Ibid., 4.
17. Ibid., 33.
18. Colin Legum, *Congo Disaster* (Harmondsworth, England: Penguin Books, 1961) 50.

THE PUSH FOR INDEPENDENCE

Several things prompted the desire for independence. The first was a proposal by A.A.J. van Bilsen of the Institute for Colonial Studies in Antwerp, who suggested granting the Congolese independence within a period of thirty years. Although van Bilsen was viewed as a radical in Belgium, his ideas were eagerly embraced by the Congolese. The first reply of the Congolese came in July 1956, with the printing of a manifesto in the periodical *Conscience Africaine*. Sponsored largely by Joseph Ileo, it asked for a thirty-year timetable for full emancipation.[20] But even this was a modest work, less aimed at attacking the Belgians for their abuses in the region than simply recognizing that the time had come for the Congolese to be granted their freedom. In part, the manifesto read:

> Belgium must not consider that there is a feeling of hostility in our desire for emancipation. Quite to the contrary, Belgium should be proud that, unlike nearly all colonized people, our desire is expressed without hatred or resentment. This alone is undeniable proof that the work of the Belgians in this country is not a failure...But to achieve that, the Belgians must realize now that their domination of the Congo will not go on forever. We protest energetically against opinion sometimes expressed in the press that does not make an essential distinction between the presence of the Belgians in the Congo and their domination of the Congo.[21]

Nevertheless, the manifesto went on to proclaim in no uncertain terms that the Congolese expected to be freed economically and socially as well as politically. It argued:

> On the one hand, existing institutions must become more and more representative by replacing progressively the present system of nominations with a system in which the population itself will designate its representatives. On the other hand, the councils which are now purely consultative must receive a true power of decision and control and increasingly extend matters in order to arrive finally at a responsible government...We are not asking only for a plan of political emancipation but for a full plan of total emancipation. At each stage of political emancipation there must be a corresponding stage of economic and social emancipation, as well as progress in education and culture. The parallel realization of these steps is an absolute necessity if political emancipation is to be sincere and effective.[22]

This was followed by a second manifesto, sponsored by the political group ABAKO, which was far less moderate in tone. Led by Joseph Kasavubu, the ABAKO advocated the development of several political parties, in contrast to the

---

19. Georges Brausch, 21.
20. Ibid. 35.
21. Alan P. Merriam, 73.
22. Ibid., 73.

first manifesto which had argued for only one. Further, it argued that the thirty-year timetable that was envisaged in *Conscience Africaine* was unacceptable in itself:

> For us, we do not wish to collaborate in the elaboration of this plan, but purely and simply to annul it because its application would serve only further to retard the Congo. In reality, it is only the same old lullaby. Our patience is already exhausted. Since the hour has come, emancipation should be granted us this very day rather than delayed another thirty years.[23]

In response to this rise of strong sentiments toward independence, the word "emancipation" crept into official Belgian terminology by 1957. The Colonial Minister Buisseret asserted that Belgian policy was "to humanize, to develop, to associate, and finally to emancipate."

THE POLITICAL PARTIES

In addition to the ABAKO party of Joseph Kasavubu, a party called the MNC (Mouvement National Congolais) was formed in August 1956. Patrice Lumumba became its standard bearer in 1958. Like the first manifesto that had been published in *Conscience Africaine*, Lumumba's early work exhibited a conciliatory attitude toward the Belgians. In *Congo, My Country*, Lumumba originally maintained:

> We would urge those who are only willing to see the bad side of colonisation to weigh up the good and the bad to see which is the greater. To whom do we owe our liberation from that odious trade practised by the bloodthirsty Arabs and their allies, those inhuman brigands who ravaged the country? At a time when our people were suffering from these atrocities, when they were being decimated by sleeping sickness and by that grim tragedy which was taking place in Manyema and throughout the Congo, when thousands of the inhabitants of the country were being carried away in chains to be sold like cattle in gruesome markets, other countries — which were more powerful than Belgium — remained indifferent to our fate and left us to perish. Belgium, moved by a very sincere and humanitarian idealism, came to our help and, with the assistance of doughty native fighters, was able to rout the enemy, to eradicate disease, to teach us and to eliminate certain barbarous practices from our customs, thus restoring our human dignity and turning us into free, happy vigorous, civilised men...As regards the mistakes which were made, I have already said that they are inherent in any human activity, be it in Africa, Europe or any other country of the world; this is virtually a truism. In my humble opinion, there is absolutely no point in constantly raking up these mistakes from the past. What matters now is to find new solutions. Does that mean that I excuse the Belgians or blindly take up their defence? No. I only excuse what is excusable

---

23. Ibid., 76.

and I only defend what can be defended. Let us stop railing against these few mistakes. [24]

But Lumumba's attitude toward the Belgians became far more militant as the country moved toward independence.

The party that most embraced the colonizers was that of Moise Tshombe in the province of Katanga. Dubbed CONAKAT (for the Confederation des Associations du Katanga), the party was based on the premise of separateness, or freedom to evolve within a loose confederation that would protect the rights of the colonizers and especially mining interests.[25]

In the beginning, there were hundreds of political parties that were based on tribal and ethnic interests. In time, these formed coalitions or became subsumed within larger parties until they represented about thirty parties in total. Between them they displayed four tendencies. The first was separatist regionalism, as embraced by Tshombe's CONAKAT. The second was federalism. The third was immediate independence as embraced by Lumumba's MNC. And the fourth was the path to independence as outlined by the Belgian government.[26]

The Parti Solidaire Africain (PSA), led by Antoine Gizenga, sent the Minister of the Congo a plan for a federal republic in September of 1957. The PSA aligned itself with ABAKO and, initially, was opposed to the MNC of Lumumba, which insisted on a unitary state. Within ABAKO, Kasavubu reiterated his demands for immediate independence. Toward the end of November, a separate branch of the MNC led by Albert Kalonji, which opposed Patrice Lumumba, formed a cartel with the ABAKO and the PSA, backing up Kasavubu's demand for a united but federal Congo.[27]

In all, Lumumba symbolized the radicals who were committed to obtaining complete independence while stressing nonalignment in the international sphere. His allies included Antoine Gizenga and Pierre Mulele, who would play important roles in the post-independence period. Kasavubu belonged to the moderates, who enjoyed the support of the Belgians, other Western governments, and politically conservative multinationals. Moise Tshombe, Albert Kalonji, Joseph Ileo, Cyrille Adoula, and Joseph Mobutu were also part of this

24. Patrice Lumumba, *Congo, My Country* (London: Pall Mall Press, 1962) 13.
25. Eds. Sandra W. Meditz and Tim Merrill, *Zaire: a Country Study* (Federal Research Division, Washington, DC: 1994) 25.
26. Colin Legum, 68.
27. Ruth Slade and Marjory Taylor, *The Belgian Congo*, 2nd ed. (London: Oxford University Press, 1961) 59.

group. And finally, the PNP was a moderate party that developed, supported by the Belgians.

The beginning of change came with the decree on the *statut de villes*, which divided the towns into communes that would elect their own communal councils. In late 1957, the first elections for these councils were held in Leopoldville, Elisabethville, and Jadotville. They were followed by elections in Bukavu, Luluabourg, Stanleyville, and two satellite towns of Leopoldville in 1958.[28] By 1958, the new Colonial Minister M. Petillon spoke openly of taking steps to initiate decolonization. [29]

Although the ABAKO party had threatened to abstain from the December elections, based upon its feeling that the elections were merely a palliative effort, the turnout in a majority of the provinces was between 80 and 90 percent. In Leopoldville, 30 percent voted, whereas the turnout was about 15 percent in the Lower Congo region. The urban elections gave ABAKO candidates 133 seats out of a total of 170, thus vesting control of the communes in the hands of those who espoused complete independence. ABAKO extremists stated that they would not recognize Belgian authority after January, even though Kasavubu gave a moderate speech in December. [30]

POLITICS GAINS MOMENTUM

Not long after this, President Charles de Gaulle gave a speech in the French Congo (Brazzaville) on August 24, 1958 in which he offered the French Congolese the chance for independence.[31] This set more of the Congolese to talking amongst themselves and was soon followed by an invitation from the Belgian government for the aspiring Congo elites to attend the World Fair in Brussels. There, people who had never met before came together and discussed the situation, giving rise to another political movement. Known by its acronym MPNC, for the Mouvement pour le Progres National Congolais, the movement was formally launched during the last few months of 1958.[32]

---

28. Ibid., 25.
29. Ibid., 20.
30. Ibid., 60.
31. Ernest W. Lefever *Crisis in the Congo: A United Nations Force in Action*, 7.
32. Colin Legum, 55.

At this time, Governor-General Petillon, who stepped in to replace Auguste Buisseret as the country's colonial minister, announced an official policy of decolonization. He appointed a commission to consult with representatives of both the Europeans and the Africans, and, based upon their findings, to outline a policy of emancipation.[33] This was followed by an All-African People's Conference in Accra (Ghana) on December 5, 1958. ABAKO leader Joseph Kasavubu failed to attend, but Patrice Lumumba was there to speak for all of the Congolese.[34] The goal that was promoted there was immediate independence.

Then, ABAKO supporters rioted at a gathering that the Force Publique attempted to disperse on January 4, 1959. There was extreme violence, resulting in the deaths of 49 Congolese and leaving 101 wounded.[35] Although the riots had a political dimension, their causes were primarily economic. The colony had fallen into financial troubles from 1956 onward and most of those who rioted were unemployed. The discontent of the population provided ABAKO with the means to co-opt the people in the cause for independence. Subsequently, Kasavubu and his chief lieutenants were arrested and flown to Belgium, though they were not imprisoned or put on trial.[36]

The Belgian government's response was to speed the course toward independence.[37] King Baudouin issued a radio message in which he stated, "It is our firm intention, without undesirable procrastination but also without undue haste, to lead the Congolese populations forward towards independence in prosperity and peace." The declaration specifically stated that elections would be held for communal and territorial councils by universal suffrage at the end of 1959.[38] And in the seven months that followed, forty acts and ordinances containing discriminatory regulations were altered or abolished.[39]

At a meeting in Elizabethville in March, Lumumba pressed again for immediate independence. Afterwards fighting broke out between his followers in Katanga, known as the Balubakat, and those of CONAKAT, Tshombe's party in Katanga. Seven people were killed, over 100 injured, and 600 arrested. For a time, martial law was declared.[40]

---

33. Ruth Slade and Marjory Taylor, 44.
34. Colin Legum, 56.
35. Eds. Sandra W. Meditz and Tim Merrill, 24.
36. Colin Legum, 58.
37. Ibid., 24.
38. Ruth Slade and Marjory Taylor, 50.
39. Georges Brausch, 21.

The Luluabourg conference, held in April 1959, was the first to include almost all the political parties. It was dominated by the MNC and Lumumba, who was supported by Ilunga and Kalonji, the MNC leaders in Kasai.[41] Kasavubu and the other ABAKO leaders who had been arrested after the Leopoldville riots did not attend the conference, as they only returned to Leopoldville in May.[42] However, dissent broke out between Lumumba and Kalonji in July, leading Kalonji to set up his own moderate party with Joseph Ileo and Cyrille Adoula that was thereafter known as the MNC-Kalonji. This had the effect of winnowing down Lumumba's bases of support in Katanga and Kasai.

By the end of September, Lumumba sent an open letter to the Minister saying that his party would no longer co-operate with Belgium. At an MNC conference in Stanleyville in October he demanded "negotiations for immediate independence; otherwise, he said, 1960 would be a year of misery and war."[43] This speech was followed by riots in Stanleyville, which led to the death of twenty Congolese. Lumumba was quickly arrested.

While he was imprisoned, another conference was held in Elizabethville, with the MNC-Kalonji presiding. The delegates approved the Belgian plan for local elections but stated that these should be preceded by a Round Table Conference between the Congolese and the Belgians. Before the conference, the MNC-Kalonji formed a cartel with the ABAKO and the PSA; the Lumumba section demanded a unitary state, whereas the Kasai branch had thrown in with the federalists.[44] As the leader of ABAKO, Tshombe had always rejected the idea of a strong central government in favor of a loose confederation. Although the PSA joined Lumumba after the Round Table Conference, the MNC-Kalonji alliance with ABAKO continued to hold.[45]

Yet there was one view that all of the parties shared. In all, they were strongly dissatisfied with the timetable that Belgium had set for the course of emancipation. The communal and territorial elections were to be held in December 1959, indirect elections for the provincial councils were to be held in March 1960, and indirect elections for a central government in September 1960.[46] They were none too pleased with the idea of indirect elections, either.

40. Ruth Slade and Marjory Taylor, 71.
41. Ibid., 60.
42. Ibid., 59.
43. Ibid., 60.
44. Ibid., 63.
45. Ibid., 64.

THE ROUND TABLE CONFERENCE

The dissatisfaction of the Congolese led to the convening of the Brussels Round Table Conference in January 1960. There, a four-year plan for independence was presented by the Belgians, but the Congolese supported Lumumba's demand for immediate independence.[47] (At the insistence of the delegates, Lumumba was freed from prison before the end of his six-month sentence, lest the Conference proceed without him.) The Belgians then announced that independence would begin on June 30, 1960. Although the Belgians made concessions, there were also many points on which the Congolese conceded. They allowed that King Baudouin would remain head of state until the day of independence, and that, after legislative elections, he would nominate the first *formateur* and the first Congolese Government. The new head of the state would be chosen by the two Congolese Houses of Parliament until the adoption of a constitution. In case of a disagreement, the President of the Senate or of the Chamber would be the head of state. The Conference also decided that an Economic Round Table should take place in April in Brussels.[48] In the end, the Round Table Conference passed sixteen resolutions which became known as the *Loi Fondamentale*, or fundamental law.[49]

Later, at the Economic Round Table, the Belgian government informed the Congolese that they had inherited a public debt of £350 million (which had been raised and guaranteed by the Belgians). As Colin Legum notes:

> The servicing and redemption of this Debt required almost 25 per cent of the Congo's annual budget, far and away the highest debt burden bequeathed to any of the former African colonies. [But] there are two softening features about the size of this Debt. First, the Congo Government inherited a Portfolio of assets valued at about £240 million, comprising a large slice of the holdings in the Union Minière, and outright ownership of several large public utilities; [though] this inheritance contributed nothing to ensuring the immediate liquidity of the new Government. Secondly, full allowance should be made for the fact that the greatest part of the Debt had been incurred in development work within the Congo."[50]

---

46. Colin Legum, 68.
47. Ernest W. Lefever, *Crisis in the Congo: A United Nations Force in Action*, 8.
48. Ruth Slade and Marjory Taylor, 69.
49. Ibid., 70.
50. Colin Legum, 82.

ELECTIONS

Finally, provincial and general elections took place in May of 1960.[51] The pro-Belgian parties, like PNP, failed badly. Aside from Katanga, where Moise Tshombe's CONAKAT cartel won just over half the seats, the nationalists swept the ballot. Patrice Lumumba's MNC emerged as the largest party, with thirty-three seats in a Parliament of 137. Thus, Lumumba became prime minister while Kasavubu, the head of ABAKO, became head of state. King Baudouin was invited to attend the celebration for independence and was welcomed warmly by Kasavubu and the crowd.[52] However, Lumumba was not so generous, having by now developed a fierce oppositional attitude. Part of his speech went as follows:

> I ask my friends, all of you who have fought unceasingly at our side, to make this thirtieth of June, 1960, an illustrious date that will be indelibly engraved upon your hearts, a date whose meaning you will teach your children with pride so that they in turn will tell their children's children the glorious story of our struggle for free-dom...We are proud of this struggle amid tears, fire, and blood, down to our very heart of hearts, for it was a noble and just struggle, an indispensable struggle if we were to put an end to the humiliating slavery that had been forced upon us. We have been the victims of ironic taunts, of insults, of blows that we were forced to endure morning, noon, and night because we were blacks. Who will forget that a black was addressed in familiar form, not because he was a friend, certainly, but because the polite form of address was to be used only for whites. We cannot forget the burst of rifle fire in which so many of our brothers perished, the cells into which the authorities threw those who no longer were willing to submit to a rule where justice meant oppression and exploitation.[53]

This was true, but it was also embarrassing to the King, all the more so when Lumumba snarled, "We are no longer your monkeys." It set the tone for their future relations, and all too soon the new government would find itself stri-dently at odds with the Belgians as the Force Publique rioted and the Belgians intervened with troops "to protect their citizens." This resulted in a protracted effort to remove the Belgian presence that would last for four years and involve the whole world in the struggle.

---

51. Ruth Slade and Marjory Taylor, 76.
52. Ibid., 80.
53. Ibid., 87.

CHAPTER 2. THE FIRST INTERVENTION

It was only days after independence that the Force Publique mutinied over extremely low pay rates and a general lack of advancement. Having been warned by their commanding officer that they could expect nothing new after independence, they held a protest meeting and demanded the Belgians' dismissal. By July 8, 1960, the Congolese seized arms in Leopoldville and drove out their Belgian officers. All Europeans were herded off the streets at gunpoint and martial law was declared. Some of the European women were raped and many men were badly beaten. There were deaths and even cannibalism in the wave of ensuing violence.

Trying to control the situation, Prime Minister Lumumba decided to Africanize the Force Publique. He renamed it the Congolese National Army (ANC), dismissed the Belgian officers, and promoted each man by one rank. But even these steps and the promise of higher pay rates did not succeed in quelling the violence. First, the police mutinied in Matadi. Soldiers looted and rampaged in the area of the Lower Congo and fighting broke out in Katanga. Then the Belgian officers were overwhelmed by soldiers in Luluabourg, the capital of Kasai.[54] Tens of thousands of Europeans were held under threat to their lives.

Alarmed by the menace to its citizens, Belgium naturally sent troops and flew in planes for evacuation. It did this reflexively, without asking for the permission of the new government. Although many observers noted that the Belgians could have been used successfully to pacify violent areas, the Congolese

---

54. Colin Legum, 110.

government viewed the incoming Belgian troops as an affront to its very sovereignty. In addition to intervening militarily, the Belgians were also supporting the secession of the Katanga province, which the president of the province, Moise Tshombe, had declared on July 11. By aligning themselves with Katanga, the center of the country's mineral wealth, the Belgians exposed themselves to the charge that they were attempting to divide the country and thereby continue their rule.

LUMUMBA CALLS IN THE UN

Faced with the threats of the ANC on the rampage and the secession of Katanga, which was quickly followed by a separatist movement in the province of Kasai, the Congolese initially appealed to the United States for help to expel the Belgians. Several cabinet ministers, headed by Vice Premier Gizenga, requested that the US Ambassador, Clare Timberlake, transmit to the US an appeal for 3,000 US troops.[55] Although Eisenhower was unwilling to see the newly independent Congo fall into the lap of the Soviets, he was equally unwilling to intervene directly for fear of instigating some form of retaliation from the Soviet Union. He therefore advised the Congolese to seek the help of the United Nations.

Lumumba did so on July 12, 1960, warning that if the UN did not take steps to immediately end the conflict that he would appeal to the Bandung Treaty powers (a group of African and Asian nations) or even the Soviet Union. Expressing great impatience, Lumumba persuaded President Kasavubu to join him in a cable to Premier Khrushchev. He stressed that the Congo was occupied by the Belgians and that the lives of the president and prime minister were in danger. The cable ended by begging the Soviets "to watch hourly over the situation."[56]

But the UN reacted quickly. UN Secretary-General Dag Hammarskjöld had already been apprised of the situation and had accordingly taken steps to recruit troops for the mission. By July 15, British transport planes had flown in 700 Ghanaians and 593 Tunisians. Within one month's time, he had recruited another 3,250 from Morocco; 2,547 from Ethiopia; 2,247 from Tunisia; 2,389 from

---

55. Joseph P. Lash, *Dag Hammarskjold, Custodian of the Brushfire Peace*, 1st ed. (Garden City, NY: Doubleday, 1961) 227.

56. Ernest W. Lefever, *Crisis in the Congo: A United Nations Force in Action*, 14.

Ghana; 1,317 from Ireland; 744 from Guinea; 628 from Sweden; 574 from Mali; 390 from Sudan; 225 from Liberia; 164 from Canada; and 73 from India. He also accepted troops from Indonesia and the United Arab Republic.[57]

In implementing the plan for UN intervention, Hammarskjöld insisted on five principal guidelines. The first was that the force should be under the exclusive control of the UN Secretary-General. The second was that the UN would not interfere in the internal affairs of the Congo. The third was that the force must have freedom of movement throughout the whole of the Congo. Point four was that the UN contingents should only be empowered to use force in self-defense. And, five was that the UN contingents should not take orders from their host countries.[58] Under these guidelines, the UN would be prohibited from taking a side in the conflict or trying to impose the type of government upon which Lumumba insisted. It would not use force to subdue the provinces of Katanga and Kasai, nor would it support any particular government faction. Finally, the UN did not adopt as part of its operative resolution any ruling on the Belgians. It refused to label the Belgian intervention as a case of international aggression, much to the disappointment of Lumumba and the Soviets.

Under the terms of a resolution that had been sponsored by the Tunisians, the UN was empowered to "take the necessary steps, in consultation with the government of the Republic of the Congo, to provide the Government with such military assistance, as may be necessary, until through the efforts of the Congolese Government with the technical assistance of the United Nations, the national security forces may be able, in the opinion of the Government to meet fully their tasks."[59] A further resolution of 20 September requested that the Secretary-General "assist the Central Government of the Congo in the restoration and maintenance of law and order throughout the territory of the Republic of the Congo and to safeguard its unity, territorial integrity and political independence in the interests of international peace and security."[60]

The UN did deploy its troops to replace the Belgian contingents in the capital city of Leopoldville and had plans to enter Katanga. At the same time that the Belgians were being ousted, the ANC was also being asked to lay down its arms and to submit to UN authority. The plan was that eventually the UN

---

57. Ibid., 29.
58. Ibid., 23.
59. Thomas R. Mockaitis, *Peace Operations and Intrastate Conflict: The Sword or the Olive Branch?* (Westport, CT: Praeger Publishers, 1999) 14.
60. Ibid.

would retrain the ANC and make it a fit military force for the Congo. But in the beginning, such thoughts were overly optimistic. The UN contented itself with merely disarming the ANC soldiers, so as to prevent further looting and rioting.

Due to the presence of organized resistance in Katanga, the UN Secretary-General had stated in his report of August 8 to the Security Council that the Council "must either change the character of the Force, which appears to me to be impossible, both for constitutional reasons and in view of the commitments to the contributing governments, or otherwise resort to other methods which would enable me to carry through the implementation of its resolution without going beyond my instructions as regards the Force."[61] Hammarskjöld was asking for clarification of his mandate. He needed to know whether the Council would approve a forcible entry into Katanga or whether he would be instructed to pursue the matter further via diplomatic means only. Since the Council at that time did not approve a forcible entry, Hammarskjöld was forced to delay his entry into Katanga.

Within Katanga and Kasai, there was resistance to the break-away movements by the people of the Baluba tribe. They fought against Tshombe's gendarmes in Katanga and were attacked by Lumumbists in Kasai. Describing the massacre of the Baluba, Hammarskjöld spoke of it as a genocide. Approximately 3,000 Baluba were killed during this time.[62] Since the mandate of the UN forces strictly proscribed the use of force for other than self-defense, they could not intervene to end the fighting.

LUMUMBA IS COMPROMISED

Lumumba had become so dissatisfied with the progress of the UN's efforts and its refusal to take up arms on behalf of ending the secession of Katanga that he turned now to the Soviets. On August 27, he arranged for an ANC invasion of Katanga using one hundred trucks and eleven IL-14 transport planes that he acquired from the Soviet Union. President Eisenhower responded that this was in flagrant violation of the UN resolutions and that it revealed Russia's "political designs in Africa."[63] The CIA was then given permission to assassinate

---

61. Arthur Lee Burns and Nina Heathcote, *Peace-Keeping by UN Forces, from Suez to the Congo* (New York: Praeger, 1963) 38.
62. Colin Legum, 24.
63. Ernest W. Lefever, *Crisis in the Congo: A United Nations Force in Action*, 40.

Lumumba, who was labeled a Soviet pawn. An agent was provided with a vial of deadly germs and a kit of hypodermic needles as the means to end his life.[64]

Before the assassination could take place, however, Lumumba was dismissed from office by President Kasavubu. This was largely due to his involvement with the Soviets but was also attributed in part to a disagreement over the system of government that was preferred for the whole of the Congo. Lumumba was a unitarist, whereas Kasavubu was a federalist who preferred a looser governing arrangement with the provinces of Katanga and Kasai. Kasavubu appointed Joseph Ileo to be the new prime minister, and Lumumba responded, in turn, by dismissing the president. The UN's immediate action was to close the radio station so that neither Lumumba nor Kasavubu could use it to incite civil war. But Kasavubu got around this by using the radio station in Brazzaville.

At first, the Parliament refused to accept the dismissals. The situation was deadlocked until Joseph Mobutu, the ANC Chief of Staff, proclaimed army rule. Some said that the CIA was behind him, while others claimed that it was a purely private initiative. Either way, Washington was pleased that Lumumba was out of the picture. Mobutu was a member of the influential "Binza group," which included Security Chief Victor Nendaka, Foreign Minister Bomboko, National Bank President Albert Ndele, and the permanent secretary of the interior ministry, Damien Kandolo.[65]

Although Mobutu said that he would continue to recognize Kasavubu as the formal head of state, he shut down the Parliament and organized a Government of University Students. At this time, the American envoy to the UN provided Mobutu with $1 million in US support to pay off the Congolese soldiers and keep them loyal to the Kasavubu faction.[66] Against the wishes of many African states, the UN accepted Mobutu's government, at least temporarily. Having started out with a policy of neutrality, the UN could not act to influence the leadership in the Congo. However, when the delegations of both the

---

64. Bill Berkley, *The Graves are Not Yet Full: Race, Tribe, and Power in the Heart of Africa* (New York: Perseus Books, 2001) 110.

65. Ernest W. Lefever, *Army, Police, and Politics in Tropical Africa* (Washington, DC: Brookings Institution, 1970) 98.

66. Carole J.L. Collins, "The Cold War Comes to Africa: Cordier and the 1960 Congo Crisis," *Journal of International Affairs*, 47.1 (1993) Questia, 1 Feb. 2005. http://www.questia.com/.

Kasavubu and the Lumumba factions asked to be seated at the UN, the UN Credentials Committee supported Kasavubu.

THE BELGIAN ROLE IN KATANGA

Meanwhile, the Belgians were building up secessionist Katanga. Between July 11 and September 8, 1960, it flew in more than 100 tons of arms and ammunition including mortars, sub-machine guns, and FN-38 automatic rifles. In addition to transferring supplies from its Congo bases, the Belgians also supplied Katanga with 25 Belgian Air Force planes. Eighty-nine Belgian officers were serving in Tshombe's guard, and 326 Belgian NCOs and technicians were acting as "volunteers."[67]

Within the United Nations, the Western bloc prevented the Afro-Asian states from passing resolutions that were strongly worded against the Belgians. But at the same time, the West, with perhaps the exception of France, did not allow the Belgians to recognize Katanga's independence. Even when Belgium threatened to withdraw from NATO over the matter, the West maintained its stance. At no time during the history of the conflict was Katanga recognized by any external state.

The UN by now was determined to enter Katanga. Having exchanged cables with Tshombe on August 10, Hammarskjöld flew into Elisabethville on August 12 with his Afro-Asian commanders, civilian UN advisers, and two companies of the Swedish battalion from the UN force. In a subsequent press release, Tshombe demanded the withdrawal of the Swedish troops, insisting that only African troops be deployed within Katanga. Although Hammarskjöld explicitly indicated that the UN was not going to interfere with the secession of Katanga, Tshombe produced a list of further demands to limit the UN's role in Katanga. These were: "that units friendly to Lumumba could not be deployed in Katanga; that the UN would not interfere with financial or administrative arrangements; that the government would retain control over entrance and exit from the nation; that the government would have the right to appoint any foreign technicians; that the UN would disarm paramilitary units elsewhere in the Congo; and that the UN would recognize the constitution of Katanga."[68] Hammarskjöld

---

67. Colin Legum, 161.
68. Thomas R. Mockaitis, 19.

declined to respond to the last two requests (which would have been impossible for the UN, under its current mandate), but reassured Tshombe that the UN force could not be used to forcibly subdue Katanga. Thus, the way was paved for the UN's peaceful entry, though this would change over time.

The Fateful Demise of Lumumba

Lumumba, as we have seen, was being opposed by the West. He remained under house arrest, with his home surrounded by pro-Mobutu troops. The Soviet Union was furious at this turn of events. On September 23, Khrushchev called upon Hammarskjöld to resign, proposing that the Secretariat should henceforth be comprised of three men instead of one, at least one of whom should be a Soviet representative. In reply, US Secretary of State Christian A. Herter pronounced that the speech was "a declaration of war" against the United Nations. But Khrushchev went still further during the Assembly debate of October 3. He accused the Secretary-General of "arbitrary and lawless behavior" that "violated the elementary principles of justice" and "supported the colonialists."[69] He called again for Hammarskjöld's resignation, and refused to pay for the Soviet portion of the UN operation.

Lumumba escaped on November 27 in a car that left his home during the night. Thinking to travel to Stanleyville, where Antoine Gizenga had taken up Lumumba's banner and started a revolt against Mobutu, Lumumba was captured near Port-Francqui on December 2 and imprisoned at Thysville. At this time, several of the UN member states that had openly supported Lumumba began to withdraw their troops in protest. Accompanying the move with an anti-colonial statement, the first to pull out were Ceylon and the UAR. Then, during the second week of December, they were followed by Indonesia, Morocco, and Guinea. Yugoslavia withdrew its technical personnel on December 21.

Kasavubu maintained that Lumumba would be brought to trial but before this could occur, he was transferred to Katanga. There, he is said to have been killed in the presence of Tshombe, allegedly by a Belgian mercenary if not a firing squad. The announcement was made public by radio on February 13, 1961.

---

69. Ernest W. Lefever, *Crisis in the Congo: A United Nations Force in Action*, 49.

FIGHTING THE DIFFERENT FACTIONS

Thereafter, the UN had to deal with four rival factions. The first was that which they considered legitimate, meaning Kasavubu's, which had about 7,000 troops in the capital city of Leopoldville. The second was Gizenga's, which had about 5,500 troops in Stanleyville. As Lumumba's preferred successor, Gizenga was then being supported by the Soviets, China, the United Arab Republic, Ghana, Guinea, Mali, Morocco, and several of the more militant African states. The third faction was that of Moise Tshombe, who had between 5,000 and 7,000 troops in Elisabethville. And the fourth faction was that of Albert Kalonji, which led about 3,000 troops in breakaway South Kasai.[70] Kasavubu, sounding much like Lumumba in earlier days, stated in a dispatch to the UN that "it is of the greatest importance that the Government should receive...military assistance within the framework of the UN, for otherwise it will be compelled to seek assistance outside the UN, despite the manifest danger that would entail of the conflict becoming international."[71]

To some extent, the UN responded to Kasavubu's demands by sponsoring the arrest and imprisonment of Gizenga during the month of January. In the main, however, its course was to pursue a policy of impartiality. It attempted to get the factions to meet with the UN Conciliation Commission which was created in November by the Secretary-General's Congo Advisory Committee. Comprised of fifteen Asian and African states with troops in the Congo, the role of the Conciliation Commission was to restore Parliament and create an inclusive government.

On February 21, 1961, the UN adopted a new resolution that broadened the force's mandate. In view of the fomenting civil strife between the different factions, it urged the UN to "take immediately all appropriate measures to prevent the occurrence of civil war in the Congo, including arrangements for cease-fires, the halting of all military operations, the prevention of clashes, and the use of force, if necessary, in the last resort."[72] Thus, the use of force was sanctioned for the prevention of civil wars.

As noted, there had been fighting in Katanga between the Baluba and the forces of Tshombe since the early days of secession. But now that the UN had an

---

70. Ibid., 53.
71. Joseph P. Lash, 255.
72. Thomas R. Mockaitis, 23.

expanded mandate, it could take steps to end the conflict. Hammarskjöld had a contingent of Indian troops transported to Elisabethville for this purpose. Tshombe's immediate response was to order the population to attack the UN troops. Riots broke out in Elisabethville, comprised of thousands of men armed with knives, sticks, and stones. They assaulted a Swedish unit that was holding the province's airport. And on April 8, Tshombe's troops attacked the Ethiopian unit in Kabalo. The UN force fought back, disarming a number of Katangan troops and mercenaries. Having proven that they were willing to use force, their actions prompted Tshombe to call a cease-fire on April 20.[73]

Under the auspices of the Conciliation Commission the factions were forced to meet, first in Tananarive and later in Coquilhatville. In Tananarive, the participants agreed to form a confederation of Congo states. In Coquilhatville, they agreed that the Congo should become a federal republic. While trying to leave the Coquilhatville airport, Tshombe was arrested by the Kasavubu faction. Kasavubu said that Tshombe would be tried for high treason and for the killing of Lumumba. He also stated that Katanga would be overcome by force and all of its Belgians expelled. Following this, six of Tshombe's Belgian aides were arrested in Leopoldville and the Katangese ministry appeared to be much more conciliatory.[74]

Tshombe was released by Mobutu on June 22. In return for his freedom, Tshombe had signed an agreement putting Katangese troops under Mobutu's command. Tshombe began trying to maneuver Kasavubu into closing the old Parliament and constituting a new government as the price that he set for ending Katanga's secession. But Kasavubu, soon realizing that Tshombe's promises were worthless and facing possible UN sanctions, went on to order Parliament to convene.

Under UN protection, the Parliament was finally reconvened at Lovanium University on July 19, 1961.[75] During the course of its first session, no one was permitted contact with the outside world and all weapons, money, and other instruments of power were explicitly forbidden.[76] In August, a new government was formed with Cyril Adoula as president and Gizenga as prime minister. The UN readily recognized the new government and agreed to support it whole-heartedly.

---

73. Ernest W. Lefever, *Crisis in the Congo: A United Nations Force in Action*, 65.
74. Arthur Lee Burns and Nina Heathcote, 93.
75. Ernest W. Lefever, *Crisis in the Congo: A United Nations Force in Action*, 49.
76. Ibid.

SUPPORTING THE NEW CENTRAL GOVERNMENT

The first thing that the UN did in support of the new central government was to impound a plane that flew regularly between Stanleyville and Cairo. This made it possible for the government to declare that there would be no further flights between Stanleyville and foreign countries, thus closing it off from the rest of the world. Gizenga, in Stanleyville, replied by taking the UN representative hostage, although this proved to no avail.

On August 24, the Congolese government adopted Ordinance No. 70. This called for the "expulsion of all non-Congolese officers and mercenaries serving in the Katanga forces."[77] Operation Rumpunch, designed to fulfill this ordinance, began on August 28, 1961. The UN moved its troops into Katanga, seizing the airport, post office, telephone system, and radio station. It also raided the army headquarters and arrested foreign personnel and mercenaries.[78] The purpose of these actions was to pave the way for the central government to disarm the Katangan army, oust and arrest Tshombe and his ministers, dissolve the Katangese Parliament, and send commissioners to rule the province.[79] By the time that it was over, the UN had arrested 338 men. Interrogation of the mercenaries revealed the existence of Belgian recruiting stations. Unlike ANC soldiers, who largely went unpaid, mercenaries recruited by the Belgians were guaranteed "generous salaries, housing and food allowances, family indemnities, hazard pay, life and disability insurance, and survivor's benefits."[80] Further UN operations were suspended because the Belgian consul agreed to repatriate its citizens thereafter voluntarily. However, this failed to take place.

Tshombe's forces responded by regaining most of their strategic positions. His army threatened the UN base at Kamina and imprisoned the Irish garrison at Jadotville. The Irish were held captive in an effort to extort terms of a cease-fire that were quite embarrassing to the UN. The provisional cease-fire was announced on September 20, restoring the status quo ante.[81]

In furtherance of its aims, the UN undertook Operation Morthor on September 13. Its purpose, as outlined by one UN official, was to "secure the post office and the radio studios and transmitters and to raid the offices of the Surete

---

77. Ernest W. Lefever, *Crisis in the Congo: A United Nations Force in Action*, 76.
78. Arthur Lee Burns and Nina Heathcote, 100.
79. Ibid., 102
80. Thomas R. Mockaitis, 26.
81. Ibid., 112.

and Ministry of Information and remove the files. Europeans and senior African personnel working in these departments were to be apprehended if possible. The flag of the Republic of the Congo [was to] be run up at the earliest appropriate moment on public buildings and on UN buildings. The Central Government would send down a Commissionare d'Etat to take over authority, in cooperation with Tshombe, if possible, in cooperation with the United Nations in any case."[82] In other words, Morthor was the logical follow-up to the UN's original commitment to the Congo's central government. But Morthor was a failure. It succeeded in capturing only one Katangan minister, who was very soon released. However, it had set Tshombe on the run.

REPLACING HAMMARSKJÖLD

Tshombe tried to negotiate another cease-fire but the UN refused him. Hammarskjöld was to attend a conference with Tshombe in Ndola, Northern Rhodesia, on September 17, but his plane was shot down, killing everyone aboard.[83] With Hammarskjöld gone, Tshombe returned to Katanga unimpeded.

On October 13, 1961, Tshombe and the UN agreed to the following terms:

> The exchange of all prisoners; the creation of joint commissions with full freedom of movement to verify compliance with the agreement; the withdrawal of UN troops from the post office and other positions in Elisabethville on condition that the provincial government would not engage in inflammatory propaganda against the United Nations; and the use of airports in Katanga to the extent permitted before hostilities, but with the understanding that technical air control would remain in UN hands.[84]

Although the government of Adoula expressed concern regarding these terms, Acting Secretary-General U Thant assured it that the terms applied only to the UN.

In the meantime, some 35,000 Baluba tribesmen were driven into a UN refugee camp that was established in Elisabethville.[85] The camp was largely controlled by Baluba thugs, but Tshombe's troops also continued to engage in harassment. They often fired into the camps and even overran the ANC troops that were under the command of Mobutu.

---

82. Ernest W. Lefever, *Crisis in the Congo: A United Nations Force in Action*, 81.
83. Ibid, 82.
84. Ibid., 89.
85. Ibid., 91.

By now, Arthur Lee Burns and Nina Heathcote report that the UN force was being seriously depleted:

> From the 19,825 men in July, it was down to 15,500 at the end of November and was expected to drop further to about 14,400 in December. The operation was also threatened with insolvency. On October 16, the UN revealed that there were only enough funds to continue ONUC for another two weeks. Out of more than a hundred UN members, only sixteen had contributed anything during 1961. Most of the expenses of the Organization were borne by the United States which, in addition to its share of $32.2 million, paid in 1961 more than 50 percent of the assessments of the small powers. The Communist countries, most of the Arab states, France, Belgium, Portugal, and South Africa refused to contribute on political grounds, while a number of Afro-Asian and Latin American countries pleaded poverty. In October imminent disaster was averted only when the General Assembly Budgetary Committee, overriding Russian opposition, voted $10 million a month for November and December, 1961.[86]

There was an effort by the Congolese central government to invade Katanga on November 2, but it was well known that the government lacked the manpower to follow through. The effort collapsed after only two days. Then, on December 5, 1961, the Katangese and UN forces clashed on the outskirts of Elisabethville and around military installations. The Katangese made a concerted effort to cut off the UN detachments from each other by setting up roadblocks throughout the province. This interfered with the UN's freedom of movement as set forth in the protocols that had been agreed to by Tshombe. The UN further obtained information that the Katangese were planning a full-scale attack. Thus, reinforcements were airlifted into Katanga on December 14, followed by a UN offensive that was geared toward removing travel restrictions.[87]

The military success of the UN resulted in talks between Tshombe and Adoula. Arranged by President Kennedy's administration, the talks at Kitona Base lasted two days. Diplomatic teams from the UN and the United States remained throughout. With pressure and guidance from both, the parties achieved an agreement which ended Katanga's secession. Upon return to Katanga, Tshombe tried to reject the Kitona agreement, claiming that it was subject to ratification by the full Katanga Parliament. On February 15, however, the Katanga Assembly approved the end of secession.[88]

The only remaining threat stemmed from Gizenga in Stanleyville. Under U Thant, with an extended mandate to prevent civil war, the UN was only too

---

86. Arthur Lee Burns and Nina Heathcote, 27.
87. Ibid., 152.
88. Ibid., 147.

happy by now to assist with removing Gizenga. Although the UN's participation did not extend to fighting, it helped to disarm Gizenga's rebels and to guard the government's prisoners, including Gizenga himself.[89] This was the first joint operation that the UN performed with the central government, and it far exceeded the ideal of absolute neutrality that had been espoused by Hammarskjöld. Gizenga was later imprisoned on an island at the mouth of the Congo River.

By then, U Thant had lost all patience with Tshombe. Watching him back away from his agreement, Thant came up with a new plan to force Tshombe's capitulation. He sent his plan to Adoula and Tshombe in August, calling for the creation of a federated state and for the reintegration of Katanga with the rest of the Congo. Tshombe was given a November 15 deadline and was threatened with a boycott of Katanga's mineral exports or UN military intervention. At the same time, U Thant had asked the Philippines, Greece, Italy, Pakistan, and Sweden to provide the UN with jet fighters.[90] The Philippines and Sweden agreed to do so. The deadline passed and nothing happened.

On December 24, UN troops were fired upon in Elisabethville. The UN, at first did little. Finally, on 28 December, Operation Grand Slam was launched to secure key points in the city and again restore freedom of movement.[91] By December 30, all the objectives of phase one had been achieved. Phase two involved advances against Jadotville and Kolwezi, the last Katangese strongholds. Unbeknownst to the UN commanders, U Thant had promised the British and the Belgians that no advance would be made on Jadotville lest it prompt Tshombe's gendarmes to attack mineral production. However, in the end the UN took Jadotville with almost no resistance. There was no retaliation on the part of Tshombe, for he had fled to Kolwezi with all of his remaining forces. Rather than suffer complete defeat, he allowed the peaceful entry of the UN into Kolwezi on January 21, 1993.[92]

Hence, the secession of Katanga was ended. The central Congolese government sent former prime minister Joseph Ileo to be the resident minister in Katanga and General Mobutu was also sent to supervise the integration of the

---

89. Ibid., 155.
90. Ibid., 195.
91. Thomas R. Mockaitis, 36.
92. Ibid., 38.

Katangan gendarmerie into the ANC.[93] But at least 10,000 of the gendarmerie disappeared into the bush with their weapons, refusing reintegration.[94]

A new threat then arose for the Adoula government in the form of the Comité Nationale de Libération (CNL or National Liberation Committee). This group included parts of the Gizenga and Lumumba factions which had organized in French Brazzaville. Upon his return to the Congo in 1963, Pierre Mulele, former minister of education in the Lumumba government, began organizing the opposition to Adoula in his home province of Kwilu.[95] Unable to deal put down the movement, Adoula resigned shortly after the withdrawal of UN forces in 1964. He was replaced by none other than Moise Tshombe, the former president of the Katanga province.

In September 1964, the rebels, under the leadership of Christophe Gbenye, a major Lumumba supporter, had succeeded in taking Stanleyville. There, many thousands of Congolese were killed simply because they were educated. With the ANC still largely ineffective, Tshombe called in his former Katanga gendarmes and recruited mercenaries to lead them against the rebels. The rebels responded by taking several hundred hostages to use as human shields. This resulted in the joint US-Belgium rescue mission, which was code-named Dragon Rouge. They evacuated about 2,000 Europeans within the space of just five days. The town was by then retaken but not before nearly 300 hostages had been killed.

Although Tshombe had acted to save Stanleyville, Kasavubu dismissed him on October 13, 1965. This then left a political vacuum which General Mobutu would fill for three unbearable decades of abominably selfish rule.

THE QUESTION OF TRUSTEESHIP

But why did the UN not stay in the Congo? Thomas Mockaitis provides part of the answer:

> If the UN were to be faulted for anything, it would have to be its failure to stay in the Congo long enough. The real work of nation building had to take place in the years (not months) following the end of Katanga's secession. Given how poorly the

---

93. Ernest W. Lefever, *Crisis in the Congo: A United Nations Force in Action,* 111.

94. Ibid., 104.

95. Winsome J. Leslie, *Zaire: Continuity and Political Change in an Oppressive State* (Boulder, CO: Westview Press, 1993) 24.

Belgians had prepared their former colony for independence, this development could have occurred only with outside help. Support for a continued mission, however, had disappeared by 1963. Like any organization, the UN may have been greater than the sum of its parts, but only slightly greater. For the major players in the Security Council ONUC had outlived its usefulness. The Soviets had failed to gain a foothold in Central Africa, Western commercial interests had been secured, and a pro-Western government ruled in Leopoldville. To make matters worse, the UN had gone deeply in debt to finance ONUC, and its members remained bitterly divided over the outcome. The organization was in no position to continue the mission. If the Western powers emerged as the winners in the Congo crisis, then the real losers were the people of the country themselves.[96]

In sum, the Congo operation was not designed for nation building. Its overtly stated purpose was to provide the military and technical assistance to assist the Congolese in pacifying the country without intervening in the Congo's internal affairs. Belgium, which could have provided the necessary personnel to train the Congolese in administering the country, was to be ousted altogether. While it is true that the United States was instrumental in the assassination of Lumumba and in the military coup by Mobutu, and had taken steps to alter the government of the country, the United States did not involve itself directly. Instead, it shouldered the majority of the cost of the UN operation and was content with the outcome of the revolts that occurred between 1964 and 1965, when the UN left the country, as this led to Mobutu's second rise to power. In the final analysis, the Western powers were satisfied because the Soviet Union was prevented from gaining a toehold in the country and the Congo's great mineral wealth remained available for Western access.

Joseph P. Lash provides another side of the picture. He writes:

> Even if Hammarskjöld had wanted it, he could not have obtained authorization for an "enforced" political solution, divided as the Assembly and Council were between partisans of different Congolese factions. And Hammarskjöld did not favor such powers. "I reject everything that would have a touch of control or direction of the Congo's internal affairs," he said. He had noted with some surprise, in view of Africa's jealous concern for its newly gained sovereignty, the proposals in this direction "from highly authoritative African sources." He did not believe that "the use of military initiatives, or pressure, is the way to bring about the political structure, in terms of persons and institutions, which at present is the first need of the Congo." Hammarskjöld was no doubt right in insisting on nonintervention. The smaller states in the UN would quickly take fright if it became an instrument for imposed solutions, especially in matters relating to their domestic affairs.[97]

---

96. Thomas R. Mockaitis, 39.
97. Joseph P. Lash, 261.

Thus, the final reason that the UN did not make the Congo a protectorate or trusteeship was because such a move would have met with resistance by other newly independent African states who were fearful of anything that might represent a precedent that could threaten their sovereignty. This was in addition to the Soviet bloc, which would have viewed such circumstances as a return to colonialism. Indeed, the Soviet Union accused the UN of having such an objective and demanded that it withdraw entirely as early as 1961.

Sadly, the Congo had endured centuries of slavery and decades of King Leopold's genocidal policies before it was birthed as a new nation in a welter of confusion and fratricidal violence. And in the years to come, under Mobutu, it would know only hunger and deprivation. This was the legacy that the developed world bestowed on the country by failing to fill the void that the Belgians had left behind, a situation that persists today.

CHAPTER 3. MOBUTU RETURNS TO POWER

Mobutu's second rise to power came on the heels of the dismissal of Prime Minister Tshombe by President Kasavubu. Although Tshombe organized a new party (CONACO) and won a total of 122 out of 167 parliamentary seats in the March 1965 elections, Kasavubu had chosen to designate Evariste Kimba to be prime minister in his stead. The Tshombe coalition then managed to block Kimba's investiture, after which Kasavuabu reaffirmed his appointment.[98]

At a meeting of the ANC high command of November 24, Mobutu decided to break the deadlock once again by assuming control of the country in another military coup.[99] The following day, it was simply announced that Kasavubu and Kimba had been replaced. Colonel Leonard Mulamba was the new prime minister, and Mobutu himself would rule as president for an emergency five-year term.[100] Speaking not only of the political rivalry between Tshombe and Kasavubu but also of the fractious state of the country, Mobutu said that he had acted "to save the nation, to put an end to chaos and anarchy."[101]

Despite this show of strength, the country was still subject to attack from without and within. There remained small pockets of insurgency in the northeast of the country and there was a mutiny in Kisangani in mid-1966. The latter threat came from a group of 600 to 800 gendarmes who had previously been loyal to Tshombe during the secession of Katanga. Having been unsuccess-

---

98. Eds. Sandra W. Meditz and Tim Merrill, 43.
99. Ibid.
100. Ibid., 44.
101. Ernest W. Lefever, *Army, Police, and Politics in Tropical Africa*, 114.

fully reintegrated into the ANC, the gendarmes mutinied and seized Kisangani on July 23, 1996.[102] This problem was resolved through negotiations by Prime Minister Mulamba and a military action in which the ANC soldiers were led by mercenaries.

A third threat then came from a mini rebellion that was led by Major Jean Schramme, a Belgian mercenary who had formerly served Mobutu and Tshombe. Apparently acting on his own rather than on behalf of a specified movement, Schramme took over Kisangani and Bukavu on July 5, 1967 with the help of 150 mercenaries and some 900 Katangan troops. Although he soon abandoned Kisangani, Schramme maintained a firm hold on Bukavu and could not be dislodged by Mobutu's ANC without outside help. In this case, the United States acted to save Mobutu with logistical support in the form of three Air Force C-130 transport planes.[103] By November 4, an agreement was negotiated by the Red Cross for the safe conduct of Schramme and his followers into the country of Rwanda, and the rebellion came to an end.[104]

Since nearly 900 ANC soldiers and their families chose to flee the country, Mobutu decided to extend a general amnesty relating to them and any of the expatriates who had left earlier, as well. Many of the Katangan gendarmes did return and Mobutu honored his promise. However, not in the case of Pierre Mulele, the leader of the 1964 Kwilu rebellion, who had been lured to return from exile in Congo-Brazzaville. Of him, Mobutu chose to make a brutal example. Mulele was publicly executed, with his eyes torn from their sockets, his genitals ripped off, and his limbs amputated. [105]

But he should have been forewarned. Just a few months before Mulele's return, Mobutu had also executed four former cabinet ministers. These were publicly hanged for what was known as the "Pentecost Plot."[106] One of the men was Evariste Kimba, whom Kasavubu had briefly appointed as prime minister in 1965. Mobutu was sending a clear signal that resistance to his regime would not be tolerated. It set the tone for his relations with the populace for many years to come; but first there would be two more invasions, this time stemming from

---

102. Ibid., 120.
103. Ibid.
104. Ibid., 121.
105. Michaela Wrong, *Living on the Brink of Disaster in Mobutu's Congo: In the Footsteps of Mr. Kurtz* (Perennial: New York, 2002) 90.
106. Winsome J. Leslie, 32.

Angola and Zambia, where a good number of the Katangan gendarmes who had participated in the 1965 rebellion had gone following their transport to Rwanda.

By then, Katanga had been renamed and was now called Shaba. Likewise, the ANC was now called the FAZ, or Forces Armées Zairoises. In what is known as the first Shaba invasion, members of the FLNC or Front for the National Liberation of the Congo invaded from bases in Angola on March 8, 1977. [107] Meeting no resistance from Mobutu's FAZ, they took the towns of Dilolo, Kisenge, and Kapanga, and were advancing toward the mining center of Kolwezi by mid-April. [108] There, they were defeated by Moroccan troops with logistical support from France, after which they retreated to Angola.

The second Shaba invasion, in 1979, was almost a replay of the first. This time, the rebel FLNC moved in from Zambia and actually took Kolwezi. Hundreds of Europeans were killed before the FLNC was defeated by French and Belgian paratoopers with American logistical support. [109] They were later replaced with an inter-African peacekeeping force of 1,000 Moroccan troops and other troops from French-speaking Africa in order to protect the region. The FAZ performed so badly that the residents of Kolwezi refused to continue to work unless they were provided with foreign protection. As a result of the second Shaba invasion, the peacekeeping force remained deployed in Kolwezi until 1979.[110]

THE CENTRALIZATION OF POWER

Recognizing that he faced threats not only from internal and external insurgents but also from the many political factions that were in existence since independence, Mobutu decided to dispense with the divisive form of government that Belgium had bequeathed to the country. On March 7, 1966, he endowed himself with legislative powers, thereafter ruling by decree and also effectively neutralizing the Chamber of Deputies and the Senate.[111] He became the head of the Army, head of state, and head of the central government, and even replaced Malumba as prime minister on December 17, 1966.[112] Following this, he

---

107. Ibid. 44.
108. Eds. Sandra W. Meditz and Tim Merrill, 57.
109. Ibid.
110. Winsome J. Leslie, 44.
111. Ibid., 32.

promulgated a new constitution on March 22, 1967, which called for a presidential system that envisioned a unicameral parliament, no more than two political parties, an independent judiciary, and provincial governors whose task would be to represent the central government.[113] The president was to be solely responsible for the appointment and dismissal of all cabinet members, the provincial governors, and all judges. The constitution also called for compulsory military service. It was submitted to ratification by a popular referendum in June 1967 and was reportedly approved by 98 percent of the population.[114]

In tandem with the release of his new constitution, Mobutu organized his Mouvement Populaire de la Revolution (MPR), which, despite the provision in the constitution that allowed for a two-party system, would be the country's sole political organization. Its specified aim was to pursue "a middle road between capitalism and communism" at home and "positive neutralism" abroad.[115] The precursor to the MPR had been the Corps des Volontaires de la République (Volunteer Corps of the Republic, or CVR) which had been formed in 1966. Mobutu absorbed the CVR at the same time that he declared all other parties illegal.[116]

In October 1967, party and administrative responsibilities were literally fused together, thereby extending the role of the party to all administrative organs as well as trade unions, youth movements, and student organizations. Further control measures included the creation of the Youth of the Popular Revolutionary Movement (JMPR), which established a link between the government and the student population, and the creation of the National Union of Zairian Workers (UNTZA), which merged existing trade unions. In both cases, the role of these bodies was changed from a potential source of confrontation to an "organ of support for government policy."[117] The MPR even extended its control to women's organizations, and also emasculated the churches in December 1971. From then on, the state only recognized the Church of Christ in Zaire, the Kimbanguist Church, and the Roman Catholic Church. Eventually, Mobutu nationalized the universities of Kinshasa and Kisangani, prohibited the use of Christian names, and mandated the establishment of JMPR sections in all

---

112. Ernest W. Lefever, *Army, Police, and Politics in Tropical Africa*, 117.
113. Ibid., 116.
114. Eds. Sandra W. Meditz and Tim Merrill, 48.
115. Ernest W. Lefever, *Army, Police, and Politics in Tropical Africa*, 116.
116. Winsome J. Leslie, 33.
117. Eds. Sandra W. Meditz and Tim Merrill, 51.

seminaries. This brought the state into conflict with the Roman Catholic Church, a situation that was only to be exacerbated as the coming years would show.[118]

Despite the formation of the JMPR, there were clashes between the government and university students in 1969. Protesting their low living allowance, rising prices, and what they considered to be extravagant government spending, the students marched from Lovanium University into the capital city of Kinshasa (Leopoldville). Reportedly, they broke through two police barricades before they were stopped in a violent clash with the Army. Five hundred students were arrested and the rest were confined to campus. Those who had been arrested were all later released with the exception of 34 students who were charged with activities against the security of the state. Before their trials, a number of the students fled to Bulgaria, whereas those who remained were sentenced to prison for as long as 20 years. These were later given amnesty on the occasion of Mobutu's thirty-ninth birthday.[119] There was, however, one further incident involving student demonstrations. On June 4, 1971, students paraded in memory of the victims of 1969, causing the Army to close the school. When sympathy demonstrations were held at Lumbumbahsi, most of the students were forced into the Army for a minimum two-year period.[120]

In May 1970 the MPR had held its first extraordinary congress and chose Mobutu as the sole candidate for the presidential elections. Mobutu was elected to serve for another seven years by a vote of 10,131,699 to 157.[121] By then, Mobutu dissolved the parliament, abolished the independent judiciary, and made provincial offices purely administrative.[122] In short, the system was so structured that nothing was allowed to operate independent of Mobutu.

As Mondonga M. Makoli states:

> By its very nature, ideology, and structure, the MPR is not only an authoritarian party-state, but it is also the condensation of what Arthur Lewis called a "totalitarian" party because of its claim to be the supreme instrument of society. The state in Zaire is, as Callaghy underscores, an authoritarian system which emphasizes the centralization of power, the flow of decisions from the top down rather than of

---

118. Ibid.

119. Margarita Dobert, "Zaire: Chapter 2A. Government and Politics," *Countries of the World*, January 1, 1991, www.highbeam.com.

120. Ibid.

121. Ibid.

122. Mondonga M. Mokoli, *State Against Development: The Experience of Post-1965 Zaire* (Westport, CT: Greenwood Press, 1992) 26.

demands from the bottom up, deference to authority, limited pluralism, and the use of violent repression when other methods of cooptation and control fail [123]

In order to ensure that provincial officers could not build up localized ethnic power bases, Mobutu directed that officials should be appointed to non-native regions, and frequently reshuffled their positions.[124] The twenty-one provincettes, which were created post-independence in order to give more people a stake in participative government, were reduced to a total of twelve provinces under Mobutu and then eight, plus the capital. These were redesignated as regions in 1972, with their functions becoming purely administrative. [125]

Because of the Shaba invasions, Mobutu announced in July 1977 that he would democratize the system. He would appoint a first commissioner of state with whom to share presidential powers. The commissioner would then appoint the members of the Executive Council. Members of the Legislative Council would no longer be nominated by the Political Bureau but directly by the people. Of the 30 members of the Political Bureau, only 12 would be nominated by the president. People were actually encouraged to run against Mobutu in the elections of November. However, "Mobutu was in fact the only candidate and he was duly elected by the 4,000 delegates to the second extraordinary congress of the MPR for another 7 years."[126]

THE AUTHENTICITY PROGRAM

Quite early in his rule, Mobutu adopted an "authenticity Program," whose main components were the traditionalization of the people and the lands of the Congo. Mobutu, as noted above, had forced the people to adopt new non-Christian names based on African tradition, and the republic was renamed Zaire in 1971. Names of important towns and cities had been changed (such as Katanga and Leopoldville, which became Shaba and Kinshasa, respectively), and the people were even forced to adopt a different mode of dress. Wearing a collarless jacket called the abacost that reflected the style of Chairman Mao, Mobutu outlawed the traditional suits and business dress of the West.[127] The ideology of

---

123. Ibid., 29.
124. Ibid., 27.
125. Eds. Sandra W. Meditz and Tim Merrill, 47.
126. Margarita Dobert.
127. Eds. Sandra W. Meditz and Tim Merrill, 50.

authenticity was presented as an attempt to "recapture the spirit of Zaire" by destroying the most obvious vestiges of the hated colonial period.[128] Mobutu himself took the name of Mobutu Sese Seko Kuku Ngbendu Wa Za Banga, which means "the all-powerful warrior who, because of his endurance and inflexible will to win, will go from conquest to conquest leaving fire in his wake." [129]

Artificial as it may have seemed, the much-touted authenticity program had far reaching goals. Tukumbi Lumumba-Kasongo has summarized its political and economic objectives as follows:

> To increase agricultural and industrial production so that the country would be self-sufficient; to advance the politics of large-scale projects; to improve conditions for individual well-being; to unite the Zaïrean people; and to promote democratic liberties, and exalt national intellectual and cultural values with respect to promoting the effective freedom of Congolese women and youth.[130]

In the first place, authenticity meant that the government was focusing on production to make the country self-sufficient. Given that the economy of Zaire was structured around the export of raw materials such as copper, cobalt, industrial diamonds, uranium, rubber, timber, coffee, palm products, cocoa, and tea, the new regime presumably focused on improving surplus conditions both for domestic consumption and exports. In January 1967, the Belgian-owned Upper Katanga Mining Union (UMHK) was nationalized, thus producing tensions between Zaire and Belgium; this was followed by the formation of a new state-owned company, the Générale Congolaise des Minerais, or GECOMINES.

Between the end of the 1960s and the early 1970s, the economic boom in copper alone accounted for a full one half of government revenues, to such an extent that it created a misleading impression. The country was suddenly expected to enjoy great prosperity and to achieve self-sufficiency without any money being expended to promote better conditions. In particular, the state invested very little money in agriculture, despite the fact that the country had received development loans from the IMF and World Bank. When the copper market sank to a near-depression level in 1974, Mobutu and his elites would simply plunder the loans to the country; in effect, their practices turned out to be as extractive and nonproductive as had been those of the Belgians before them.

---

128. Winsome J. Leslie, 33.
129. Ibid., 34.
130. Tukumbi Lumumba-Kasongo, 93.

In the second place, "authenticity" also addressed the school system in furtherance of Mobutu's aim to indoctrinate the people. The students were henceforth to receive a civic and political education that was based on the Manifeste de la N'sele (Manifesto of N'sele) instead of the Christian religion. Because Christianity was perceived as a representative of colonialism par excellence, it was attacked with vehemence.[131]

By late 1972, the "regime had banned all religious radio and television broadcasts and prohibited the activities of all religious youth movements in order to further strengthen the impact of the MPR ideology. A ban on the printing, sale, and distribution of thirty-one religious publications followed. Further, all religious groups were required to publish detailed information on their membership. Things came to a climax at the end of 1974 when all religious school networks were nationalized and the government declared that Christmas would no longer be a public holiday."[132] Diplomatic relations with the Vatican were broken in 1972.

Finally, Mobutu called for a "reexamination of the school's monopoly on education, advocating even a 'de-schooled' society." The main objectives of his educational reform have been recorded by Galen Hull:

> To achieve universal basic education of six years by 1980; to increase the professional emphasis of secondary and higher education so that they can provide the nation with trained personnel necessary for development; to act so that the school is no longer the sole means of advancement in society; to establish the government's control over the entire education system, including schools run by churches, replacing religious instruction with political and civic education and; to introduce a year of mandatory national service before entrance to the university.[133]

In addition to mandatory national service, Mobutu also instituted a policy of obligatory civil work that was known as the Salongo. Being, in effect, a system of forced labor, the Salongo called on the Zairean people to perform collective work in a way that was ironically reminiscent of the earlier colonial system.[134] Not surprisingly, people reacted to the system with bitterness and resistance. They did only so much work as they could legally get away with, and the work that they did perform was often not held to standards.

---

131. Ibid., 95.
132. Winsome J. Leslie, 51.
133. Tukumbi Lumumba-Kasongo, 98.
134. Eds. Sandra W. Meditz and Tim Merrill, 53.

ZAIRIANIZATION

Amidst rising mineral prices in 1973, Mobutu announced a new program that was geared toward transferring the national wealth from foreign ownership to the hands of the Zairian people. By presidential decree, most foreign-owned companies were expropriated, including 2,000 small businesses, plantations, farms, and fisheries.[135] Transfer of these holdings to the Zairians was determined on the basis of their membership and standing within the MPR. Mobutu awarded ownership to those whose loyalty he wanted to buy and was also quite generous with members of his own ethnic group, which was based in Equateur Province, in the east. The principal objective behind Zairianization was to enlarge the size of the middle class but its effect in practice was to enrich those who were in influential political positions rather than redistributing national wealth to the general populace.

Speaking in 1973, Mobutu proclaimed that his desire to transfer foreign holdings to the hands of the Zairean people was motivated because "Zaire is the country that has been the most heavily exploited in the world. That is why farms, ranches, plantations, concessions, commerce, and real estate agencies will be turned over to sons of the country." As Sandra Meditz and Tim Merrill note, "At first, 'the sons of the country' consisted essentially of high-ranking party members and government officials, in all approximately 300 people. Major plantations and ranches and large commercial enterprises were allocated to the top political elite. Smaller enterprises were allocated to local notables. Army officers, judges, members of the regional administration, and ambassadors failed to qualify as potential recipients."[136]

Dissent over who got what and on the basis of what conditions eventually prompted Mobutu to announce that all enterprises would henceforth be sold through the state. But, as before, it emerged that the new owners would be those with top political positions, as these people had access to sources of wealth and privilege that common people lacked. It also resulted in mayhem, as those who acquired properties and business enterprises were unskilled in management and business relations. They often sold off their assets or bankrupted their businesses, such that major shortages and layoffs resulted.[137] The plantation sector

---

135. Tukumbi Lumumba-Kasongo, 96.
136. Eds. Sandra W. Meditz and Tim Merrill, 53.
137. Mondonga M. Mokoli, 30.

was brought to a standstill and Mobutu was forced to change his policy of Zairi-anization by 1974.

On December 30, 1974, shortly after his return from the People's Republic of China and the Democratic People's Republic of Korea, Mobutu announced a "ten-point radicalization program intended to bring about a revolution in the revolution."[138] "Party leaders were expected to turn their properties over to the state and devote themselves to agricultural activities. [They] were chastised for their mercenary behavior and lack of civic sense. More importantly, the large-scale Belgian-owned corporations that had been left untouched by the Zairian-ization decrees were now targeted for nationalization."[139] Simultaneously, however, Mobutu announced that there would be a partial retrocession, allowing for up to 40 percent of ownership to be returned to foreign hands, excepting those industries which were considered vital to the state such as energy, timber, and large-scale transportation.[140] In time, foreign owners were allowed to regain as much as 60 percent equity, due to the disastrous impact that possession by the country's local plunderers had had on the Zairian economy.[141]

MOBUTU'S FOREIGN POLICY

As discussed in Chapter 2, Mobutu had been less than friendly to the Communists, having demanded the expulsion of the Soviet envoys soon after he had taken power the first time. His suspicion of them would continue until 1968, when he reestablished formal diplomatic relations with Moscow.[142] However, Mobutu's overall relations would be most firmly centered on the West.

Between 1960 and 1969, approximately 100 Congolese military personnel were trained in the United States. The US also provided $198.5 million in mil-itary assistance to Congo-Zaire during the space of this time. (This includes the $170.7 million that the US had contributed to the UN operation between 1960 and 1964.[143]) In addition, Mobutu received support from the CIA. As noted earlier, the CIA provided over $1 million in funds to ensure the loyalty of the

---

138. Eds. Sandra W. Meditz and Tim Merrill, 54.
139. Ibid.
140. Tukumbi Lumumba-Kasongo, 97.
141. Eds. Sandra W. Meditz and Tim Merrill, 55.
142. Ernest W. Lefever, *Army, Police, and Politics in Tropical Africa*, 118.
143. Ibid., 124.

Army to the Kasavubu faction, which Mobutu had then recognized as the nominal head of state. But in the years that followed, Mobutu himself received as much as an additional $25 million through the CIA to ensure his loyalty to the West.[144] He also pocketed at least $1.4 million that was channeled through his hands for support of the anti-Communist Angolan rebels.[145] Further, the CIA provided technical assistance for the presidential bodyguard and the security apparatus. And, finally, throughout the three decades of his rule, the US is said to have provided Mobutu with upwards of $2 billion in foreign assistance.[146] In exchange, Mobutu provided the US with a secure base at Shaba from which to conduct operations that were aimed at bringing down the Communist government in Angola. Mobutu himself was also active in Angola, hoping to see that his relative Roberto Holden was installed in the government at Luanda.

The Mobutu regime also relied heavily on Western creditor institutions. Although the price of copper exports in 1967 was such that Mobutu did not need Western aid, the situation changed by 1975. Then, the fall in copper prices caused the government's foreign debt to escalate to an outstanding $887 million, forcing Mobutu to turn to the International Monetary Fund.[147] By 1982, the situation worsened still further, so that Zaire was on the verge of default. He was then offered a stringent package of IMF economic austerity measures. Although IMF funds were forthcoming, the failure of copper prices and the absence of increased bilateral foreign aid impelled Mobutu to limit debt repayment to 20 percent of the national budget by 1986.[148] Yet, the IMF and the World Bank still continued to deal with Mobutu, given Western support for his regime in view of his anti-Communist leanings. This was despite the fact that Mobutu's personal use of loans and aid, together with theft by government ministers, was predominantly responsible for the increased severity of the debt crisis.

---

144. Mark Hubbard, *The Skull beneath the Skin: Africa after the Cold War* (Boulder, CO: Westview Press, 2001) 12.
145. Ibid., 19.
146. Bill Berkeley, 116.
147. Mark Hubbard, 18.
148. Ibid.

THE FATHER OF KLEPTOCRACY

Mobutu was born on October 14, 1930, in the central town of Lisala, as a member of the Ngbandi tribe.[149] As one of his ruling myths of legend, he promoted a story about his youth which describes him as having slain a leopard at the urging of his grandfather, who had cautioned him not to be afraid. "From that day on," Mobutu noted, "I am afraid of nothing."[150] Although he claimed to be devoutly Catholic, due to his parish schooling, he was also highly dependent on African marabouts or witch-doctors.[151] During his thirty-two years in office, he was further said to be most dependent on and magnanimous toward his own ethnic group, which hailed from the province of Equateur. He selected most of his security personnel from the region, surrounding himself with only native Lingala speakers, and he chose Lingala as the language of national discourse.[152] The people of Equateur were also recipients of Mobutu's largesse, becoming land-holders and business owners during the period of Zairianization in a way that was markedly disproportionate to the favors he bestowed on others.

Fashioning his image as that of the supreme African chief, Mobutu wished to be seen as the leader who was chosen by God to lead the Zairian people. His most preferred titles were the "Father of the nation, the Guide, the Messiah, the Helmsman, the Leopard, the Sun-President, and even (because of his excessive philandering) the Cock who Jumps on Anything That Moves."[153] Given his inflated opinion of himself, Mobutu felt not only that he had the right to rule by decree and to control all aspects of life, but also that he should be entitled to a standard of living that has been matched by few other despots. His standing placed him in a position where he was able to literally bilk the country and foreign aid as well.

Winsome J. Leslie provides a summary account of Mobutu's early thieving as follows:

> Throughout the 1970s...as much as 20 percent of the government's operating budget went directly to the office of the president without any financial control. A 1988 study of Zaire's 1986 budget still revealed amounts going to the office of the president representing six times the budgetary appropriations allotted for that purpose, while the funding of crucial areas such as education and health was virtually

---

149. Michaela Wrong, 70.
150. Ibid., 71.
151. Ibid., 72.
152. Mark Hubbard, 223.
153. Bill Berkeley, 109.

ignored. Copper, cobalt, and diamonds from Zairian mines and lucrative agricultural products such as coffee have consistently been sold abroad illegally in secret deals, costing Zaire millions of dollars in foreign exchange earnings. In one such interesting development leaked to the press in 1989, $300 million to $400 million in foreign exchange receipts largely from the state mining company GECOMINES could not be accounted for by International Monetary Fund (IMF) and World Bank officials. Even development aid funds, including the agricultural products under the US PL 480 program, channeled through government institutions have been stolen by prominent government officials.[154]

Mobutu also tended to treat the Zairian central bank as his personal cash reserve. He and his family withdrew a total of $71 million in 1977, three years after the collapse of the price of copper and the beginning of the country's decline. When he was not handing out properties and offices, it was his custom to deal in cash, which was dealt out to his extensive patronage network, Mobutu's small, close-knit family, and the 10,000-strong Presidential Guard.[155] Mobutu also used his stolen funds to pay for the allegiance of Western politicians, including a former Belgian prime minister.

In a report that was completed by IMF officials in 1982 under the leadership of Erwin Blumenthal, Blumenthal stated that the mismanagement and theft was such that there was "no, I repeat no, chance on the horizon for Zaire's numerous creditors to get their money back.... Mobutu and his government show no concern about the question of paying off loans and the public debt.... [There] was, and there still is, one sole obstacle that negates all prospect: the corruption of the team in power."[156] Blumenthal had also identified seven special bank accounts in Brussels, Paris, Geneva, London, and New York into which money was being channeled.

Nevertheless, IMF figures show that Zaire continued to receive funds during the period when Blumenthal's report was being compiled and long after it was released. Zaire received $231 million between 1967 and 1982. This was in addition to bilateral aid that Zaire received from the West. In large part, the investment in Zaire was justified (despite the blatant and abysmal poverty in which most of the people lived while Mobutu was in power) by the force of the Communist threat. And, the other half of the coin was that no one wanted to see Zaire dissolve, as it had in the first half of the 1960s, in fratricidal strife. Mobutu was viewed as the only man who could hold the country together.

---

154. Winsome J. Leslie, 36.
155. Mark Huband, 18.
156. Ibid., 19.

In the meantime, Mobutu's graft continued, in clear view of all observers. In 1978, GECOMINES, the state-owned copper and cobalt conglomeration, was instructed to deposit its entire export earnings, which approached $1.2 billion, into an extrabudgetary presidential account. Budgetary appropriations for the president that were granted by Zaire's parliament continued to account for 30-50 percent of capital investment from the late 1960s, reaching $65 million a year in 1988. In a World Bank report that covered the period of 1980-1987, it was revealed that the presidency spent $94 million and the political institutions $172 million within the space of a given year. When even that was not enough, the government simply appropriated more money under the all-encompassing category of "other goods and services."[157]

This example of thievery from the top down encouraged people under Mobutu to steal as well. As Sandra Meditz and Tim Merrill note:

> A survey of government personnel in Lumbumbashi in 1982 documented the variety of means by which state employees supplemented their irregular and inadequate salaries. Embezzlement including direct payroll theft, payoffs, forgeries of official signatures and seals, sale of false documents of certification, illegal taxation, second jobs, and foodstuff production and sale. Other analysts have added false bills and profit-margin cheating on the allowed rate of profit for business; import, export, and excise stamp fraud; sale of merchandise quotas; postal and judicial fraud and extortion at military barricades. Bribery too is commonplace.[158]

Another author adds:

> Government service is also seen as the primary vehicle for entering business. Political influence allows one to negotiate bureaucratic red tape, obtain seed money, and gain access to contracts—often through bribes. The system has spawned the development of a "political aristocracy," an elite that contributes nothing to the productive process of the state but exists to maximize its own wealth. Systematic corruption originates with Mobutu and his clique, but it permeates the entire society through patron-client networks. Since the 1970s this situation has been aggravated by economic crisis. Economic scarcity and uncertainty have encouraged personal enrichment by those in positions of power at the expense of the majority. Kleptocracy in Zaire is viewed by some as a pyramidal system based on patrimonial redistribution. The process begins with the relatively small presidential clan linked to Mobutu through familial or personal ties.[159]

The complete and utter recklessness with which people enriched themselves under Mobutu was acknowledged by the ruler himself in a speech that he gave in 1977. He then advised his countrymen that they should "steal just a little,"

---

157. Ibid., 21.
158. Eds. Sandra W. Meditz and Tim Merrill, 106.
159. Ibid.

or perhaps "steal wisely and that they should invest the proceeds in the country rather than stowing it abroad." [160] But, as many authors show, it was the uncertainty of Mobutu's system that encouraged politicians and officeholders to plunder and steal as they did. With Mobutu's constant reshuffling of his cabinet and all-too-frequent dismissals, it was unclear how long any of them would be allowed access to sources of wealth. "It is this uncertainty coupled with the relative scarcity of economic resources, particularly foreign exchange, that results in corruption and 'grabbing.'"[161]

As we shall see in the following chapter, stealing and extortion were by no means limited to Mobutu and his ministers. It was also a way of life for the police at all levels who preyed on the Zairian populace in a reign of terror and extraction. Being paid in money that was virtually worthless, due to outrageous rates of inflation, if, in fact, they were paid at all, the police, the Army, and the JMPR (Youth Brigade) were to become the bane of Zaire's existence, issuing false fines and making arbitrary arrests, even as they terrorized the population with beatings, imprisonment without charge, and also outright murder.

---

160. Ibid.
161. Winsome J. Leslie, 35.

CHAPTER 4. TERROR AND DISSENT

If the rule of Mobutu is best known for his patron-client networks and the degree to which he bilked the country in order to support his regime, it is also well known for the outright rule of terror that he imposed on the Zairian people. One of the president's first priorities when he took power in 1965 was to centralize the police forces that had been organized by the Belgians. In existence at the time were the ANC (the Army), the Surete (the Intelligence Services), and the local and regional police. Mobutu nationalized these forces in 1966 and initially placed them under the direction of the Interior Ministry. By 1970, he had set the number of police at a total of 20,000 and stated that their purpose was to perform all ordinary police functions including the "prevention and detection of crime, the apprehension and prosecution of offenders, the maintenance of public order, and the protection of citizens and property." [162]

But in 1972, Mobutu created the Gendarmerie Nationale (National Police Force), which militarized the police force and removed local accountability.[163] Since all police would henceforth report to the military, local officials could no longer call on them directly but instead had to place their requests through a burdensome chain of command. This meant that the police seldom responded to calls, such that the local officials increasingly relied on the CADER, which was the security arm of the JMPR, Mobutu's established youth movement.[164]

---

162. Lawyers Committee for Human Rights, *Zaire: Repression as Policy: A Human Rights Report* (New York: Lawyers Committee for Human Rights, 1990) 42.
163. Ibid.

The CADER was primarily created to carry out the security functions of the JMPR, whose tasks in the 1970s were to monitor political matters relating to Zairian youth, to replace religious youth movements, and to oversee schools with particular sensitivity to gathering political information for government security forces. Its influence was pervasive, but it was staffed by incompetent and untrained youths. As the economic situation in Zaire worsened, it was not uncommon to hear of theft, arbitrary arrest, and extortion taking place during patrols. The youths were also responsible for uncovering financial irregularities in the administrations of local officials, so that there were dual grounds for suspicion by local administrators. Due to the predatory status that the CADER developed, it was dissolved in later years, only to reemerge as the Corps des Activistes pour la défense de la Révolution, which showed the same tendencies and abuses.[165]

Mobutu, however, relied on the CADER, especially in times of his absence from the country. Recognizing that coups most commonly occur when a leader is away from command, Mobutu insisted that the CADER patrol every night and maintain a high and constant state of alert.[166]

In all, Mobutu's main preoccupation can be seen not in the prevention of crime but in the development of the intelligence and security services as they evolved over time. The Surete, for example, was renamed the CND during the 1970s. The CND was characterized as being highly effective in ensuring that no one gathered enough political support to ever challenge Mobutu. CND agents were especially active in the exile groups, making sure that any contacts with such people were immediately reported to the presidential palace.[167] Since CND agents were attached directly to the presidency and could only be prosecuted with the consent of the political police, their independence from the law and judiciary was obvious. Although the local authorities tried in the 1970s to find a way to bring the CND under their control by creating CND committees, CND members continued to elude the control of the party.[168]

---

164. Eugene K. Keefe, "Zaire: Chapter 5C. The Police System," *Countries of the World*, January 1, 1991, www.highbeam.com.
165. Winsome J. Leslie, 49.
166. Michael G. Schatzberg,*The Dialectics of Oppression in Zaire* (Indianapolis, IN: Indiana University Press, 1988) 32.
167. Eugene K. Keefe.
168. Michael G. Schatzberg, 39.

The CND was dissolved in 1980, to reemerge as two separate wings: the CNRI (National Center for Research and Information) and the SNI (National Intelligence Service). By 1982, these two branches were merged to form what was called the AND, the nation's principal security force. The main tasks of the AND were collecting and interpreting information relevant to state security and "investigation and determination of violations of state security, and surveillance of people suspected of exercising activities of a nature that may threaten the security of the state."[169]

Operating through a countrywide network of informers, the AND was often seen as the most coercive arm of the state. Reports by Amnesty International and the Lawyers Committee for Human Rights documented such phenomena as arbitrary arrest and detainment by the AND, and beatings, torture, and even death while in the custody of AND officials. It was common knowledge that the AND also intercepted the regular mail and monitored those officials who were suspect of designs against the state. [170] Mistreatment of political prisoners included such things as electric shock, submergence in septic tanks, having one's legs literally welded to chairs, and being suffocated in bags. The ways of the AND made ordinary Zairians afraid to receive mail or even to engage in the most superficial of discussions for fear of being overheard and punished. In later years, the AND was renamed SNIP, but it persisted in its ways as before.

There arose a multiplicity of agencies whose activities were redundant to those of SNIP. Within the Gendarmerie Nationale, there was a special investigative wing called the Special Intelligence and Surveillance Brigade (BSRS).[171] The BSRS and SNIP shared common features with the Military Intelligence and Action Service (Service d'Action et de Renseignements Militaires, or SARM). SARM's principal duty was to ensure the Army's loyalty to Mobutu.[172] Other principal security forces included the Garde Civile and the Special Presidential Division (DSP).[173]

The Garde Civile (Civil Guard) was created in 1984 "to be responsible for guaranteeing public security, ensuring public order, and assisting the Gendarmerie Nationale (National Police Force) in controlling mineral smuggling out of Zaire."[174] It, like other security forces, has been accused of political repression

---

169. Lawyers Committee for Human Rights, 44.
170. Winsome J. Leslie, 47.
171. Lawyers Committee for Human Rights, 43.
172. Winsome J. Leslie, 48.
173. Lawyers Committee for Human Rights, 40.

and human rights abuses. Still worse, however, is the Division Spéciale Presidentielle (DSP), which was organized to protect Mobutu and his family. The DSP is an elite Israeli-trained force with sophisticated technology for surveillance, daily monitoring, and the administration of pain. Its members are well paid in contrast to the FAZ, or regular Army, and are reputed to be of Mobutu's own tribe, the Ngbandi.[175]

Finally, there was the FAZ itself, which, though lacking in skills and motivation to prevent armed insurrections, as demonstrated by its extremely poor showing in the first and second Shaba invasions, was quite effective at instilling fear in the population. "Poor morale and resentment stemming from pay irregularities, poor living conditions, and lack of equipment are taken out on civilians, who have no recourse or protection. Harassment can take the form of roadblocks allegedly to check for papers but that in reality are a shakedown for money." The FAZ, too, resorted to arbitrary arrest and detainment, with human rights abuses.[176] In 1989, there were reports that FAZ members also raped schoolgirls and physically assaulted women who participated in a demonstration in the capital of Kinshasa. [177]

As was often Mobutu's custom, he even called attention to the abuse of the Army and the police during the course of a public speech in 1977. Ostensibly castigating them, he remarked:

> These abuses of power are ascertained almost everywhere...agents abuse their titles and intimidate citizens by saying: "Attention I am with the CND; I am a soldier; I am a magistrate; I am the friend of the President."...Know that Zaire belongs to 25 million Zairian men and women. It does not belong to the friends of Mobutu, neither to a few privileged people, nor to their collaborators, nor to the soldiers, nor to the magistrates, nor to the agents of the CND.[178]

Nonetheless, their abuses only increased as Zaire became a growing hotbed of political opposition.

---

174. Winsome J. Leslie, 46.
175. Ibid., 48.
176. Ibid., 44.
177. Ibid., 45.
178. Michael G. Schatzberg, 41.

EARLY DISSENT

The FLNC was among the earliest of those groups which chose to chal-lenge Mobutu. Responsible for the Shaba invasions, the group relied heavily on the former Katangan gendarmerie for its military endeavors. Although their leader, Mbumba, claimed that the group's function was political rather than mil-itary, it was responsible for the deaths of over 100 Europeans in the second Shaba invasion.

The FLNC was also said to have received support from the PRP (Parti Rev-olutionarie du Peuple), which was created in 1964 by none other than Laurent Kabila. Kabila would go on to become the dictator of the Congo after the over-throw of Mobutu, but was best known at the time for the kidnapping and ransom of four foreign students, three of whom were Americans. Kabila was among the most faithful of Lumumbists, with a left-leaning ideology that embraced the ideal of a people's revolution. The PRP was said to control some enclaves in remote portions of Kivu and had conducted guerilla activity in the Sud Kivu-Shaba area near Lake Tanganyika. [179]

Also of Lumumbist orientation were the Democratic Forces for the Liber-ation of the Congo (FODELICO) and the Congolese National Movement-Lumumba Revived. The first was led by Antoine Gizenga, who had been active in the 1961 rebellion, leading a movement from Stanleyville while Lumumba was imprisoned. Once this had been quashed by the United Nations, he ceased to be an overt threat to Mobutu; and the Congolese National Movement-Lumumba Revived was equally harmless. Its spokesman Paul Roger Mokede claimed that the movement only wanted a more liberal regime where criticism of the pres-ident was possible, rather than the overthrow of Mobutu.[180]

Another source of resistance continued to manifest itself in the students. In 1979, there were strikes at all university campuses, protesting terrible living conditions and Mobutu's autocratic leanings. Then, teachers and students joined together to demand a more liberal regime and the creation of at least two addi-tional political parties. They persisted in these demands through 1989, even to the extent that they demanded Mobutu's resignation. This resulted in a political

179. Winsome J. Leslie, 55.
180. Margarita Dobert, "Zaire: Chapter 2B. Political Participation and National Priorities," *Countries of the World*, January 1, 1991, www.highbeam.com.

crackdown wherein twenty-five students were jailed and the universities were closed.[181]

Finally, there was dissent within the Parliament, which, as discussed, was not an independent body but rather an arm of the MPR, which carried out Mobutu's wishes. On November 1, 1980, a group of thirteen dissidents published an anonymous open letter to the President, partly charging him as follows:

> You [Citizen President-Founder] are in the habit of affirming that there are no small and big Zairians. But, of a population of 25 million inhabitants, only fifty individuals "occupy the most lucrative positions and control the entire political apparatus." This is the same as saying that in "authentic" Zairian society, the percentage of those who control the economy and politics reaches 0.0002%!!! There is not, that we know of, any country in the world in which the concentration of economic and political power is as scandalous.[182]

Not long after this letter was disseminated in Europe, the thirteen members of Parliament were arrested and, with minimum legal formalities, sentenced to five years of house arrest. Amnesty International reported on the plight of these parliamentarians and Mobutu's practices in general in May of 1980, stating that Mobutu was guilty of:

> the detention without charge or trial of suspected opponents of the government for long periods; the imprisonment of political prisoners convicted at trials which did not conform with internationally recognized standards; the use of torture; the frequency of deaths in detention resulting from torture, ill treatment and harsh prison conditions; and the use of the death penalty in both criminal and political cases and extrajudicial executions. [183]

THE REVOLT OF THE INTERNATIONAL COMMUNITY

By August 1983, Mobutu was beginning to run into trouble with the foreign aid community as well. Between 1981 and 1983, the US Congress stubbornly refused to approve the president's request for increased aid to Zaire. This was due to the evidence of widespread corruption which stemmed from Mobutu himself. Yet, in typical Mobutu fashion, he attempted to deflect such criticism by making over 100 arrests that were supposedly aimed at stemming the tide of graft and by replacing a number of government officials.[184] He also announced,

---

181. Winsome J. Leslie, 53.
182. Michael G. Schatzberg, 8.
183. "Where Mobutu's Millions Go," *The Nation*, May 19, 1984.
184. "Administration to Seek Aid for Zaire," *Syracuse Post Standard*, August 5, 1983, A-6.

as far back as December of 1979, that Zaire was adopting austerity measures in order to please the IMF and World Bank. From then on, the Zairian people would not be able to spend their savings or to convert Zairian money into foreign currencies.

But in the same year, Mobutu himself withdrew approximately $13 million from the Central Bank in addition to the $209,000 that was withdrawn by his family. Mobutu was also acquiring enormous funds from European and US businessmen who were willing to pay bribes and commissions for their contracts with Zaire. And he continued to receive income from GECOMINES through "off the books" sales of copper and cobalt.

As the IMF explained in an interview with the *New York Times*, the only thing that was holding the economy together were the illegal transactions at all levels. Explaining what appeared, inexplicably, to be a rate of 1.8 percent growth in the Zairian economy, one economist said, "the reason was that goods could be imported with black money, and the economy grew." Soberly realistic, the IMF finally stated that "graft may be the only thing that can bail out Zaire."[185]

By the year 1990, the United States and the IMF had officially suspended loans to Zaire. With the Cold War at an end, there was simply no reason to maintain Mobutu in the style to which he aspired. His country had run up an arrears of $70 million in debt service and had already fallen off the IMF austerity wagon an astounding seven times. Zaire, as a result, continued to be a country where the underground economy was a vital fact of life. It remained a haven for mercenaries, counterfeiters, money launderers, and diamond smugglers, and even the Central Bank had to resort to the black market to buy and sell hard currency.[186]

An article in *US News and World Report* reveals just how bad things were:

> The only place in Kinshasa where local currency is readily obtainable is Wall Street, a nickname for a one-block area between the Belgian and American embassies. There, dozens of Zairian women sit on upturned bottle crates fondling purses stuffed with Z notes. Soldiers armed with machine guns stand nearby as the women sell the Z's for dollars and other Western currencies. Lately, the Z has all but collapsed as a valid currency. In January 1990 it traded at 300 to the dollar; now a dollar commands 800,000 Z's. Hoarding by Mobutu and his cronies, coupled with 16,500 percent inflation, has caused a cash-flow crisis of epic proportions. At the Banque Credit d'Agricole, a teller burst into fits of laughter when asked to cash a traveler's check. Producing a credit card provokes a similar response. The economy is cash only, and most banks have either run out of or refuse to dispense currency

---

185. "Where Mobutu's Millions Go.".
186. Bill Berkeley, 113.

without a kickback. "We have more than 5 billion Z's in the bank," says one frustrated businessman, "and we can't get more than 5 million without paying a 'withdrawal fee' of 30 to 50 percent." The meltdown of the Z's value has had some near-comic side effects. Dinner at one of Kinshasa's Belgian owned restaurants now requires almost a pound of bank notes. The situation is so bad that one Western embassy recently paid out its $28,000 local monthly payroll in notes worth one half of a US cent. Some businesses have taken to weighing bank notes, others use the quick-counting machines favored by drug dealers. [187]

According to Winsome J. Leslie, the only official sources of revenue continued to be the head tax (a pernicious holdover from the colonial regime), fines and fees for legal infractions, extraordinary taxes, and a yearly contribution to the MPR. The head tax applied to all nonsalaried employees, making rural farmers a particular target. Taxes levied by force were often simply pocketed by those who enforced their collection. [188]

AUTHORIZED DISSENT

In January 1990, Mobutu conducted a two-month tour of Zaire to engage in what he termed a "direct dialogue with the people." Zairians were encouraged to submit their ideas on how to run the government to a new Bureau National de la Consultation, and over 6,000 did. As part of this "Zairian perestroika," pamphlets and letters began to circulate in Kinshasa which openly criticized the president and called for his resignation. The protest march became common, resulting in crackdowns by the Special Presidential Brigade, the paramilitary Civil Guard, and a newly created antiterrorist corps, the Special Intervention Regiment. However, the final offshoot of this unrest was that Mobutu announced the end of the single-party state and the creation of a multiparty system on April 24, 1990, to coincide with what he called the birth of the Third Republic. [189] Henceforth, two parties would be permitted to operate alongside the MPR. [190] In addition to the tri-party system, Mobutu also advocated constitutional reform, the dissolution of MPR institutions (particularly the Central Committee), depoliticization of the Army and security forces, and free and fair elections. [191]

---

187. "In Zaire, a Big Man still rules the roost," *US News and World Report*, August 10, 1992.
188. Winsome J. Leslie, 40.
189. Ibid., 50.
190. Mark Hubbard, 116.
191. Winsome J. Leslie, 57.

Given the switch to a multiparty system, he was compelled to open a Sovereign National Conference to prepare the country for change. Opposition parties proliferated and old leaders in exile returned. In October 1990, Mobutu lifted the three-party limit, allowing over 100 parties to emerge. Yet, multiparty reform was somewhat emasculated because Mobutu subsequently took measures to exert control over the parties by mandating that they must register with the Supreme Court after depositing a fee of Z5 million in order to be recognized. [192] Even registered parties were prohibited from meeting without permission from municipal authorities. Further, Mobutu announced that he would remain in power as a person "above the parties." Though he initially stepped down as the head of the MPR, he resumed that post in 1991.[193] The MPR was resuscitated under a new name, the Mouvement Populaire pour le Renouveau (Popular Movement for Renewal).

THE OPPOSITION PARTIES

The Union for Democracy and Social Progress (UDPS) was formed by the original thirteen parliamentarians who were responsible for an open letter to Mobutu that was highly critical of the regime. Its members had subsequently been placed under house arrest for a full five year period.[194] When a popular demonstration was held to celebrate the release of Etienne Tshisekedi, the movement's most popular leader, it was violently repressed. Five people were said to have been killed, and Tshisekedi himself wound up in the hospital after being attacked by security forces in May.

Former political leaders and rebels Joseph Ileo Nsongo Amba (formerly Joseph Ileo) and Christophe Gbenye, the leader of one of the rebellions that had occurred in 1965, also formed their own parties; Ileo founded the Democratic and Social Christian Party (PDSC) while Gbenye announced the formal establishment of the Congolese National Movement-Lumumba (MNC-Lumumba).[195]

About 130 parties came together to form a united front that is known as the Union Sacrée (Holy Alliance). The former prime minister Nguza Karl-i-bond was head of the Union des Fédéralistes et des Républicains Indépendents

192. Ibid.
193. Eds. Sandra W. Meditz and Tim Merrill, 211.
194. Winsome J. Leslie, 55.
195. Eds. Sandra W. Meditz and Tim Merrill, 213.

(UFERI), one of the three main opposition parties within the Union Sacrée.[196] Mobutu himself has also funded the creation of several so-called opposition groups. The most prominent of his loyalists is the Forces Démocrates Unies (United Democratic Forces). Finally, there was talk of the formation of a third political force, separate from both the Union Sacrée and the Forces Démocrates, that would be comprised of the remaining liberal parties.[197]

Due to Mobutu's manipulation and the extent of the disagreement between the parties, it looked as though little of significance would happen. Few of the opposition parties had any plan for an economic recovery, and fewer still put forth ideas on how to end the systemic corruption. Mobutu continued to exploit the opposition's disarray, while standing in the way of any government reforms that could have had real meaning for the country. In the meantime, repression continued.

Unrepresented by the party system, there remained the problem of the students. For some time before the announcement of liberalization, the student bodies in Kinshasa and Lumbumbashi clashed repeatedly with police over unapproved demonstrations. On May 9, 1990, the most serious altercation occurred in Lumbumbashi, involving students who attacked known informers of Mobutu's police system. This was in response to the "disappearance" of some of their members, and also was a measure of the students' willingness to risk their lives in order to ensure a democratic transition. After weeks of demonstrations, the Special Presidential Brigade acted. It cut off the electricity and moved through the dormitories, slitting the throats of those whom they believed to have been involved in the attacks on their informers. Only those students who originated from the president's Equateur region were specifically spared from the onslaught. They had been removed from campus prior to the offensive. In the wake of the government's own investigation of the incident, Amnesty International and the Belgian press reported that between 100 and150 students had been slaughtered.[198]

In the spring of 1991, Mobutu asked the prime minister of the first transitional government, Lunda Bululu, to resign, and appointed a new prime minister, Professor Malumba Lukoji. March was also the month during which the police attacked a peaceful Christian demonstration, leaving 35 dead and dozens

196. Bill Berkeley, 122.
197. Winsome J. Leslie, 58.
198. Ibid., 54.

wounded. This was followed by another attack on a political meeting in Mbuji Mayi in April, where another 45 died and another 30 were wounded.[199]

Despite this spate of repressive actions, tens of thousands of Zairians flocked to a Kinshasa football stadium in July to witness the first real gathering of Zaire's political parties. Ignoring the government's refusal to authorize their rally, opposition leaders such as Etienne Tshisekedi of the UDPS and former prime ministers Kengo wa Dondo and Nguza Karl-i-Bond of UFERI came together in opposition. Also present was Joseph Ileo of the PDSC, a former minister in the government of Patrice Lumumba.[200]

Their gathering preceded the Sovereign National Conference (CNS), which was finally convened in August. Represented at the Conference were over 2,800 political, religious, and civic leaders, whose demand was for the establishment of a new constitution prior to the elections. Despite very great odds, the conference managed to reject pro-Mobutu candidates and elect Monsignor Laurent Monsengwo Pasinya, the Catholic archbishop of Kisangani, as chairman of its Interim Bureau.[201] However, despite a strong showing of representatives, the Conference was boycotted by some of the opposition groups, and Mobutu elected on August 15 to suspend it indefinitely.[202]

THE PILLAGE

Any talk of reconvening the conference was stifled by the pillage that followed. In September 1991, some 3,000 paratroopers in Kinshasa went on a rampage, protesting low wages and lack of pay.[203] What started at the N'Dijili airport soon spread to Camp Kokolo (Kinshasa's largest army barracks) and from there to the commercial areas in the capital and the affluent suburbs of Binza and Ma Campagne. The soldiers were joined by regular citizens who engaged in massive looting and plundering, particularly targeting those businesses that belonged to Lebanese, Greeks, and Portuguese traders.[204] "In 72 hours of anarchy, $1 billion worth of property was looted or destroyed and more

---

199. Eds. Sandra W. Meditz and Tim Merrill, 214.
200. Mark Hubbard, 224.
201. Winsome J. Leslie, 59.
202. Eds. Sandra W. Meditz and Tim Merrill, 215.
203. Bill Berkeley, 121.
204. Winsome J. Leslie, 45.

than 200 people were killed."[205] Then, France and Belgium intervened with paratroopers who received American logistical support.

Not long after the pillage, Mobutu was pressed by foreign governments to come to terms with the opposition. He appointed Etienne Tshisekedi of the UDPS to be the country's newest prime minister, but he refused to relinquish control over four vital areas. These were: defense, finance, foreign affairs, and mining, all of which formed the underpinnings of Mobutu's autocratic regime.[206] Not surprisingly, Tshisekedi lasted just six days. With the backing of Western governments, Tshisekedi had sought control over the Central Bank, one of the principal means by which Mobutu enriched himself and his friends and often co-opted his enemies.[207] Tshisekedi was dismissed and replaced by Bernardin Mungul-Diaka, head of the Rassemblement des Democrates pour la Republique (RDR), a small party of the Sacred Union (which was prominently pro-Mobutu).

After being dismissed, Tshisekedi established a rival government. But by late November 1991, Mobutu had established a third transition government, led by Prime Minister Nguza Karl-i-Bond. Nguza and UFERI were subsequently expelled from the Union Sacrée and Nguza reacted, in turn, by suspending the Sovereign National Conference in January 1992.[208] The government under Nguza included ten ministers from the opposition, although not from the UDPS and PDSC, which boycotted his government and called for general strike.[209]

Following a march that involved tens of thousands of people in the capital of Kinshasa and after being subjected to significant pressure from Belgium, France, and the US, Mobutu agreed to reconvene the Conference at the start of the month of April. When it met on April 6, the 2,800 delegates declared that they had the power not only to forge a new constitution but also to legislate for a multiparty system. By August, the Conference had passed a Transitional Act to serve as a provisional constitution and had created a transitional government. Tshisekedi was nominated to return to the post of prime minister and he appointed a government of national unity that included Mobutu's opponents.[210]

---

205. "In Zaire, a Big Man still rules the roost."
206. Winsome J. Leslie, 59.
207. Bill Berkeley, 121.
208. Winsome J. Leslie, 59.
209. Eds. Sandra W. Meditz and Tim Merrill, 216.
210. Bill Berkeley, 123.

Mobutu's response was to reconvene the former legislature and to entrust it with drafting a rival constitution that would be more to his personal liking. [211]

But the opposition proceeded without him. On December 6, 1992, the CNS (Sovereign National Conference) was reorganized as the HCR (High Council of the Republic) to be headed by Archbishop Monsengwo. It was authorized to proceed with drawing up a new constitution and to organize legislative and presidential elections.[212] By mid-January 1993, the HCR was ready to charge Mobutu with treason and even threatened to impeach him unless he recognized the new transitional government. [213]

THE SECOND PILLAGE

Another round of looting and pillage occurred in January 1993, as soldiers rioted over payment in the inflationary Z5 million banknotes which Mobutu's government had issued. It began again in Camp Kokolo and spread rapidly to Lumbumbashi and Kisangani. The French ambassador, Philippe Bernard, was killed in the confusion and overall at least 300 deaths resulted.[214]

According to Michaela Wrong, this pillage and the one that occurred before it were so violently significant that they became historical landmarks. She says, "events are labeled as being 'avant le premier pillage' or 'après le deuxième pillage,' before and after the lootings. It is the Congo's version of BC and AD."[215]

In the aftermath of the pillage, Mobutu attempted to reassert his authority by convening a special conclave of pro-Mobutu forces. The HCR and Sacred Union chose to boycott it. During the conclave, Mobutu dismissed the Tshisekedi government, despite the fact that under the rules of the Transitional Act he did not have the power to do so. The result was that there were now two governments, with Faustin Birindwa named as the new prime minister of Mobutu's rival faction.

While the Tshisekedi government was legal and was internationally recognized, Mobutu continued to stand in the way of it gaining power and resources. Tshisekedi's frustration with the state of the economy and his own

---

211. Eds. Sandra W. Meditz and Tim Merrill, 218.
212. Ibid.
213. Ibid., 219.
214. Winsome J. Leslie, 46.
215. Michaela Wrong, 20.

impotence finally became so great that he requested UN intervention to restore the country to normalcy. The UN Secretary-General did appoint a special envoy to Zaire in July 1993, but he took no significant action.[216]

Of all the international bodies that supported the Tshisekedi government, the first to do so openly was the government of Belgium. It attempted to isolate Mobutu politically and economically, and refused to invite Mobutu to King Baudouin's funeral when the leader passed away in July.[217]

Finally, the two rival governments reached an agreement in October. They established firm plans for a transitional constitution, a joint transitional parliament, and an electoral schedule that would address presidential and legislative elections to be held in December 1994.[218] But since the replacement of Faustin Birindwa with Kengo wa Dondo in July 1994, Mobutu continued to hamper the functioning of the government institutions. As a result, reform of the administration and the establishment of an independent electoral commission remained blocked.[219]

RESULTING SOCIETAL DECAY

An analysis of the state of life in Zaire, by 1994, could only present a pessimistic picture. Inflation had risen to more than 6,000 percent and the figures for unemployment were reported at 80 percent, with most people engaged in subsistence activities. The growth rate in GDP had been negative since 1989, estimated at -8.0 percent in 1992.[220] According to World Bank statistics, Zaire's economy had shrunk to the level of 1958 while the population had tripled. [221] The average life expectancy was fifty-two, but AIDS and other diseases threatened even this figure. "Infectious and parasitic diseases including malaria, trypanosomiasis (sleeping sickness), onchocerciasis (river blindness) and schistosomiasis were now a major health threat. Measles, diarrheal diseases, tetanus, diphtheria, pertussis, poliomyelitis, tuberculosis, and leprosy were also prev-

---

216. Eds. Sandra W. Meditz and Tim Merrill, 219.
217. Tukumbi Lumumba-Kasongo, 79.
218. Eds. Sandra W. Meditz and Tim Merrill, 219.
219. "Zaire: troika demarche to political leadership (protests from the US, France and Belgium on the slowness of political reform in Zaire)," US Department of State Dispatch, May 8, 1995.
220. Eds. Sandra W. Meditz and Tim Merrill, xxvii.
221. Michaela Wrong, 214.

alent. And the majority of the population was infected with intestinal worms."[222] Only 14 percent of the population had access to safe drinking water and malnutrition was widespread.[223] Relying on subsistence farming, barter, hawking, and illegal trade, most Zairians were eating just one meal a day or a meal every other day.[224]

Most hospitals were closed, with private sources of health care available to only 50 percent of the population. In those hospitals which did operate, such as that of Mama Yemo, the practice of "impounding the ill" in order to guarantee payment for services was common. The FAZ regularly "patrolled" the hospitals to ensure that those indebted could not escape. [225]

As to the state of the school system, most of the state-run schools were closed. Enrollment was gauged to be 78 percent for primary school and 23 percent for secondary school. Only 56 percent of primary school-aged children were reported to reach fourth grade.[226] Teachers in Likasi were constantly on strike, as their average monthly salary of 30 million Zaires was worth less than four bottles of beer.

Further, few of Zaire's 36 million people had any idea of what was happening in their country since Mobutu had turned off the government radio in 1990. The postal system had collapsed, few telephones worked (the people in power relied mainly on Motorola cellular phones), gasoline was in short supply, and the national news agency had run out of paper. Zaire, in sharp contrast to the state in which the Belgians had left it, now had only 3,000 miles of paved roads.[227] In the capital city of Kinshasa, gendarmes manned roadblocks where motorists were given the choice of paying a bribe or being taken to jail, and roaming gangs were common. The effect of economic disaster was even seen at the zoos, where the weaker animals were regularly fed to those that were more aggressive.

Finally, the endemic sickness of the Zairian economy gave rise to alternate forms of subsistence and expressions of rebellion. As Sandra Meditz and Tim Merrill note, faced with low producer prices and dishonest state marketing boards, farmers:

---

222. Eds. Sandra W. Meditz and Tim Merrill, xxvii.
223. Ibid.
224. Bill Berkeley, 128.
225. Michaela Wrong, 137.
226. Eds. Sandra W. Meditz and Tim Merrill, xxvii.
227. "In Zaire, a Big Man still rules the roost.".

sabotaged cotton production by diverting fertilizer intended for cotton production to their own food crops, by failing to space plants appropriately, and by refusing to replant their fields as instructed. Farmers then redirected their energies to the cultivation of more profitable crops such as corn, cassava, and peanuts. Low wages for palm oil plantation workers and low prices for palm nuts purchased from petty producers resulted in workers deserting plantations. They abandoned commercial production in order to concentrate on producing food crops. Illicit mining of gold in the Kivu regions and Haut-Zaire occurs on both an individual and group basis. People engaged in illicit mining protect themselves with private militias against government soldiers and officials or local officials are paid off. Similar arrangements exist for diamond mining. Illicit trade flourishes in all commodities that can be sold for foreign currencies, among them gold, coffee, ivory, diamonds, cobalt, tea, cotton, and palm oil. Finally resistance is expressed linguistically in the labels used to deflate state institutions and ideologies and to create an alternative folk consciousness. The army's national slogan of "always out front" is transformed into "always behind," the national airline Air Zaire has become known as "Air Maybe," and the national highway authority is called the "Department of Potholes."[228]

And Michaela Wrong observes that the CNS (Sovereign National Conference) was now said to stand for "Connerie Nationale Souveraine," or Sovereign National Bullshit.[229] People had lost all faith in the institution due to Mobutu's power to deadlock the legislation and block every significant reform.

Even Prime Minister Kengo wa Dondo's economic reforms were seen as the same old game in 1996. He announced that privatization measures would be increased, allowing a group of European airlines, for example, to purchase 49.5 percent of Air Zaire for $33 million. But donors were still uncomfortable with the $47 million (5.7 percent of the entire budget) that was still being allotted for government spending. Whereas inflation had been projected to decrease to a rate of 20 percent, it was more than 461 percent in 1995. Moreover, the country's foreign debt was estimated at varying between $7 and $8 billion, $1.4 billion of which was currently owed.[230] As a result, the World Bank reaffirmed its position that it would no longer lend to Zaire, stating that, "Zaire will remain in remission until it does two basic things. First, it must put its house in order and then deal with its international debt. To put its house in order, Zaire must set an election timetable and have a new government which will decide on how to go about stabilizing the economy. The current government is a long way from this. They keep on setting deadlines for election that they are not meeting." [231]

228. Eds. Sandra W. Meditz and Tim Merrill, 108.
229. Michaela Wrong, 108.
230. "Zaire: Still Outside World Bank Books," *Inter Press Service English News Wire*, February 27, 1996.
231. Ibid.

In sum, the country was cut off from foreign aid, wracked with internal strife, and ready for rebellion. As we shall see in the following chapter, this paved the way for a movement called the AFDL, which began predominantly in Zaire's Kivu region.

CHAPTER 5. THE FINAL END OF MOBUTU

At this time, it is prudent that we diverge from our study of the Congo to explain the genocide in Rwanda, as this had tremendous bearing on the situation in Zaire. The confrontation between the Tutsis and the Hutus, the two main (and somewhat arbitrarily defined) ethnic groups that reside within Rwanda, was markedly a feature of colonial occupation. When the Belgians took over the country, they established an ethnic classification system that distinguished the Tutsis from the Hutus by their more "European" features. Identification cards were issued to concretize the system, with the main differences being that they served as a passport to education and jobs within the civil service for those who were fortunate enough to be classified as Tutsis. The Hutus, even though they were numerically superior to the Tutsis, had no choice but to accept these arrangements. They were also brutally treated within a system of forced labor that the Belgians implemented (albeit not nearly as badly as in the Congo) in order to speed the construction of railways; beatings and whippings were common.[232] As a result, thousands of Hutus fled the country into nearby Tanzania.

But by 1957, a revolution had begun in the Hutu way of thinking. With Belgian power waning and with the rise of a new breed of intellectuals within the Hutu community, a manifesto was published that decried the oppression of the Hutus and demanded power sharing. Now that the country was moving toward independence, there was simultaneously a revolution in the way that the

---

232. Linda Melvern, *Conspiracy to Murder: The Rwandan Genocide* (New York: Verso, 2004) 5.

Belgians treated the Hutus: all Tutsi officials were replaced with Hutu candidates. The response to this turn of events, in 1959, was the first outbreak of violence between the Tutsi and the Hutu.

This was immediately preceded by the demise of the Tutsi king in what were viewed as suspicious circumstances, and was followed by the death of hundreds of Tutsis, whose houses were also burned. Thousands fled in panic to exile in Tanzania, Burundi, and Uganda.[233] Others sent petitions to the UN warning that the violence against Tutsis was highly organized and that they remained in fear for their lives. The UN General Assembly sent a special commission to Rwanda which found that "racism bordered on Nazism against the Tutsi minorities and that the government together with the Belgian authorities was to blame."[234] Those who fled would return time and again to attack the Hutu government in an effort to regain power. However, the Hutus drove them back and, in reprisal for their offensives, committed further violence against the Tutsis who remained in Rwanda.[235]

In the year 1960, the Belgians established a provisional Rwandan government headed by a Hutu named Gregoire Kayibanda, whose party had swept the country's elections. He was to be the nation's first leader when Belgium granted the country self-rule in 1962. But as Rwanda failed economically, so did Kayibanda. Clutching at the straw of ethnic solidarity to retain his hold on power, Kayibanda countered the threat to his rule by inciting violence against the Tutsis. Thousands more were killed, and, between 1959 and 1973, some 300,000 Rwandans fled the country.[236]

Nevertheless, popular discontent with Kayibanda remained an outstanding feature, and in 1973 Rwanda's senior army commander General Juvenal Habyarimana seized power in a bloodless coup. In this, he was backed by the Rwandan Armed Forces (FAR) and his own elite force, the Presidential Guard.[237] Yet, again in 1986, the economy began to falter. Opponents called for a multiparty democracy to replace the one-party system that Kayibanda had instituted, and the call was strongly echoed by Rwanda's primary aid donors.

---

233. Elizabeth Neuffer, *The Key to My Neighbor's House: Seeking Justice in Bosnia and* Rwanda (New York: Picador, 2002) 90.
234. Linda Melvern, 7.
235. Elizabeth Neuffer, 90.
236. Ibid., 90-91.
237. Ibid., 93.

In October 1990, Rwanda came under attack from the Tutsis in Uganda. Under pressure from the government of Uganda, which had by no means welcomed the flood of refugees that had sought sanctuary within its boundaries, Habyarimana agreed to establish a joint commission to study repatriation. His promises proved empty. The Rwandan Patriotic Front (RPF), which had sprung up in Uganda, continued to fight with Rwanda for another three years before Habyarimana took any measures aimed at conciliation. The RPF was comprised mostly of 4,000 second-generation Rwandan refugees who had joined Uganda's National Resistance Army (NRA). The RPF invasion was a failure in Rwanda due to the fact that France and Zaire sent forces to protect Habyarimana. Zaire sent troops belonging to the hated DSP (Division Speciale Presidentielle) and France sent two contingents of paratroopers. It was the French who saved Habyarimana by setting up a blockade against a potential attack on the capital and staying on in Rwanda to provide the financial and military guarantees that were not forthcoming from Belgium.[238]

According to Linda Melvern, the aid community at large was also partly responsible for the flow of loans to the country that allowed Habyarimana to arm the FAR and the general public. She states that Rwanda was the subject of a World Bank and IMF Structural Adjustment Program as early as October of 1990. Experts who studied the government's spending noted that some US $112 million of the money that was earmarked for Rwanda was spent on weapons and tools.[239]

In the meantime, Habyarimana launched a series of government crackdowns. Some 13,000 Tutsi and moderate Hutu were arrested, and every clash with the RPF resulted in the retaliatory killing of Tutsis. Again, thousands more were killed between 1990 and 1994.[240] What was seen to be the most violent of Habyarimana's militias was the Mouvement Révolutionaire pour le Développement party (MRND), which was also known as the Interahamwe. Another was the Coalition pour la Défense de la République (CDR). When Habyarimana initially signed a cease-fire with the RPF and agreed to share power with it, the Rwandan Army (FAR) revolted. As a result, Habyarimana denounced the accords and the trouble started all over.[241]

---

238. Linda Melvern, 14.
239. Ibid., 57.
240. Elizabeth Neuffer, 97.
241. Ibid., 99.

THE RWANDAN GENOCIDE

Finally, Habyarimana signed the Arusha Accord in August, 1993. At that time, the UN decided to send a peacekeeping force to oversee the integration of the RPF within the FAR and to ensure that there would be a smooth political transition. But, largely because this was in the wake of the Somalia debacle, only a small force of 2,548 military personnel and 60 civilian police was approved for Rwanda. UNAMIR, the UN Assistance Mission to Rwanda, gathered information early on which pointed to another action against the Tutsis, and General Romeo Dallaire swiftly asked the UN command for reinforcements and a change in mandate. The information that he had received was that weapons were being stockpiled and that lists of persons slated for assassination were being drawn up by militant Hutus. In response, however, the UN command insisted that Dallaire was to act within his present mandate, and, accordingly, that he should share his findings with Habyarimana. The result was that by mid-January Rwanda was the scene of violent political assassinations, grenade attacks and more ethnic strife.[242]

Then, on April 6, 1994 the plane carrying Habyarimana from a meeting in Tanzania was shot down, allegedly at the instruction of Paul Kagame, the leader of the RPF.[243] It sparked the beginning of a genocide as the Interahamwe militia massacred the Tutsis and the RPA (the militant wing of the RPF) battled the Rwandan Army. In this, the Interahamwe was aided by widespread propaganda stemming from Radio Mille Collines (a private extremist Hutu radio station) and Radio Rwanda. Because of this, and the highly structured nature of Rwandan village society wherein every cell was armed and activated by the militant Hutu extremists, the "elite" Tutsis were being killed at the incredible rate of 4,000 per day.[244]

During this time, Elizabeth Neuffer notes that the UN Security Council met constantly but there was little or no agreement among diplomats about what to do. The UN was apparently under the impression that what was occurring in Rwanda was a matter of civil war rather than organized genocide. Madeleine Albright, the US representative to the UN, told Security Council representatives that Washington was opposed to the mission being reinforced

---

242. Ibid., 102-3.
243. Yaa-Lengi M Ngemi, *Genocide in the Congo (Zaire): In the Name of Bill Clinton, and of the Paris Club, and of the Mining Conglomerates, So It Is!* (New York: Writers Club Press, 2000) 61.
244. Linda Melvern, 19.

under any circumstances. If anything, the desire of the US was to pull out alto-gether.[245] President Clinton is notorious for having warned at the time that "the UN must know when to say no."

Given the weight of American pressure, the Council voted on April 21 to decrease the number of troops to a paltry 270. But after six more weeks of slaughter left 300,000 dead, the US and the UN agreed to a new proposal. On May 17, 1994, the Council voted to expand the number of troops to 5,500 with the proviso that it would do so under a highly restricted mandate. In addition, only 850 troops and 150 observers would be deployed in the first phase of the operation.[246] It took the deaths of nearly half a million Rwandans before UN Secretary-General Boutros Boutros-Ghali was willing to label the episode a genocide in May. Finally, the French dispatched troops in June for a humani-tarian mission. Dubbed "Operation Turquoise," the French operation was cen-tered on creating a safe area for the majority Hutus, who were by then being driven out of the country by the Tutsi RPA. In so doing, they provided shelter for those who had engineered the genocide, and allowed hundreds of thousands of killers, together with many more innocent victims, to escape to nearby Zaire.[247] In all, 2 million Rwandans were said to have fled to Zaire, Burundi, and Tan-zania. Of these, nearly 50,000 died when cholera and dysentery raged through their camps in Zaire.[248]

THE MOBUTU-HUTU ALLIANCE

Mobutu allowed the refugees to stay in Zaire. Styling himself as the savior of the Hutus, he allowed them to regroup and rearm within the refugee camps.[249] The camps were quickly overrun by the Hutu genocidaires who were responsible for the killings in 1994. Humanitarian and aid agencies could not prevent the most murderous and vicious among them from wielding power over the innocent, which meant that the refugees were yoked to the cause of returning, again and again, in violence to their country of origin. Rwanda suf-fered attacks on the border regions and quickly warned Zaire that it would not

---

245. Elizabeth Neuffer, 123.
246. Ibid., 127.
247. Ibid.
248. Ibid., 128.
249. Bill Berkeley, 140.

tolerate such instances. Mobutu, turning a deaf ear to Rwanda, even thought at one time that he would extend the vote to the Hutus, as he considered the transition to a multi-party system. In showing preference for the Hutus, he also turned against the native Tutsi population in Zaire. With his support and encouragement, the Tutsis were labeled as "vampires" and "vermin" who were to be forcibly expelled.

In tandem with the president's urgings, the Hutu in the Zairian refugee camps conducted raids in the outlying areas of the Kivus, where the Tutsi had lived for generations. They were responsible for mass killings and violence, particularly in the Masisi region where tens of thousands of Tutsi died. As David Rieff notes, these killings did not spark the international indignation that had been so inflamed by the treatment of Hutus in the Zairian refugee camps. Most reports on the subject were confined to internal memos and obscure journals that were inaccessible to the general public. The government of Zaire was not only complicit in these massacres, it also acted under Mobutu to revoke the citizenship of the Tutsis and to provoke further actions against them.[250] Soon, the Tutsis came to the realization that they would have to fight for their right to remain in Zaire.

The Rebel Partnership with Rwanda, Uganda And Angola

Sympathetic to their cause, Rwanda supplied the Zairian Tutsis with arms, training, and support. All that it took to mobilize the Tutsi was an invasion by the Rwandan RPA in 1996. In no time at all, the RPA had occupied the town of Uvira and the nearby city of Bukavu. The RPA then made common cause with the enemies of Mobutu, which, in addition to the Zairian Tutsi, included four obscure political parties that had come together in Lemera, South Kivu in October of 1996.

The first group was represented by the Congolese Tutsi and was led by Deogratias Bugera. The second was a group of Lumumbists led by Kisase Ngandu. The third was a Marxist guerrilla group led by Laurent Kabila. And the fourth group was led by Anselme Masasu, a former Rwandan soldier.[251] Calling themselves the Alliance des Forces Démocratiques pour la Libération du Congo

---

250. David Rieff, "Realpolitik in Congo: should Zaire's fate have been subordinate to the fate of Rwandan refugees?" *The Nation,* July 7, 1997.

(AFDL), the rebels seized on the Rwandan invasion as their cue to revolt against Mobutu.[252]

Soon to join Rwanda were Uganda and Angola. Uganda, too, was Tutsi-led and sympathized with Rwanda. Uganda had also suffered assaults by rebel groups which were based inside Zaire. Anti-Museveni movements that were supported by Sudan were attacking from the region. Likewise, Angola had been struggling for years with the UNITA rebel movement which had been conducting border raids from Zaire with Mobutu's help and support. Thus, these three governments banded together with the goal of crippling the insurgent movements that had mobilized against them. Reportedly, Angola airlifted at least 1,000 Zairian insurgents from camps in Angola into eastern Zaire.

The first act of this coalition of forces was to break up the refugee camps in order to drive the Hutus back to Rwanda where they could be tried for crimes of war or resettled under the new government. Tens of thousands of Hutus did return to Rwanda, thus allowing the United States to withdraw its offer of troops to police and repatriate refugees.

As it crossed the country, the AFDL drew further support from Zaire's disillusioned youth. Having been viewed as superfluous within their own communities, young Zairian boys joined the rebels in force. The AFDL advanced northward along the Ugandan border and westwards toward the River Zaire. Ugandan troops simultaneously occupied the strategic Beni area to allow the rebels to advance to the north. When Mobutu returned to Zaire in December 1996, after having sought treatment for his prostate cancer in Switzerland, the rebels had already made spectacular gains in the north, east, and south. Mobutu made a last-ditch effort to separate the Zairian Tutsis from the rebels by proclaiming that they would finally be granted full citizenship in Zaire, but the promise of ready, tangible gains and the imminent fall of Mobutu prompted the Tutsis to remain on the rebel side. On April 7, 1997, many government troops disarmed and offered their support to the AFDL as it advanced upon Lumbumbashi. Similarly, the political opposition in Kinshasa aligned with the rebel group.[253]

---

251. International Crisis Group, "Congo at War: A Briefing on the Internal and External Players in the Central African Conflict," International Crisis Group, November 17, 1998.

252. Musifiky Mwanasali, "5 Civil Conflicts and Conflict Management in the Great Lakes Region of Africa," *Zones of Conflict in Africa: Theories and Cases*, eds. George Klay Kieh and Ida Rousseau Mukenge (Westport, CT: Praeger, 2002) 59.

By 1997, a group called the Katangan Tigers had also joined the rebels. Originally organized by Moise Tshombe, the Tigers consisted of the gendarmes who had fled to Angola rather than be integrated into the Army following Katanga's final defeat in 1964. Between 1996 and 1997 approximately 2,000 Tigers had returned to fight on behalf of the rebellion.

In the meantime, the rebels had already seized the best mineral-producing regions. Foreign mining consortiums quickly jumped on the rebel bandwagon and struck deals with the AFDL for mining rights in the country. For the most part, the AFDL left the mines untouched. As long as it received taxes from the wealthy regions, it was prepared to allow business to continue unimpeded. The population itself was also a source of wealth, as many contributed voluntarily to the sweeping rebel advance. Thus, Mobutu was being hit where it hurt the most. Deprived of the country's wealth and stricken with prostate cancer, he was swiftly losing power.

THE INTERNATIONAL VIEWPOINT

As early as March of 1997, the American flag had been publicly burned in Zaire to protest US continued involvement with one of the world's most hated dictators.[254] Citizens of small towns and cities prepared for the coming of the rebels with the view that they were being liberated from decades of misrule. They tossed handfuls of sweet breakfast cereals to the crowds of advancing fighters, which included a great number of *kadogos*, or child soldiers. The US and other foreign countries, with the notable exception of France, held a purely pragmatic view toward the rebels' continued success. Many thought that international negotiations would speed and ease the fall of Mobutu and prepare the country for change. Although France initially demanded active intervention to save and prop up Mobutu, it finally backed down in the face of US demands.

The US was fully aware that Rwanda was training and aiding the rebels. There was a strong pro-Rwanda lobby in Washington which backed the Rwandan invasion for purposes of dismantling the ex-FAR and Interahamwe

---

253. Heinrich Matthee, "State collapse or new politics? The conflict in Zaire 1996-1997 (Statistical Data Included), *Strategic Review for Southern Africa*, June 1, 1999.

254. Tukumbi Lumumba-Kasongo, *The Dynamics of Economic and Political Relations between Africa and Foreign Powers: A Study in International Relations* (Westport, CT: Praeger Publishers, 1999) 78.

militias that had caused so much carnage since 1994. Rwanda continued to receive arms and economic assistance from the international community and, in particular, the US. The US had been retraining the Rwandan army for "humanitarian purposes" since Kagame had taken over.

By March 1997, it was no longer clear who ruled the country. The rebels were advancing on Kinshasa from three fronts, and already had cut the supply lines into the city. While the rebels were said to display great restraint in much of the territory that they covered, it was to be otherwise with Mobutu's FAZ. Running in the face of danger, Mobutu's army plundered and looted, and also engaged in rape as it retreated toward Kinshasa.

Under the guidance of South Africa's Nelson Mandela, an effort was made to negotiate the terms of a hand-off of power to rebel leader Laurent Kabila, who had by then emerged as the spokesperson for the AFDL (due to the assassination of his rival, Kisase Ngandu under highly suspect conditions). Kabila and Mobutu met on a ship in international waters to discuss the situation but nothing could be done to stop the rebel movement. It would neither accept Mobutu as the head of a transitional government nor allow him to resign with dignity. By the time that the rebels approached Kinshasa, Mobutu was met by four of his commanders, who advised him to leave the city. The Army conceded defeat and quickly turned toward the rebels. Mobutu's plane was fired upon as it left for Gbadolite. From Gbadolite, Mobutu and his family would swiftly fly to Morocco, where Mobutu died in exile of prostate cancer.

It was not until Kabila had seized power and installed himself in office that the international community began to demand an investigation of the rebels' military exploits. Particularly highlighted were the attacks on the Hutu refugee camps, which were said to have resulted in mass slaughter and carnage. Kabila himself denied this but refused permission for the UN to conduct an inquiry into the matter. He instructed airlines not to sell the UN tickets to suspected massacre sites, and, outside Kisangani, rebels barred aid workers from entry to sprawling camps while soldiers hunted down more people with machine guns and machetes. According to observers, many thousands of Hutus were reputed to have died at the hands of the rebels and the invasion coalition, with their bodies buried in mass graves or left to rot in the forests. Despite Kabila's stonewalling, however, the UN did issue at least an incomplete report on the matter, recommending that the Security Council establish a formal UN tribunal to prosecute those responsible.[255] Disappointingly, world leaders who were eager to normalize relations did not wish to adopt this recommendation for fear that Kabila would be tried for war crimes.

KABILA IN POWER

The first thing that Kabila did when he took over the country was to sack the government ministry and imprison its crooked participants, and also to demand full investigations into their holdings and possessions.[256] Most pro-Mobutists had already fled the country, and their assets in Zaire were simply seized and redistributed by Kabila's new Office for Ill-gotten Gains (Office des Biens Mal Acquis, OBMA). The OBMA seized businesses worth over 200 million dollars and 350 houses and apartments in Kinshasa. Wealthy Zairians had formerly paid bribes to Mobutu's system in order to be protected; they now found that they were subject to losing their homes and possessions without any form of recourse. Kabila launched an extensive campaign to seize assets that were held abroad, and he was particularly incensed that Mobutu was said to have amassed a huge fortune in foreign properties and bank accounts. While foreign banks and governments proved to be quite receptive to Kabila's inquiries, little was actually done to secure these foreign assets. At best, Mobutu's cronies were subjected to a preliminary freeze on their holdings, but this was quickly lifted as Kabila's government lost interest.

All too soon, it seems, Kabila was to prove himself the equal of Mobutu. Like Mobutu, he renamed Zaire the Democratic Republic of the Congo. He also adopted the same system of patronage and was particularly prone to rewarding Rwandans, without whose help the rebels would never have seized control of the government. James Kabare, a Rwandan soldier, was made military commander in Kinshasa and then Chief of Staff. It was Rwandan Tutsi soldiers who provided for Kabila's personal security, and the Rwandan RPA that policed the streets of Kinshasa. Kabila's favoritism toward Rwandans and also the Banyamulenge (Zairian Tutsis) was to have the effect of discrediting his regime in the eyes of many people. The Congolese complained of being ruled from abroad and anti-Tutsi sentiment deepened. Some Rwandan soldiers were assassinated in

---

255. Bill Berkeley, 251.
256. Michaela Wrong, 32.

Kinshasa and Kabila was forced to recall his AFDL troops from other regions in order to redress the imbalance of Rwandans who were stationed in Kinshasa.

Within Kinshasa itself, Kabila made a concerted effort to crack down on crime and rampaging soldiers. Whereas the population had once feared the FAZ, with its practices of arbitrary arrests, detentions, torture, and establishing road-blocks that were shakedowns for money, the Army (renamed the FAC, or Forces Armées Congolaises, under Kabila) was less predatory and more disciplined than before. This gained Kabila support among Kinshasa's poor people, who had been preyed on in previous years. Unfortunately, however, this new regime of safety did not extend beyond Kinshasa. In other parts of the country, Kabila's reforms had little effect, if any.

Among the Congolese who welcomed Kabila were Kasaiens who had been forcibly expelled from southern Katanga by members of a Katangan political party that was led by Gabriel Kyungu wa Kumwanza. During Mobutu's reign, many Kasaiens had lost family members and property simply because they were not native Katangese. The success of Kabila raised hopes that they could regain what they had lost and that the Katangese would be prosecuted. However, Kabila only appointed criminals like Kyungu to high posts in the government and within the business community.[257] Kabila also banished Etienne Tshisekedi, the head of the nation's largest political party, to his native village in Kasai.

As for political reforms, Kabila decided early on that the country must be "reeducated" before elections could be held. Much as Mobutu had done with the MPR, he declared all parties other than the AFDL to be illegal in the eyes of the government and without rights in the country. The new law declared that those wishing to continue to operate as a party must register with the Ministry of Interior within thirty days. For an application to be accepted, it would need to be signed by 150 founding members of the party, who, in turn, had to be resident in the DRC. A nonrefundable fee of 30,000 Congolese francs ($10,000 US dollars) would also have to be paid. The decree of January 31 explicitly pro-hibited political activity for those who had not continuously resided in the DRC for at least the past two months, thus aiming to restrict the Mobutists who had fled the country from legal participation.[258]

---

257. Musifiky Mwanasali, 61.
258. Inter Press Service English News Wire, "DR Congo: Kabila's Decision to Ban Existing Parties Criticized," *Inter Press Service English News Wire*, February 5, 1999.

By now, there were over 400 parties, whose largest stakeholders were as follows: the Union for Democracy and Social Progress (UDPS) whose leader was Etienne Tshisekedi; the Parti democrate-social chrétien (Christian Social-Democratic Party-PDSC); and Olegankoy's FONUS (Forces Novatrices de l'Union Sacrée). There also remained the National Congolese Movement/Lumumba.[259] Eventually, Kabila let himself be pressured into declaring that elections would be held in 1999. But his promises led to delays, and few doubted that they meant much. Polls conducted in Kinshasa showed that fewer than 1 in 5 would vote for Kabila, and he surely knew this.[260]

In order to combat his opposition, Kabila established a Court of Military Order in 1997 via presidential decree No. 019. The Court's initial purpose was to restore military discipline in the capital and its environs, but its position became more ominous in August 1998. Then, its jurisdiction was expanded to include Katanga, Kasai, and Bas Congo, and roving courts were added. Decree Law 171 of January 2, 1999 expanded the Court's rights further and also declared a state of emergency due to a new rebellion. The Court was given the right to replace civilian authorities, appropriate private property, and to forcibly recruit civilians for military endeavors. Death sentences became common and the only means of appeal in such instances was a plea to the president, who appointed all of the judges. Court officials and prosecutors expressed strong support for the death penalty, saying that it was necessary to eliminate "suspected rebels, common criminals, ill-disciplined military, and collaborators with the enemy."[261] Since its inception, the Court conducted more than 250 executions, and was increasingly used by the government to punish nonviolent opposition and outspoken critics.

Although the security regime of Mobutu was effectively disbanded, it only resulted in the outgrowth of new agencies whose main preoccupation was the potential for internal insurrection. Thus, there emerged a new national police force under the Ministry of the Interior, a National Security Council (CNS), and a number of other agencies with the power to arrest, detain, and investigate, including the Rapid Intervention Police (PIR), the National Informationa Agency (ANR), the Military Detection of Anti-Patriotic Activists (DEMIAP), the National Security Directorship (DESN), and others.[262]

---

259. International Crisis Group.
260. Stefan Lovgren; Kevin Whitelaw, "Mobutuism without Mobutu," *US News & World Report*, November 24, 1997.
261. Africa News Service, "Congo Conducting Mass Executions," *African News Service*, February 10, 2000.

The Kabila regime also established a track record of opposing non-governmental organizations (NGOs). Suspecting that their reason for existence was to incite opposition against the State by protecting anti-government elements within the refugee camps, Kabila took a number of actions against local human rights organizations. One of the country's main groups, AZADHO (later ASADHO), was banned, and other local organizations were required to register with the Justice Ministry. Asylum Law reports that more than 100 groups were denied recognition and that the government has been involved in harassing human rights organizations. Local offices have been raided and human rights activists have been arrested or received death threats or other forms of intimidation.

During his first year in office, Kabila made two cabinet reshuffles. The first, in September, was minor. The second, in November, was substantial. Then Deputy Minister of Economy, Commerce, and Industry, Jean Amisi Kalondaya, was elevated to finance minister to replace Mawampanga Mwana Nanga, whom Kabila held responsible for the country's economic collapse. Also replaced was his controversial foreign minister, Abdoulaye Yerodia Ndombasi, who had had an arrest warrant issued against him by an outraged judge in Belgium for inciting ethnic hatred. Ndombasi was replaced by Human Rights Minister Leonard She Okitundu.[263]

To support the new Congolese franc that was introduced in June of 1998, Kabila outlawed all transactions in any form of foreign currency, including US dollars, which had been the one secure basis for commerce up until then. Diamond producers and other exporters preferred to smuggle their goods abroad rather than be paid in nontransferable Congolese francs; as a result, the ban on foreign currency had a severe impact on the country's export earnings and crippled the new government in terms of collected revenue. To make matters worse, inflation was riding high at 240 percent and there was little if any confidence that the regime would bring better results.[264]

As for government investment in social services, spending for health under Kabila was less than one percent of the budget. The DRC was suffering from a severe shortage of medical staff and hospitals, and average life expectancy was

---

262. Asylum Law, "Democratic Republic of Congo Assessment," Version 4, September, 1999, http://www.asylumlaw.org/docs/congodemocraticrepublic/ind99b_congodr_ca.htm.
263. Kenneth Ingham, "Year in Review 2000: world-affairs Congo, Democratic Republic of the (the former Zaire)," Encyclopaedia Britannica, www.britannica.com.
264. Ibid.

estimated at 52 and 50.4 years for males and females respectively. Likewise, less than one percent of central government spending was aimed at education. Although primary education for those aged between 6 and 12 years was officially compulsory, a high percentage of children did not have access. The official levels of enrollment were placed at half for primary school children and 20 percent for those who were in the secondary school age group of 12 to 18 years.

In the international sphere, there was a meeting at the World Bank in Brussels where the US urged the governments of 14 countries to grant financial assistance to the DRC in the form of a $4 billion trust fund, and the US also asked that these countries resume bilateral assistance. When a World Bank official was asked about the political implications of assisting a regime that had come to power through bloodshed, one interviewed official replied that "the bank does not take a position on how a regime comes to power, and that, as an apolitical institution, massacres are beyond the bank's mandate."[265]

In the course of preparing to rule, Kabila was also said to have established contacts with the Hutu ex-FAR and Interahamwe. He did this as early as 1997, at the same time that he met with the Mayi-Mayi (a cross ethnic group native to the Congo that had aided the AFDL) and those rebel groups that were plaguing Uganda and Angola, including the Ugandan ADF (Allied Democratic Forces) and the Burundian FDD (Forces pour la Défense et de la Démocratie). In meeting with the enemies of his supporters, he is said to have laid the groundwork for expelling his erstwhile allies: Rwanda, Uganda, and Angola. And this he did in 1998, after demoting James Kabare, his Rwandan Chief of Staff. Without formality or preamble, Kabila demanded that all Rwandans leave the country on July 27, 1998.

This sparked varying reactions. By now, Uganda and Rwanda had already concluded that Kabila was an incompetent leader. He was not willing to forge an inclusive government that would include his opposition, nor would he take steps to stabilize the economy. Moreover, attacks by the rebels that opposed Rwanda and Uganda from Congolese territory continued unabated. Kabila demanded that they leave, but they were already working to find a candidate they could support to replace him.

---

265. David Aronson, "America's myopic Africa policy: CONGO GAMES," *The New Republic*, January 5, 1998.

THE SECOND CONGO WAR

Within the FAC, tensions were already high between soldiers of Tutsi origin and other Congolese ethnicities. It took no more than Kabila's announcement to expel their foreign allies to set off a chain of rebellions. There were open clashes within the Army as the Tutsi FAC refused to lay down their arms. A pogrom against Tutsis resulted, and it was conducted against men, women, and children throughout the whole of the Congo.[266] Tutsis were massacred, arrested, and even publicly lynched in Kinshasa, Lumbumbashi, and Kisangani. A loyalist army broadcast from a radio station in Bunia proclaimed that "People must bring a machete, a spear, an arrow, a hoe, spades, rakes, nails, truncheons, electric irons, barbed wire, stones, and the like, in order, dear listeners, to kill the Rwandan Tutsis."[267]

In the meantime, two of the best and largest Army units mutinied. These were stationed in the east and were in close contact with Rwanda, which intervened to support them. This was followed closely by the incident of August 4, in which a plane load of Rwandans and Ugandans was hijacked and landed at Kitona army base within the western Congo where between 10,000 and 15,000 former Mobutu soldiers were being reeducated. These joined the Rwandans and Ugandans who had been on board the plane, and, after swiftly overwhelming Kitona, began a march on Kinshasa.[268]

By then, Uganda and Rwanda had convened a meeting in Goma (in the east of the Congo) where they brought together the anti-Kabila forces to form a new rebel movement called the Rassemblement Congolais pour Démocratie (RCD). Among the RCD's first founders was Arthur Zaidi Ngoma, the first person nominated to lead the rebellion. The RCD also included the Banyamulenge (Zairian Tutsi) faction of the FAC and former Mobutists who had been scorned and harassed by Kabila. The RCD immediately took Bukavu and Uvira, two towns in the Kivus, while Rwanda, Uganda, and Burundi were moving in northeastern Congo. By August 13, the rebels held the Inga hydro-electric station that provided power to Kinshasa in addition to the port of Matadi through which most of Kinshasa's food passed.[269] Christian Scherrer reports:

---

266. Tatiana Carayannis, "The complex wars of the Congo: towards a new analytic approach," *Journal of Asian and African Studies*, August 1, 2003.
267. Wikipedia, http://en.widipedia.org.
268. Ibid.
269. Ibid.

Inconvenience in the dark city and insecurity were greatly exacerbated by radio hate propaganda and an all-out ethnicization campaign: the result were state-sponsored genocidal atrocities in the Kinshasa city area and across the government-held territory. In Kinshasa alone some twelve hundred victims were hunted by Kabila's newly created Force de l'Autodéfense Populaire (FAP) and were publicly and brutally killed. The destiny of five hundred fifty Tutsi, who were taken from the Kokolo military camp to an unknown destination, is still unknown. The moral order was seriously disturbed; the dehumanization of the victims went that far that even acts of cannibalism were reported by human rights and victims organizations.[270]

Kabila himself had transmitted televised appeals to the public, saying, "In every village the people must get armed, be it with spears, bows and arrows and other weapons, and exterminate the enemy, [to avoid] becoming the slaves of the Tutsi." His foreign minister, Abdoulaye Yerodia, also incited violence by telling the public that "they [the Tutsi] are like insects, and even microbes must methodically and resolutely be exterminated."[271]

But now, Angola defected from its former alliance with Rwanda and Uganda. It attacked from its bases in Cabinda and put a halt to the advance of Rwandan and Ugandan forces in the western Congo. Angolan air power protected Mbuji Mayi and Mbandaka, and Kabila also responded by mobilizing the ex-FAR and Interahamwe. He further appealed for help to the members of the SADC (South African Development Community). In addition to Angola, Zimbabwe, Namibia, Libya, Chad, and Sudan responded.

The diamond center of Kisangani fell on August 23. In September 1998, Zimbabwean forces were flown into Kinshasa. While they protected the capital of the Congo, Angola attacked northward and eastward from its borders. Uganda, in retaliation, conspired to form a new rebel movement called the MLC (Movement for the Liberation of the Congo). When a peace summit was held at Windhoek, Namibia on January 18, 1999, Rwanda, Uganda, Angola, Namibia, and Zimbabwe participated but neither the RCD nor the MLC was invited. Thus, the peace agreement came to nothing.

The Roman Catholic Church reported a massacre of 500 people that took place at the start of the New Year within the eastern Congo. Occurring in Makobola, the massacre was said to be the largest since the start of the rebellion. It was reportedly conducted by Tutsis who were driven off by the Mayi-Mayi; they returned when the latter retreated and committed further murders.[272]

---

270. Christian P. Scherrer, 254.

271. Ibid., 255.

272. Seattle Post-Intelligencer, "Massacre of 500 People Reported in East Congo," *Seattle Post-Intelligencer*, January 6, 1999.

Ugandan forces traveled deep into the country to secure the airports at Kisangani and Kindu, lest the towns be used as bases for the bombing of Uganda. The RCD confirmed that it had taken the town of Lubao in Kasai Oriental and that it had used the towns of Samba and Kabao to launch this invasion. Although the FAC declined to fight the RCD, it reportedly encountered strong resistance from Katangese extremists and Rwandan Interahamwe. Lubao, in turn, was seen as a starting-point for an invasion of Mbjui Mayi, a key target due to its mineral wealth.[273] In retaliation, the Zimbabwe air force started the indiscriminate bombing of rebel-held towns and cities over a period of months.

In April of 1999, Libya brokered a further agreement between Uganda's Museveni and the government in Kinshasa. The RCD and Rwanda refused to take part in the process, and this led to trouble in the RCD. Tensions which had been simmering within the RCD due to the dominance of the Banyamulenge resulted in a split among its members. Ernest Wamba dia Wamba was ousted as the head of the RCD and replaced by a pro-Rwanda figure. Wamba subsequently moved to Kisangani, where he established a new movement called the RCD-K/ML. The remainder of the RCD resettled in the region of Goma, and took the name of RCD-Goma.

Rwanda now announced that it would unilaterally observe a ceasefire on May 28, 1999. This gave momentum to a DRC-Ugandan initiative that was aimed at drawing up a plan to withdraw Uganda's troops while providing for joint defensive arrangements along their respective borders. With that in mind, a team of Libyan peacekeepers arrived in Kampala. Then, on June 7, 1999, a summit was held in Harare. There, the presidents of Angola, Namibia, and Zimbabwe declared that Rwanda's cease-fire announcement was void due to the fact that it had begun a new campaign to support the RCD within the eastern Congo.[274]

On June 1999, the RPA captured Lusambo in Kasai Oriental and threatened to move on to the diamond mines of Mbuji Mayi. The situation worsened as forces of the MLC also threatened Mbandaka. By now, the government was straining to control the Congo through an alliance of many disparate groups, which also included the ex-FAR/Interahamwe. A complete list of the many engaged groups is provided here, as follows.

---

273. Chris Simpson, "DR Congo: Rifts Within the rebel Movement Appear to be Widening," *Inter Press Service English News Wire*, February 1, 1999.

274. MONUC, Peacekeeping in the DRC: The Lusaka Ceasefire Agreement," (New York: UN Documents, October 2001) Monograph No. 66.

THE CONGOLESE REBEL PARTIES

RCD (Congolese Assembly for Democracy): As mentioned, the RCD was created by Uganda and Rwanda to both legitimize their invasion and to embrace the Congolese insurgents. In addition to Arthur Zaidi Ngoma, a lawyer in the field of human rights who was elected to lead the rebellion, the movement was comprised of such prominent political figures as Bizima Karaha (former minister of foreign affairs under Kabila); Shambuyi Kalala (formerly in charge of propaganda for the AFDL); Emile Ilunga (who wanted to be president of the political wing of the Katangan Tigers); Moise Nyarugamo (formerly Kabila's private secretary); Deogratias Bugera (formerly secretary-general of the AFDL); Wamba dia Wamba (a professor of history who would be elected to replace Ngoma as the RCD's leader); Alexis Tambwe (who previously held office in the Tshisekedi government that opposed Mobutu); and Lundu Bululu (Mobutu's prime minister in May 1990). The RCD split into two groups in 1999 when Wamba dia Wamba was expelled from command.[275]

RCD-Goma: One of the two parties resulting from the split of the RCD in 1999. Called RCD-Goma because it was headquartered in Goma, it is said to have been supported by two armed factions, the ANC (Armée Nationale Congolaise) and an auxiliary militia known as the Forces de Défense Locales (FDL). RCD-Goma is an ally of Rwanda. Headed by Emile Ilunga, its strength was gauged at between 17,000 and 20,000 men in 2000. It exercises control over parts of south Kivu, Maniema, North Kivu, Oriental and Katanga, and has created an administrative government in order to rule these areas.

RCD-K/ML (Rassemblement Congolais pour la Démocratie-Kisnagania/ Mouvement de Libération): The second party resulting from the split of the RCD in 1999, it was founded by Wamba dia Wamba and eventually led by Mbusa Nyamwisi. The RCD-K/ML initially allied itself with the MLC (below) and Uganda to counter the influence of RCD-Goma (supported by Rwanda) within parts of eastern Congo. Its armed wing is called the Armée Populaire Congolaise (APC), and its headquarters is situated in the Beni region of North Kivu. Its strength was gauged at 2,500 in 2000. In 2001, the RCD-K/ML became an ally of the Kinshasa government.

RCD-N (Rassemblement Congolais pour la Démocratie-National): The RCD-N split off from the RCD-K/ML (above) when the latter abandoned its

---

275. International Crisis Group.

alliance with Uganda to join the Kinshasa government in 2001. The RCD-N has remained faithful to Uganda and is led by Robert Lumbala. It is also aligned with the MLC (below).

UPC (Union des Patriotes Congolaises): Led by Thomas Lubanga, the UPC, like the RCD-N, also split off from the RCD-K/ML but it did so in June of 2002. Led by Thomas Lubanga, it was loyal to Uganda until that country withdrew its support in January of 2003, at which time Lubanga sought alliance with RCD-Goma (above).

MLC (Mouvement de Libération du Congo): Led by Jean-Pierre Bemba, its areas of influence are the province of Equateur, as well as large portions of Orientale province with a strength of approximately 6,000-7,500 fighters. Its supporters are primarily Uganda and former allies of Mobutu. It was allied with RCD-K/ML (above) until the latter became an ally of Kinshasa in 2001.

The Banyamulenge (Congolese Tutsis): Having lived in the Congo for centuries, the Tutsi who originally came from Rwanda have had to fight for their rights in Zaire. They were denied citizenship under Mobutu and they have fared no better under Kabila, who, after originally showing them favor during the 1996 rebellion, created an exceedingly hostile environment toward them, resulting in mass murder and lynchings.

THE FOREIGN REBEL SUPPORTERS

FAB (Forces Armées Burundaises): The Burundian armed forces joined the Congolese rebellion in order to fight against its own insurgent groups who were stationed in the Congo. The FAB was allied with Rwanda and RCD-Goma, and occupied a portion of South Kivu until September 2002. In the year 2,000, Burundi had approximately 2,000 soldiers in the Congo.

FPR (Front Patriotique Rwandais): The FPR is the army of Rwanda, which invaded from Uganda in 1990 to take power in Kigali by 1994. The FPR first crossed the Congolese border in 1996 to fight against the ex-FAR and Interahamwe who were sheltering in the country. Its cause remains the same today. The FPR helped to create the RCD in 1988, and was to be allied with RCD-Goma when the split in the RCD occurred in 1999. Rwanda's strength in the Congo was gauged at between 17,000 and 25,000 fighters at the end of the year 2000. After the FPR became a political party, its armed wing was known as the RPA (Rwandan Patriotic Army)

UDPF (Ugandan People's Defense Force): Commanded by Brigadier Katumba Wamala, the UDPF had some 10,000 troops in Equateur Province, acting from a headquarters in Gbadolite. The rationale for this Ugandan presence in the Congo is much like that of the Burundi and Rwanda forces: to fight against the insurgents. Uganda, with Rwanda, contributed to the formation of the RCD; in the wake of the split in the RCD in 1999 it became the main supporter of RCD-K/ML. Other Congolese parties that it sponsored include the MLC, the RCD-N, and, until January 2003, the UPC. Uganda was said to have 10,000 soldiers in the Congo by the end of the year 2000.

GOVERNMENT FORCES AND ALLIES

The FAC (Forces Armées Conglaises): The army of the Congo, it commanded between 45,000 and 55,000 soldiers at the end of the year 2000. It is made up of former soldiers from Mobutu's FAZ and rebel elements of Kabila's AFDL.

The Katangan Tigers: Comprised of former gendarmes of Katanga who fled to Angola in 1964, the Katangan Tigers has split into two wings in the present. One is led from Angola by Henri Mukatshung Mwambu and the other was led from Brussels by Dr. Emile Ilunga. Ilunga went on to oppose Kabila by joining the RCD, at which time the Katangan Tigers united and chose to support Kabila.

People's Civil Defense (Défense civile et populaire): In Kinshasa and elsewhere, "people's" roadblocks are set up to check identification papers. They are especially venal toward Congolese Tutsis, since Kabila's policies and embrace of the ex-FAR/Interahamwe have created an anti-Tutsi hysteria.

Mayi-Mayi (also called Mai-Mai): Cross-ethnic Congolese who object to the invasion by Rwanda and Uganda. In general, they have been allied with Kabila; however, certain factions such as the Mudundu 40 have sided with the Rwandans. In September 1999, Kabila named a Mayi-Mayi commander Sylvestre Louetcha as head of the army general staff.

FDLR (Forces Démocratiques pour la Liberation du Rwanda): A union of Hutu extremists formerly belonging to the ex-FAR and the Interahamwe. The Kinshasa government supported the FDLR which opposes Rwanda and RCD-Goma. As of October 2002, the government would cut ties with the FDLR in exchange for the withdrawal of Rwanda's forces. Its strength, when allied with the ALiR (below) was said to be between 30,000 and 40,000, as of the year 2000.

ALiR (Armee de Libération du Rwanda): A collection of Hutus who oppose the Tutsi government in Kigali, but are not associated with the genocide of 1994. They have, however, joined hands with the FDLR (above). The ALiR began as a guerrilla movement in May 1997 before being pushed into the Congo in 1998.

FDD (Forces pour la Défense de la Démocratie) and FNL (Front National de Libération): The FDD is a movement that was founded by Leonard Nyagoma following the assassination of President Melchior Ndadaye in 1993. Originating in Burundi, FDD and the FNL are the main guerrilla movements that have been fighting the Burundian government from Congolese soil. Its strength in 2000 was said to be 16,000 soldiers. But, as of December 2002, these factions signed ceasefires with Burundi and agreed to cooperate with the formation of a transitional government.

ADF (Allied Democratic Front), West Nile Bank Front, and the LRA (Lord's Resistance Army): Three insurgent rebellions that are directed against Uganda. The LRA is led by Joseph Kony, a self-proclaimed mystic who has conducted a campaign of terror against the population of northern Uganda, particularly recruiting children. (Sudan had backed these groups in retaliation for Uganda's support of the Sudan People's Liberation Army (SPLA).)

Zimbabwe: President Robert Mugabe's interests coincide with power and wealth. He is, on the one hand, determined to outshine South Africa as the leader of the SADC (South African Development Commission) and, on the other, to strip the Congo of mineral wealth. Mugabe and Kabila are linked due to their Marxist pasts, and they were known to each other before the start of the war. The size of Zimbabwe's forces in the country (gauged at 11,000 in 2002) is second only to Rwanda's.

Angola: The government of Luanda is, of course, critical of the Kabila regime for allowing UNITA rebels to operate from its territory. It joined the second Congo war on the side of Kabila, having helped to bring him to power, and also to eliminate any prospect of support for UNITA. President dos Santos was criticized for intervening in the Congo as his troops are badly needed at home. In 2002, dos Santos had between 2,000 and 2,500 soldiers in Congo.

Namibia: The Namibian government, too, has interests in Congolese mining. It also has an interest in diverting water from the Congo River across Angola to Namibia. The Namibian public is opposed to intervention in the Congo and has been alarmed by the presence of UNITA on its borders. UNITA threatened to invade Namibia if it did not withdraw from the Congo. In 2000,

Namibia had between 1,600 and 2,000 soldiers in Congo, and it had supplied the DRC with about twenty tons of weaponry.

Sudan: Sudan did not contribute a significant military presence, even though it was said to be fighting in Orientale province against the rebels. It did, however, continue to offer extensive support to the three Ugandan rebel movements: the LRA, ADF, and the West Nile Bank Front, in retaliation for Ugandan support of the Sudan People's Liberation Army.

Chad: Chad was persuaded by France to supply the Congo with 1,000 troops. France apparently saw this as the only credible means to become reengaged in the region after its 1994 action in Rwanda.

Libya: Muammar al-Qaddafi provided the planes to transport the Chadian soldiers. Some say that he means to profit financially, but his attempts at being a negotiator for the DRC point to something different. It is likely that he saw this as a way to emerge from international ostracism after the Lockerbie, Scotland incident.

SIGNING THE LUSAKA ACCORD

It was not until June 17 that South Africa arranged for a summit to take place in Lusaka with the purpose of signing another ceasefire. The meeting, which got moving on July 2, was to mark the start of a direct dialogue between the government and the three main rebel groups: the RCD-Goma, the RCD-K/ML, and the MLC. After a third week of negotiations, the summit produced the Lusaka ceasefire agreement, which was signed by the DRC, Zimbabwe, Namibia, Angola, Rwanda, and Uganda, but not by the rebel groups.[276] Executed on July 10, 1999 the agreement called for:

- A cessation of hostilities and the disengagement/redeployment of foreign forces.
- The orderly withdrawal of all foreign forces.
- A national dialogue and reconciliation.
- Reestablishment of state administration over the territory of the DRC.
- Disarmament of armed groups.
- The formation of a national army.
- The normalization of the security situation along the common borders between the DRC and its neighbors. [277]

---

276. MONUC, "Peacekeeping in the DRC: The Lusaka Ceasefire Agreement."

On August 1, 1999, Jean-Pierre Bemba signed the Accord on behalf of the MLC. This was followed, on August 31, by signatures from the fifty founding members of the RCD. A Joint Military Commission (JMC) was established to regulate and monitor the cessation of hostilities on behalf of the agreement's signatories in preparation for the deployment of UN and OAU (Organization of African Unity) observers. Sir Ketumile Masire, former president of Botswana, was appointed as facilitator for the OAU negotiations. The JMC's observers were to be responsible for peacekeeping functions until the UN arrived. The entire text of the Lusaka Ceasefire Agreement is provided here as follows:

The Lusaka Cease-fire Agreement

Preamble

We the parties to this Agreement;

Considering Article 52 of the UN Charter on regional arrangements for dealing with matters relating to the maintenance of international peace and security as are appropriate for regional action;

Reaffirming the provisions of Article 3 of the OAU Charter which, inter alia, guarantee all Member States the right to their sovereignty and territorial integrity;

Reaffirming further Resolution AHG/16/1 adopted by the OAU Assembly of Heads of State and Government in 1964 in Cairo, Egypt, on territorial integrity and the inviolability of national boundaries as inherited at independence.

Recalling the Pretoria Summit Communique dated 23rd August, 1998 reaffirming that all ethnic groups and nationalities whose people and territory constituted what became Congo (now DRC) at independence must enjoy equal rights and protection under the law as citizens.

Determined to ensure the respect, by all Parties signatory to this Agreement, for the Geneva Conventions of 1949 and the Additional Protocols of 1977, and the Convention on the Prevention and Punishment of the Crime of Genocide of 1948, as reiterated at the Entebbe Regional Summit of 25 March, 1998;

---

277. MONUC, "Peacekeeping in the DRC: The Lusaka Ceasefire Agreement."

Determined further to put to an immediate halt to any assistance, collaboration or giving of sanctuary to negative forces bent on destabilizing neighbouring countires;

Emphasizing the need to ensure that the principles of good neighbourliness and non-interference in the internal affairs of other countries are respected;

Concerned about the conflict in the Democratic Republic of Congo and its negative impact on the country and other countries in the Great Lakes Region;

Reiterating the call made at the Second Victoria Falls Summit held from 7 to 8 September, 1998, as contained in the Joint Communique of the Summit, for the immediate cessation of hostilities;

Cognisant of the fact that adressing the security concerns of the DRC and neighbouring countries is central and would contribute to the peace process;

Recalling the mandate, contained in the Victoria Falls II Joint Communique, given to the Ministers of Defence and other officials working in close cooperation with the OAU and the UN to establish the modalities for effecting an immediate ceasefire and put in place a mechanism for monitoring compliance with the ceasefire provisions;

Recalling the United Nations Security Council Resolution 1234 of 9 April, 1999 and all other Resolutions and Decisions on the DRC since 2 August, 1998;

Recalling further the Summit meetings of Victoria Falls I and II, Pretoria, Durban, Port Louis, Nairobi, Windhoek, Dodoma and the Lusaka and Gabarone Ministerial peace efforts on the DRC conflict;

Recalling further the Peace Agreement signed on 18 April, 1999 at Sirte (Libya);

Recognising that the conflict in the DRC has both internal and external dimensions that require intra-Congolese political negotiations and commitment of the Parties to the implementation of this Agreement to resolve;

Taking note of the commitment of the Congolese Government, the RCD, the MLC and all other Congolese political and civil organizations to hold an all inclusive National Dialogue aimed at realizing national reconciliation and a new political dispensation in the DRC;

Hereby Agree as Follows:

Article I

The Cease-Fire

The Parties agree to a cease-fire among all their forces in the DRC.

The cease-fire shall mean:

• the cessation of hostilities between all the belligerent forces in the DRC, as provided for in this Cease-fire Agreement (hereinafter referred to as "the Agreement");

• the effective cessation of hostilities, military movements and reinforcements, as well as hostile actions, including hostile propaganda;

• a cessation of hostilities within 24 hours of the signing of the Cease-fire agreement;

• The Ceasefire shall entail the cessation of:

• all air, land, and sea attacks as well as all actions of sabotage;

• attempts to occupy new ground positions and the movement of military forces and resources from one area to another, without prior agreement between the parties;

• all acts of violence against the civilian population by respecting and protecting human rights. The acts of violence include summary executions, torture, harassment, detention and execution of civilians based on their ethnic origin; propaganda inciting ethnic and tribal hatred; arming civilians; recruitment and use of child soldiers; sexual violence; training and use of terrorists; massacres, downing of civilian aircraft; and bombing the civilian population;

• supplies of ammunition and weaponry and other war-related stores to the field;

• any other actions that may impede the normal evolution of the cease-fire process.

Article II

Security Concerns

On the coming into force of this Agreement the Parties commit themselves to immediately address the security concerns of the DRC and her neighbouring countries.

Article III

Principles of the Agreement

The provisions of paragraph 3 (e) do not preclude the supply of food, clothing and medical support for the military forces in the field.

The cease-fire shall guarantee the free movement of persons and goods throughout the national territory of the Democratic Republic of Congo.

On the coming into force of the Agreement, the Parties shall release persons detained or taken hostage and shall give them the latitude to relocate to any provinces within the DRC or country where their security will be guaranteed.

The Parties to the Agreement commit themselves to exchange prisoners of war and release any other persons detained as a result of the war.

The Parties shall allow immediate and unhindered access to the International Committee of the Red Cross (ICRC) and Red Crescent for the purpose of arranging the release of prisoners of war and other persons detained as a result of the war as well as the recovery of the dead and the treatment of the wounded.

The Parties shall facilitate humanitarian assistance through the opening up of humanitarian corridors and creation of conditions conducive to the provision of urgent humanitarian assistance to displaced persons, refugees and other affected persons.

The United Nations Security Council, acting under Chapter VII of the UN Charter and in collaboration with the OAU, shall be requested to constitute, facilitate and deploy an appropriate peacekeeping force in the DRC to ensure implementation of this Agreement; and taking into account the peculiar situation of the DRC, mandate the peacekeeping force to track down all armed groups in the DRC. In this respect, the UN Security Council shall provide the requisite mandate for the peace-keeping force.

The Parties shall constitute a Joint Military Commission (JMC) which shall, together with the UN/OAU Observer group be responsible for executing, immediately after the coming into force of this Agreement, peace-keeping operations until the deployment of the UN peace-keeping force. Its composition and mandate shall be as stipulated in Chapter 7 of Annex 'A' of this Agreement.

The final withdrawal of all foreign forces from the national territory of the DRC shall be carried out in accordance with the Calendar in Annex B of this Agreement and a withdrawal schedule to be prepared by the UN, the OAU and the JMC.

The laying of mines of whatever type shall be prohibited.

There shall be immediate disengagement of forces in the areas where they are in direct contact.

Nothing in the Agreement shall in any way undermine the sovereignty and territorial integrity of the Democratic Republic of Congo.

The Parties re-affirm that all ethnic groups and nationalities whose people and territory constituted what became Congo (now DRC) at independence must enjoy equal rights and protection under the law as citizens.

The Parties to the Agreement shall take all necessary measures aimed at securing the normalization of the situation along the international borders of the Democratic Republic of Congo, including the control of illicit trafficking of arms and the infiltration of armed groups.

In accordance with the terms of the Agreement and upon conclusion of the Inter-Congolese political negotiations, state administration shall be re-established throughout the national territory of the Democratic Republic of Congo.

On the coming into force of the Agreement, the Government of the DRC, the armed opposition, namely the RCD and MLC as well as the unarmed opposition shall enter into an open national dialogue. These inter-Congolese political negotiations involving les forces vives shall lead to a new political dispensation and national reconciliation in the DRC. The inter-Congolese political negotiations shall be under the aegis of a neutral facilitator to be agreed upon by the Congolese parties. All the Parties commit themselves to supporting this dialogue and shall ensure that the inter-Congolese political negotiations are conducted in accordance with the provisions of Chapter 5 of Annex 'A'.

In accordance with the terms of the Agreement and upon the conclusion of the national dialogue, there shall be a mechanism for the formation of a national, restructured and integrated army, including the forces of the Congolese Parties who are signatories to this Agreement, on the basis of negotiations between the Government of the Democratic Republic of Congo and the RCD and MLC.

The Parties affirm the need to address the security concerns of the DRC and her neighbouring countries.

There shall be a mechanism for disarming militias and armed groups, including the genocidal forces. In this context, all Parties commit themselves to the process of locating, identifying, disarming and assembling all members of armed groups in the DRC. Countries of origin of members of the armed groups, commit themselves to taking all the necessary measures to facilitate their repatriation. Such measures may include the granting of amnesty in countries where such a measure has been deemed beneficial. It shall, however, not apply in the case of the suspects of the crime of genocide. The Parties assume full responsibility of ensuring that armed groups operating alongside their troops or on the territory under their control, comply with the processes leading to the dismantling of those groups in particular.

The Parties shall ensure the implementation of the terms of the Agreement and its Annexes 'A' and 'B' which form an integral part of the Agreement.

The definitions of common terms used are at Annex 'C'.

The Agreement shall take effect 24 hours after signature.

The Agreement may be amended by agreement of the Parties and any such amendment shall be in writing and shall be signed by them in the same way as the Agreement.

In Witness Whereof the duly authorized representatives of the Parties have signed the Agreement in the English, French and Portuguese languages, all texts being equally authentic.

Done; at Lusaka (Zambia) on This __ Day of ____ _____

For the Republic of Angola
For the Democratic Republic of Congo
For the Republic of Namibia;
For the Republic of Rwanda;
For the Republic of Uganda;
For the Republic of Zimbabwe;
For the Congolese Rally for Democracy (RCD);
For the Movement For the Liberation of the Congo (MLC);

As Witnesses:

For the Republic of Zambia;
For the Organization of African Unity;
For the United Nations;
For the Southern African Development Community

Annex 'A' to the Cease-fire Agreement

Modalities for the Implementation of the Cease-fire Agreement in the Democratic Republic of Congo

Chapter I

Cessation of Hostilities

The Parties, shall announce a cessation of hostilities, to be effective 24 hours after the signing of the Cease Fire Agreement. The announcement of cessation of hostilities shall be disseminated by the parties through command channels, and it shall concurrently be communicated to the civil population via print and the electronic media.

Until the deployment of United Nations/Organisation of African Unity (UN/OAU) observers, the cessation of hostilities shall be regulated and monitored by the Parties through the Joint Military Commission. With the deployment of UN/OAU observers, the responsibility of verification, control and monitoring of the cessation of hostilities and subsequent disengagement shall be reported through UN/OAU.

Any violation of the cessation of hostilities and subsequent events shall be reported to the Joint Military Commission and to the UN/OAU mechanisms through the agreed chain of command for investigation and action as necessary.

Chapter 2

Disengagement

The disengagement of forces shall mean the immediate breaking of tactical contact between the opposing Military Forces of the Parties to this Agreement at places where they are in direct contact by the effective date and time of the Cease-Fire Agreement.

Where immediate disengagement is not possible, a framework and sequence of disengagement is to be agreed by all Parties through the Joint Military Commission/UN and OAU.

Immediate disengagement at the initiative of all military units shall be limited to the effective range of direct fire weapons. Further disengagement to pull all weapons out of range, shall be conducted under the guidance of the Joint Military Commission/UN and OAU.

Wherever disengagement by movement is impossible or impractical, alternative solutions requiring that weapons are rendered safe shall be designed by the Joint Military Commission/UN and OAU.

Chapter 3

Release of Hostages and Exchange of Prisoners of War

Upon the cease-fire taking effect, all Parties shall provide ICRC/Red Crescent with relevant information concerning their prisoners of war or persons detained because of the war. They shall subsequently accord every assistance to the ICRC/Red Crescent representatives to enable them to visit the prisoners and detainees and verify any details and ascertain their condition and status.

On the coming into force of the Agreement, the Parties shall release persons detained because of the war or taken hostage within three days of the signing of the Cease-fire Agreement and the ICRC/Red Crescent shall give them all the necessary assistance including relocation to any provinces within the DRC or any other country where their security will be guaranteed.

Chapter 4

Orderly Withdrawal of all Foreign Forces

The final orderly withdrawal of all foreign forces from the national territory of the Democratic Republic of Congo shall be in accordance with Annex 'B' of this Agreement.

The Joint Military Commission/OAU and UN shall draw up a definitive schedule for the orderly withdrawal of all foreign forces from the Democratic Republic of the Congo.

Chapter 5

National Dialogue and Reconciliation

On the coming into force of the Cease-fire Agreement in the DRC, the Parties agree to do their utmost to facilitate the inter-Congolese political negotiations which should lead to a new political dispensation in the Democratic Republic of the Congo.

In order to arrive at a new political dispensation and national reconciliation arising from the inter-Congolese political negotiations, the Parties agree upon the implementation of the following principles:

- the inter-Congolese political negotiations process shall include the Congolese parties, namely the Government of the Democratic Republic of Congo, the Congolese Rally for Democracy and the Movement for the Liberation of the Congo, the political opposition as well as representatives of the forces vives;
- all the participants in the inter-Congolese political negotiations shall enjoy equal status;
- all the resolutions adopted by the inter-Congolese political negotiations shall be binding on all the participants;

The Parties agree that the Organisation of African Unity shall assist the Democratic Republic of Congo in organizing the inter-Congolese political negotiations under the aegis of a neutral facilitator chosen by the Parties by virtue of his/her moral authority, his/her international credibility and his/her experience.

For the success of the all inclusive inter-Congolese political negotiations leading to national reconciliation, the facilitator shall be responsible for:

- making the necessary contacts pertaining to the organization of the inter-Congolese political negotiations within an environment which will cater [to] to the security of all participants;
- organizing, in conjunction with the Congolese Parties, consultations with a view to inviting all the major organizations and groups of the recognized representative political opposition as well as the main representatives of the forces vives;
- conducting, in accordance with the timetable the discussions leading to the establishment of a new political dispensation in the Democratic Republic of Congo.

Without prejudice to other points that may be raised by the participants, the Congolese Parties shall agree [to]:-

- the timetable and the rules of procedure of the inter-Congolese political negotiations;
- the formation of a new Congolese National army whose soldiers shall originate from the Congolese Armed Forces, the armed forces of the RCD and the armed forces of the MLC;
- the new political dispensation in the DRC, in particular the institutions to be established for good governance purposes in the DRC;
- the process of free, democratic and transparent elections in the DRC;
- the draft of the Constitution which shall govern the DRC after the holding of the elections;

The calendar of the inter-Congolese political negotiations shall be as follows:

i. Selection of a facilitatorD-Day + 15 days

ii. Beginning of a national dialogueD-Day + 45 days

iii. Deadline for the close of the national dialogueD-Day + 90 days

iv. Establishment of new institutionsD-Day + 91 days

Chapter 6

Re-Establishment of the State Administration Over the Territory of the Democratic Republic of Congo

In accordance with the terms of the Agreement and upon conclusion of the Inter-Congolese political negotiations, state administrations shall be re-established throughout the national territory of the Democratic Republic of Congo.

On the coming into force of the Agreement, there shall be a consultative mechanism among the Congolese Parties which shall make it possible to carry out operations or actions throughout the national territory which are of general interest, more particularly in the fields of public health (e.g. national immigration campaign), education (e.g. marking of secondary school leavers examinations), migrations, movement of persons and goods.

Chapter 7

The Joint Military Commission

The Joint Military Commission shall be answerable to a Political Committee composed of the Ministers of Foreign Affairs and Defence or any other representative duly appointed by each Party.

The Joint Military Commission shall be a decision making body composed of two representatives from each Party under a neutral Chairman appointed by the OAU in consultation with the Parties.

The Joint Military Commission shall reach its decisions by consensus.

The mandate of the Joint Military Commission shall be to: -

- establish the location of Units at the time of the Cease-fire;
- facilitate liaison between the Parties for the purpose of the Cease-fire;
- assist in the disengagement of forces and the investigation of any cease-fire violations;
- verify all information, data and activities relating to military forces of the Parties;

- verify the disengagement of the military forces of the Parties where they are in direct contact;
- work out mechanisms for disarming armed groups;
- verify the disarmament and quartering of all armed groups;
- and verify the disarmament of all Congolese civilians who are illegally armed; and
- monitor and verify orderly withdrawal of all foreign forces.

The Parties commit themselves to providing the JMC with any relevant information on the organization, equipment and locations of their forces, on the understanding that such information will be kept confidential.

Chapter 8

United Nations Peace-Keeping Mandate

The UN in collaboration with the OAU shall constitute, facilitate and deploy an appropriate force in the DRC to ensure implementation of this Agreement.

The mandate of the UN force shall include peacekeeping and peace enforcement operations as outlined below:

- Work with the JMC/OAU in the implementation of this Agreement;
- Observe and monitor the cessation of hostilities;
- Investigate violations of the Cease-fire Agreement and take necessary measures to ensure compliance;
- Supervise disengagement of forces of the Parties as stipulated in Chapter 2 of this Annex;
- Supervise the re-deployment of forces of the Parties to Defensive Positions in conflict zones in accordance with Chapter 11 of this Agreement.
- Provide and maintain humanitarian assistance to and protect displaced persons, refugees and other affected persons;
- Keep the Parties to the Cease-fire Agreement informed of its peace-keeping operations;
- Collect weapons from civilians and ensure that the weapons so collected are properly accounted for and adequately secured;
- In collaboration with JMC/OAU, schedule and supervise the withdrawal of all foreign forces;
- Verify all information, data and activities relating to military forces of the Parties.

8.2.2 Peace Enforcement

a. Tracking down and disarming Armed Groups;

b. Screening mass killers, perpetrators of crimes against humanity and other war criminals;

c. Handing over "genocidaires" to the International Crimes Tribunal for Rwanda;

d. Repatriation;

e. Working out such measures (persuasive or coercive) as are appropriate for the attainment of the objectives of disarming, assembling, repatriation and reintegration into society of members of the Armed Groups.

8.3 Composition of the UN Peace-keeping forces shall be selected from countries acceptable to all of the Parties.

8.4 The Joint Military Commission shall, immediately upon the coming into force of the Agreement, be responsible for executing peace-keeping operations until the deployment of the UN Peace-keeping force.

Chapter 9

Disarmament of Armed Groups

The JMC with the assistance of the UN/OAU shall work out mechanisms for the tracking, disarming, cantoning and documenting of all armed groups in the DRC, including ex-FAR, ADF, LRA, UNFRll, Interhamwe, FUNA, FDD, WNBF, UNITA, and put in place measures for:

- handing over to the UN International Tribunal and national courts, mass killers and perpetrators of crimes against humanity; and
- handling of other war criminals.

The Parties together with the UN and other countries with security concerns, shall create conditions conducive to the attainment of the objective set out in 9.1 above, which conditions may include the granting of amnesty and political asylum, except for genodicaires. The Parties shall also encourage inter-community dialogue.

Chapter 10

Formation of a National Army

In accordance with the terms of the Agreement and following the inter-Congolese political negotiations, there shall be a mechanism taking into account, among others, the physical check of troops, the precise identification of troops, the precise identification of all elements with regard to their origin, date of their enlistment, the units to which they belong, as well as the identification of terrorists and the count of weapons of war distributed in the framework of irregular ("parallel") civil defence groups, for the formation of a national army, restructured and integrated, including the forces of the Congolese Parties signatories to the Agreement, on the basis of negotiations between the Government of the Democratic Republic of the Congo, the Congolese Rally for Democracy and the Movement for the Liberation of the Congo.

Chapter 11

Re-Deployment of Forces of the Parties to Defensive Positions in Conflict Zones

Following disengagement, all forces shall re-deploy to defensive positions.

The positions where units are located shall be identified and recorded by the JMA/OAU and UN.

Upon re-deployment to defensive positions, all forces shall provide relevant information on troop strength, armaments and weapons they hold in each location, to the JMC, OAU and UN mechanisms.

The JMC shall verify the reported data and information. All forces shall be restricted to the declared and recorded locations and all movements shall be authorized by the JMC, OAU and UN mechanisms. All forces shall remain in the declared and recorded locations until:

- in the case of foreign forces, withdrawal has started in accordance with JMC/OAU, UN withdrawal schedule; and
- in the case of FAC and RCD/MLC forces, in accordance with their negotiated agreement.

Chapter 12

Normalisation of the Security Situation Along the Common Borders Between the Democratic Republic of Congo and its Neighbours

Normalisation of the security situation along the common borders between the Democratic Republic of Congo and its neighbours requires each country:

Not to arm, train, harbour on its territory, or render any form of support to subversive elements or armed opposition movements for the purpose of destabilizing others;

To report all strange or hostile movements detected by either country along the common borders;

To identify and evaluate border problems and cooperate in defining methods to peacefully solve them;

To address the problem of armed groups in the Democratic Republic of Congo in accordance with the terms of the Agreement.

Chapter 13: Calendar for the Implementation of the Cease-Fire Agreement

The Calendar for the implementation for the Cease-Fire Agreement is contained in annex B.

Annex 'B' to Cease-Fire Agreement

Calendar for the Implementation of the Cease-Fire Agreement
Major Cease-fire EventsProposed Calendar

1. Formal signing of the Cease-fire	D-Day
2. Announcement of and dissemination of information on cease-fire by all parties	D-Day + 24 hours
3. Cessation of Hostilities, including cessation of Hostile Propaganda	D-Day + 24 hours
4. Release of Hostages	D-Day + 3 days
5. Establishment of Joint Military Commission and Observer Groups	D-Day + 0 hours to D-Day + 7 days
6. Disengagement of Forces	D-Day + 14 days
7. Selection of a facilitator	D-Day + 15 days
8. Redeployment of the Forces of the Parties in the conflict Zones	D-Day + 15 days to D-Day + 30 days
9. Provide information to the JMC, OAU, and UN Mechanism	D-Day + 21 days
10. Mobilisation of OAU Observers	D-Day + 30 days
11. Release/Exchange of Prisoners of War	D-Day + 7 days to D-Day + 30 days
12. Beginning of National Dialogue	D-Day + 45 days
13. Deadline for the closure of the National Dialogue	D-Day + 90 days
14. Establishment of New Institutions	D-Day + 91 days
15. Deployment of UN Peace-keeping Mission	D-Day + 120 days

16. Disarmament of Armed Groups	D-Day + 30 days to
	D-Day + 120 days
17. Orderly Withdrawal of all ForeignForces	D-Day + 180 days
18. Verification and Monitoring	D-Day + 7 days to
	+ 180 days (renewable)
19. Re-establishment of State Administration	D-Day + 90 days to
	D-Day + 270 days
20. Disarmament of Non-Military Personnel	D-Day + 360 days
21. Measures to normalize the security	D-Day + 30 days to D-Day
situation along the international borders	+ 360 days

Annex 'C' to the Ceasefire Agreement

Definitions

"Armed groups," means forces other than Government forces, RCD and MLC that are not signatories to this agreement. They include ex-FAR, AFF, LRA, UNRF II, NALU Interahamwe militias, FUNA, FDD, WNBF, UNITA and any other forces

"Forces of the parties," means the forces of the signatories to the Agreement

"Parties," means signatories to the Agreement.

"Great Lakes Region," means the groups of states within or bordering the Great Rift Valley system of East and Central Africa.

"National Dialogue," means the process involving all stakeholders in the inter-Congolese political negotiations with a view to installing a new political dispensation which will bring about national reconciliation and the early holding of free and fair democratic elections.

"*Forces vives*," means all the stakeholders representatives of the civil society such as the churches, Trade Unions, etc.

"Cease-fire Agreement," means this document and its Annexes.

"Interahamwe," means armed militias who carried out genocide in Rwanda in 1994.

This concludes the basic text of the Lusaka Cease-fire Agreement.

THE ESTABLISHMENT OF MONUC

In mid-July 1999, UN Secretary-General Kofi Annan informed the Security Council that the mandate for a UN force (Mission de l'Organisation des Nations Unies en Republique Democratique du Congo, or MONUC) to help implement the Lusaka Agreement, would have to hold the following powers:

- To observe and monitor the cessation of hostilities.
- To investigate violation of the ceasefire agreement and to take necessary measures to ensure compliance.
- To supervise the disengagement of forces.
- To supervise the redeployment of forces to defensive positions within the conflict zones.
- To provide and maintain humanitarian assistance to and to protect displaced persons, refugees, and other affected groups.
- To keep the parties to the ceasefire agreement informed of its peacekeeping operations.
- To collect weapons from civilians and ensure that the weapons so collected were properly accounted for and adequately secured.
- To schedule and supervise the withdrawal of all foreign forces in collaboration with the JMC and the OAU.
- To verify all information, data, and activities relating to military forces of the parties.[278]

Annan did not include in his report any mention of tracking down armed, dangerous groups, nor screening the refugees and fighters for human rights abusers and violators of the Genocide Conventions. Despite the fact that the need for these precautions had been discussed by the signatories to the Lusaka ceasefire agreement, they were overlooked for the time being. Perhaps it is true that in the wake of the Somalia debacle and even after the Rwandan horror, Annan could not have garnered the support that he needed had he expanded the UN's mission beyond what he stated above. As it was, he was also extremely cautious in outlining three distinct phases in which he thought that the UN should be deployed. The first was to be a deployment of unarmed military liaison officers to the capitals of the signatories and to the rear headquarters of the rebel groups. The second phase was to involve a deployment of up to 500 military observers within the DRC. The third phase was to be dedicated to the deployment of a larger peacekeeping force.[279]

---

278. MONUC, "Peacekeeping in the DRC: MONUC Phase I," (New York: UN Documents, October 2001) Monograph No. 66.

Accordingly, the Security Council approved the deployment of up to 90 liaison officers. These were sent to Kinshasa, Kigali, Kampala, Harare, Windhoek, Bujumbura, Lusaka, and Addis Ababa. By January 2000, small teams of four liaison officers had also been deployed to locations within the DRC, including Kinshasa, Kananga, Kindu, Goma, Boende, Lisala, Gemena, Gbadolite, and Isiro.[280]

But, as we shall see in the following chapter, the UN initiative was not well received. It faced resistance from all of the belligerent parties, and most of all from Kabila. Thus, fighting would continue and many more of the Congolese would meet with death, disfigurement, mutilation, and rape, concomitant with the destruction that war always brings.

---

279. Ibid.
280. Ibid.

CHAPTER 6. CORRUPTION AND REBELLION

Recognizing that there was an inverse relationship between the likelihood of peace in the DRC and the inability to rein in corruption and other illegal practices in mineral exploitation, United Nations Secretary-General Kofi Annan recommended that a panel of experts be convened to study the ways that the rebels funded their exploits. It was found, early on, that much of the tension between Rwanda and Uganda was structured around mineral exploitation, and that it had erupted in pitched battles for control of the regions with the most mineral wealth. This was particularly true in the Kivus.

To reiterate conditions, it should be mentioned that Katanga contains one-third of the world's known cobalt and one-tenth of its copper reserves. The DRC possesses 50 percent of African timber reserves, and accounts for 80 percent of reserves of coltan (which, when refined into tantalum, is used in cellular phones, satellites, and computers). In Ituri and South Kivu, it possesses extensive gold reserves, and it is also known to possess uranium and diamonds.[281]

Rwanda and Uganda seized mineral stockpiles in the areas that they controlled, and also looted the local banks. Thousands of Congolese civilians were tortured and killed during military takeovers of mineral-rich regions, and some hundreds of thousands more were driven from their homes. Bereft of their own communities, the displaced often died of malnutrition and inadequate access to humanitarian aid and health agencies. Children as young as 12 were forced to

---

281. Phillipe Tremblay, "The Transition in the Democratic Republic of Congo: A Historic Opportunity," (Montreal, Quebec: Droits et Democratie, April 2004) 54.

work in the mines under conditions of hard labor, and many were killed or muti-lated in punishment for resistance. It is estimated that more than three quarters of the killings in the DRC have taken place in the east, and that this region also accounts for 90 percent of the internally displaced.[282]

But these factors were very lucrative for those who controlled the guns. Dena Montague notes that, "Between 1996 and 1997, Rwanda's coltan pro-duction doubled bringing up to $20 million a month in revenue. The volume of Rwanda's diamond exports rose from 166 carats in 1998 to some 30,500 in 2000...From 1997-1998 the annual volume of Uganda's diamond exports jumped from 1,500 carats to about 11,3000...[and] since 1996 Ugandan gold exports have increased tenfold. The final destination for these minerals is largely the United States."[283]

According to a report from the International Crisis Group, "Uganda's gold exports shot up from $12.4 million in 1994-5 to $110 million in 1996...Major General Salim Saleh, the president's brother...was deeply involved in buying gold in UPDF controlled areas...Brigadier Kazini is accused of distributing diamond and cobalt concessions while he was commander of the UPDF operations in the DRC...Ties between front-line UPDF commanders and businessmen [also] fuelled much of the Hema-Lendu violence which may have claimed some ten thousand lives in the Ugandan controlled northeast since the war's out-break."[284] Another report claims that a full 50,000 died in clashes between Hema and Lendu in a bid to dominate Ituri's diamond, gold and coltan reserves.[285]

In the UN report itself, the panel cited Ali Hussein as playing a major role in diamond and gold deals in Bukavu and Kisangani. The second chief looter is Colonel James Kabarebe, and the third looter is Tibere Rujigiro, a member of the RPF who is considered to be one of the Army's main money providers. Another is a woman named Aziza Kulsum Gulamali, who has acknowledged past involvement in the war in Burundi. She has built new alliances with Rwanda and·

---

282. Amnesty International, "Democratic Republic of the Congo: Our brothers who help kill us — economic exploitation and human rights abuses in the east," (New York: Amnesty International, April 2003).

283. Dena Montague, "The Business of War in the Democratic Republic of Congo: Who Benefits? — Statistical Data Included," www.findarticles.com.

284. MONUC, "Peacekeeping in the DRC: Causes of Conflict and Key Protagonists."

285. Diamond Intelligence Briefs, "65 bodies discovered in DRC's Ituri region," *Diamond Intelligence Briefs*, October 13, 2003.

RCD-Goma, and deals mainly in gold, coltan, and cassiterite controlled by the Rwandans. She was recently appointed by RCD-Goma as general manager of SOMIGL, a conglomerate which obtained the monopoly for commercialization and export of coltan, in exchange for which RCD-Goma expects that she will contribute $1 million monthly to its coffers.[286]

There were also allegations that an Australian mining consortium was involved in a massacre of over 100 people because of a mining concern during 2004. Although Australian lawyer Richard Meeran said that Anvil Mining Limited played no part in the killings, a secret United Nations probe revealed that the soldiers who protected the mine launched their attack with vehicles provided by Anvil Mining.

In response to these violations and in light of the link between mineral exploitation and the ongoing conflagration, the UN recommended that the Security Council declare a temporary embargo on the import or export of various goods including timber, gold, and diamonds, from or to Burundi, Rwanda, and Uganda. It also recommended that the Security Council should freeze the assets of the rebel movements, their leaders, and companies or individuals who were in league with any of these agents.[287]

The UN also urged that world leaders enforce the Kimberley Process, whereby certification for diamonds is required from the point of the mine of origin to the hands of the final seller. Undertaken in 2000, when ministers from a group of African countries met in Kimberley, South Africa, the plan has allegedly succeeded in containing the illicit trade in diamonds to about 4 percent of the market. But the Kimberley Process was only slowly embraced by law within the United States. Although House Ways and Means Committee Chairman Bill Thomas (R-Calif) introduced a bill on conflict diamonds at the 108th Congress, and it passed the House in 2001, it was rejected by the Senate. The same was also true after House Representative Amo Houghton (R-N.Y.) introduced the Clean Diamond Trade Act (HR 2722) in August, 2001; it passed by a vote of 408-6 in Congress but was then allowed to languish when it passed to the Senate.[288] This took place even though the Congress had noted that:

---

286. Africa News Service, "The Systematic Looting of the Congo," *Africa News Service*, April 19, 2001.

287. MONUC, "Peacekeeping in the DRC: MONUC Phase II: Progress and Revised Concept" (New York: UN Documents, October 2001) Monograph No. 66.

Funds derived from the sale of rough diamonds are being used by rebels and state actors to finance military activities, overthrow legitimate governments, subvert international efforts to promote peace and stability, and commit horrifying atrocities against unarmed civilians. During the past decade, more than 6,500,000 people from Sierra Leone, Angola, and the Democratic Republic of the Congo have been driven from their homes by wars waged in large part for control of diamond mining areas.[289]

The Clean Diamond Trade Act was only passed by an executive order of President George W. Bush in July, 2003.

Based on the history of prosecutions of industries involved in war crimes and supporting criminal regimes (largely gleaned from the experience of World War II), Luis Moreno Ocampo, the chief prosecutor of the International Criminal Court (ICC), said that persons involved in the trade of "blood diamonds" may be subject to charges of complicity in war crimes and genocide.

However, much of the mineral exploitation in the DRC being conducted with the consent of the Kinshasa government in order to finance its foreign backers. The government of the DRC has allowed Zimbabwe to exploit its diamond mines, while committing serious violence and human rights violations. Zimbabwe had some 13,000 troops in the DRC, most of which were deployed in and around Mbuji Mayi where between 3,000 and 5,000 soldiers were active in mining the Shaba and Kasai Oriental provinces (Pweto, Kabinda, Ikela). They were also active at Mbandaka in Equateur. [290] In another deal, Zimbabwe Defense Industries (ZDI) was to provide arms and munitions in return for which the Zimbabwean mining company Ridgepointe would take over the management of GECOMINES and receive a 37.5 percent share of the DRC's state mining. "Between 20 and 30 percent of the DRC's 62.5 percent of the firm's profits was to be used for financing the Zimbabwean war effort."[291] There is also a joint venture between the DRC and the Zimbabwean firm Osleg (Operation Sovereign Legitimacy) for purchase of diamonds and gold which are sold in Kin-

---

288. Sheila R. Cherry, "Conflict Diamonds could lose sparkle: an international tracking and certification plan should significantly decrease the trade in 'conflict diamonds' used by rebel movements to finance armed conflicts," *Insight in the News*, February 4, 2003.

289. Kyle Rex Jacobson, "Doing business with the devil: the challenges of prosecuting corporate officials whose business transactions facilitate war crimes and crimes against humanity," *Air Force Law Review*, January 1, 2005.

290. MONUC, "Peacekeeping in the DRC: Causes of Conflict and Key Protagonists," (New York: UN Documents, October 2001) Monograph No. 66.

291. Ibid.

shasa. Zimbabwe has a contract to cut down 33 million hectares (over 75 million acres) of Congolese trees in three years of operation with anticipated profits of US $300 million. And, finally, there are other agreements between them for the exploitation of electric power and agriculture.

These factors indicate that the war would continue in the DRC so long as both the rebels and government backers were permitted to plunder the country. If the first action of the UN had been to install a peacekeeping mission and take over the mining towns, kicking the rebels out and sealing them off from exportable goods, perhaps it could have brought the war to a halt sooner from lack of funds for munitions. But such was not to be the case. Instead, the UN proceeded meekly with the implementation of the Military Liaison Officers (MLOs), whose only responsibility was to establish contact between the signatory governments of the Lusaka Peace Accord and the main rebel groups.

MONUC PHASE II

In his report of January 17, 2000, Secretary-General Kofi Annan asked for the existing force of 77 MLOs to be expanded to 5,537 military observers and peacekeepers. The enhanced MONUC force would be responsible for "military liaison; the monitoring of cessation of hostilities; the investigation of ceasefire violations; and the verification of disengagement of various forces."[292] Again, the UN would not be empowered to serve as an interposition force, nor would it act to track down and disarm irregular militant forces or seize human rights abusers. With regard to eventual plans for disarmament and demobilization of armed groups, Annan envisioned that this would take place with an even further expanded mission under what he categorized as Phase III of deployment.

The Security Council did act to expand MONUC's forces to a total of 5,537, but stated in its February 25 Resolution that deployment would be delayed until such time as Annan had received the requisite security guarantees from all of the warring parties; the DRC had assured MONUC's freedom of movement; and conditions on the ground were peaceable enough to warrant nonviolent intervention. Nevertheless, it also approved an extended mandate, under which the Security Council stated that "MONUC may take the necessary

---

292. MONUC, "Peacekeeping in the DRC: MONUC Phase II," (New York: UN Documents, October 2001) Monograph No. 66.

action, in the areas of deployment of its infantry battalions and as it deems it within its capabilities, to protect United Nations and co-located JMC personnel, facilities, installations and equipment, ensure the security and freedom of movement of its personnel, and protect civilians under imminent threat of physical violence."[293]

For two months, the country remained wracked with terror. Fighting continued around Mbandaka where government troops were heavily engaged against the rebels. In February, Zimbabwean, Namibian, and Congolese troops responded to the encirclement of an allied force and clashes between armed groups and Rwandan rebels continued in the east. Also in February, reports trickled in regarding an assault on the Hema community by ethnic Lendu fighters, resulting in the deaths of approximately 7,000 people — a situation that the UN classified as a genocide. And an estimated 150,000 Banyamulenge were surrounded and at risk of massacre in South Kivu.[294]

In March, RCD-Goma and the Rwandan army attacked Kasai province, seizing the town of Idumbe. Moving further eastwards toward Longa and Lodi, they also attacked the town of Bena Leka. Simultaneous with this thrust, they continued their efforts to cut off Kabinda from Mbuji Mayi. But the MLC, too, had interests in Ilebo and Bandaka, and were said to be preparing to attack in April.[295]

THE KAMPALA CEASEFIRE

On April 9, 2000, with pressure from the JMC and the United Nations, a ceasefire agreement materialized at a meeting in Kampala. Sponsored by the JMC, the plan called for a complete cessation of hostilities, disengagement on both sides of the front line to establish a security corridor, and the redeployment of forces.[296] Troops were to be pulled back to 15 kilometers from the front lines

---

293. M2 Presswire, "Security Council expands mission in Democratic Republic of Congo, unanimously adopting resolution 1291 (2000); Extends mandate until 31 August, authorized 5,537 troops to help implement Lusaka ceasefire agreement," *M2 Presswire*, February 25, 2000.
294. Kofi Annan, "Second Report of the Secretary-General on the United Nations Organization Mission in the Democratic Republic of the Congo" (New York: UN Documents, April 18, 2000).
295. Ibid.
296. MONUC, "Peacekeeping in the DRC: MONUC Phase II."

and remain there for three months while the UN deployed peacekeepers in the buffer space between them. This would pave the way for a total withdrawal of foreign forces.

However no progress was made in respecting these conditions or creating an otherwise suitable environment for the enhanced deployment of MONUC. There was heavy fighting in Kisangani, causing the deaths of over 150 civilians and more than 1,000 casualties, with severe property damage.[297] The targets most affected were the power station, the hydro-electric dam, the cathedral, one hospital, and large numbers of houses that had been occupied by UN observer staff. There was a cessation of hostilities on May 21, when the military commanders signed an agreement with MONUC to demilitarize Kisangani in accordance with the plan laid out in Kampala. Ugandan and Rwandan troops began pulling back to positions that were 100 kilometers away from the city.

But the violence spread elsewhere. The MLC began to advance along the Ubangi River, and government forces attacked to stem the rebel movement. There was also fighting in the Kivus, where inter-ethnic clashes were rampant. Conducted by the ex-FAR and Interahamwe as well as Rwandan and Burundian rebel groups, attacks on civilians were especially widespread. The Mayi-Mayi were also partly responsible, displacing some 35,000 people out of a population of 80,000. In Kilambo and the neighboring villages of Masisi, people have suffered attacks by both sides in the war. First, the RCD and the RPA conducted indiscriminate massacres and burned houses in Kibirangiro, Buabo, Mafuo, Kihuma, Kilambo, Camarambo, Bushuwi, Kanii, Lwanguba, and Busekeri. Observers reported that after this spate of violence, the people would try to return, only to be set upon by ex-FAR and Interahamwe who accused them of supporting the RCD and the RPA.[298] Thus, the civilian population was caught between two sides, and largely remained in the forest where it suffered in desperate conditions.

As far as MONUC was concerned, it had no power to persuade the armies to stop these disastrous exploits. MONUC itself had no freedom of movement, as it was denied the right to deploy in Basankusu (Equateur Province) by the marauding MLC. For its part, the RCD refused MONUC permission to land at Kongolo airport and to deploy a military observer either there or in Kabalo. In

---

297. Hrvoje Hranjski, "Congo War Continues Despite Deal," *AP Online*, June 9, 2000.
298. Human Rights Watch, "Democratic Republic of Congo: Eastern Congo Ravaged Killing Civilians and Silencing Protest," Vol. 12, No. 3(A), May 2000.

government-controlled territory, MONUC was denied permission to land at Mbandaka even for a medial evacuation. Similarly, it was refused entry into Mbuji Mayi.[299]

After blocking the progress of the MLC along the Ubangi River, the government took the town of Imese. From there, the FAC captured Dongo and finally reached Libenge. There, it was met and halted by the MLC, which demanded that it retreat to the Kampala ceasefire lines. The MLC proceeded to capture Dongo, while the government withdrew to Mbandaka. Fighting occurred on a lesser scale around the town of Ikela (Equateur Province) and the government was also said to be engaged in Kabalo.

Rwanda and Uganda continued to hold to the ceasefire lines that had been declared for Kisangani, and also began to withdraw some of their troops in accord with the Kampala agreement. Uganda withdrew five UPDF battalions on June 22, and Rwanda announced the return of 1,000 troops on August 8, 2000.[300]

In Kinshasa, the UN was coming under fire by inflammatory propaganda. This resulted in organized demonstrations and the continued refusal of the government to allow UN penetration in those areas where it had requested deployment permission. In a public statement of July 21, Kabila accused MONUC of being inactive and facilitating external aggression. He asked the UN not to deploy any armed troops to Kinshasa and Mbandaka, insisting that MONUC should deploy exclusively to rebel-controlled regions. On July 27, Kabila actively blocked deployment on government-held territory.

Kofi Annan also noted, in his Fourth Report to the Security Council, that government use of the death penalty persisted. The UN accused the government of breaking a moratorium on the death penalty, executing nine soldiers and imprisoning 60 others who are also under death sentence.[301] Over 80 journalists had been jailed since Kabila took power on May 17, 1997. One publisher was given 150 lashes by state security forces after distributing copies of his newspaper on a street corner in Kinshasa. Journalists and political opponents continued to be tried for crimes in violation of international law, and the Minister of

---

299. Kofi Annan, "Third Report of the Secretary-General on the United Nations Organization Mission in the Democratic Republic of the Congo" (New York: UN Documents, June 12, 2000).

300. Kofi Annan, "Fourth Report of the Secretary-General on the United Nations Organization Mission in the Democratic Republic of the Congo" (New York: UN Documents, September 21, 2000).

301. AP Online, "Congo Accused of Executing Soldiers," *AP Online*, February 15, 2000.

the Interior had announced that the government would prosecute for "high crimes against State security persons not affiliated with a registered political party who make political statements."[302] Ten members of the Democratic Union and Social Progress Party had been arrested and detained for holding party meetings, and the leader of the People's Revolutionary Movement had likewise been arrested.

Approaching the end of 2000, *World Investment News* reported that the country had all but collapsed. Its real per capita GDP (Gross Domestic Product) had sunk from $224 in 1990 to $85 in 2000 (or 23 cents a day). In the meantime, consumer prices had risen at "an annual average rate of 107 percent in 1998, 270 percent in 1999, and 554 percent in 2000."[303] As for the country's external debt, it had escalated to 280 percent of GDP (almost US $13 billion), with about 75 percent of that total outstanding as arrearage.

The main activity during December took place in Equateur Province, Katanga Province, and within the eastern Congo. There were aerial bombing raids against Gemena, Moba and other rebel-held locations, and fighting was also reported in the vicinity of Pweto. The latter drove 60,000 people into refugee status in Zambia. The government also launched a major offensive against the northeastern Katanga Province.[304]

THE ENTRY OF JOSEPH KABILA

Laurent-Désiré Kabila was assassinated by one of his bodyguards on January 16, 2001. He was replaced by his 29-year-old son Joseph on January 26. Joseph consented to disengaging the FAC from the front lines according to a plan devised in Harare, which allowed two weeks for completion of the verification phase once the parties had disengaged and moved to new positions well behind the established front lines. He also agreed to more than a token deployment of MONUC and to accept Sir Ketumile Masire as facilitator of the Inter-Congolese Dialogue that had been mandated by the Lusaka Accord.[305]

302. Kofi Annan, "Fourth Report of the Secretary-General on the United Nations Organization Mission in the Democratic Republic of the Congo."

303. World Investment News, "Congo (DRC): Paving the reconstruction," http://www.winne.com/congo/bf06.h6tml.

304. Kofi Annan, "Fifth Report of the secretary-General on the United Nations Organization Mission in the Democratic Republic of the Congo" (New York: UN Documents, December 6, 2000).

On February 22, 2001, the Security Council authorized an updated concept of operations that was to include the establishment of further military observer teams and four different headquarters in Kisangani, Mbandaka, Kananga, and Kalemie. The joint military commissions, which were located at Lisala, Boende, Kabinda, and Kabalo, were to be relocated to the MONUC headquarters. The new plan envisaged "up to 550 military observers...as well as up to 1,900 armed personnel to guard equipment facilities and supplies at the sector headquarters and support bases. Two riverine units comprising some 400 troops were also requested as well as necessary rotary and fixed-wing air assets. Total military personnel required was approximately 3,000 officers and other ranks."[306]

Under Resolution 1341, the parties were given two weeks, starting on March 15, to withdraw from their front-line positions. Although the RCD and MLC initially tried to block this decision and the deployment of UN forces, they were quickly overcome by diplomatic pressure. The ceasefire was generally respected, with the exception of FAC and FLC skirmishes in Bolomba, and attacks by non-signatory armed groups in the areas of the eastern provinces. By April 2000, Rwandan leader Paul Kagame had offered to enact a strategic withdrawal in the Kivus by February 2001. Namibia, too, was planning to withdraw its forces by the end of August 2001.[307] Perhaps most feared at this time was the possibility that Zimbabwe would decide to privatize its forces in order to provide for continued mining exploitation and selective security in the region. It was believed that this would set a dangerous precedent for Rwanda and Uganda, and was undesirable in any case.

Since April 2001, the UN had verified the compliance of the parties in redeployment to 86 of the 96 new deployment points. By August 2001, Uganda's defense minister expressed hope that Ugandan troops would be out by the end of the year, with the exception that he would maintain a presence in Buta, Bunia, and the Wenzori mountain area. Zimbabwe had signaled its willingness to withdraw, but there was great concern that this should be timed to coincide with the withdrawal of Rwanda and Uganda. Namibian forces, for their part, had already withdrawn in August. The only country to actually reinforce its troops was Angola. This was true even though Rwanda had unilaterally withdrawn 1,000 of its troops early in the year.[308]

---

305. MONUC, "Peacekeeping in the DRC: MONUC Phase II."
306. Ibid.
307. MONUC, "Peacekeeping in the DRC: MONUC Phase II: Progress and Revised Concept."

For Rwanda, the Kivus remained a problem. Although the area was technically under the control of RCD-Goma, which was allied to Rwanda, fighting still continued between Mayi-Mayi/Interahamwe and RPA/RCD forces. It was evident that the ex-FAR/Interahamwe, FDD, and FNL continued to receive substantial support from the Kinshasa government until at least June 2001, such that the RPA disengagement had necessarily been reversed.[309] Further, instability in the region was heightened by the presence of some 35,000 Rwandan and 15,000 Burundian refugees.

During August, the RCD announced that it had appointed a 70-member provincial assembly in keeping with its plans to establish a federal system of government in the areas that it controlled. It went on to organize an inter-Kivu dialogue in Bukavu from September 25 to 29. Although it was attended by representatives from both North and South Kivu, it was boycotted by many church and civil society groups.[310] Fighting continued meanwhile between the Burundian rebels and the RCD/RPA.

On November 16, RCD-K/ML took over administrative control of Bunia, forcing MLC troops to retreat. This had the effect of provoking further clashes between these two groups within Oriental Province. MLC troops forced the RCD-K/ML to withdraw toward Isiro, where RCD-K/ML sought UN support to stop MLC's advance. Aided by the Mayi-Mayi, the MLC then moved further eastward toward the remaining RCD-K/ML strongholds of Bunia, Beni, Butembo, and Bafwasende.

The RCD and MLC announced, on November 4, 2001, that they would create a joint military force to disarm irregular armed groups in the eastern DRC. By the end of January 2002, they had assembled between 2,500 and 3,000 troops in Kindu to pursue that purpose. Catching the spirit of the movement, Kabila, too, announced that he was sponsoring the disarmament of armed groups. He presented 3,000 unarmed combatants who were said to be Rwandans for the UN to screen and demobilize. This was followed, in December, by the formal decommissioning of 2,600 child soldiers (*kadogos*).[311] There remains strong evidence, however, that all warring parties continue to recruit and use child soldiers,

308. Ibid.
309. MONUC, "Peacekeeping in the DRC: MONUC and the Road to Peace: The Situation in the Kivus" (New York: UN Documents, October 2001) Monograph No. 66.
310. Kofi Annan, "Ninth Report of the Secretary-General on the United Nations Organization Mission in the democratic Republic of the Congo" (New York: UN Documents, October 16, 2001).

including the DRC. RCD-Goma accepted children as young as 8, and the UN Secretary-General's report of November 26, 2002 identified no fewer than 10 armed groups engaging in child recruitment.[312]

THE INTER-CONGOLESE DIALOGUE

In accordance with the terms of the Lusaka Accord, which provided for an Inter-Congolese Dialogue that would include the opposition to Kabila and be geared toward national reconciliation, Joseph Kabila had affirmed his commitment to the Inter-Congolese Dialogue, publishing a statement dated May 4, 2001, in which he declared that he was committed to the following:

- The sovereignty and territorial integrity of the DRC.
- The inclusion of the government, RCD, MLC, and the political opposition and representatives from civil society to participate in the Inter-Congolese Dialogue.
- The freedom of the Congolese parties in all the provinces to elect their representatives to the Inter-Congolese Dialogue in a just and equitable manner, as witnessed and verified by an independent authority.[313]

Accordingly, a team assigned to the Inter-Congolese Dialogue was dispatched throughout all eleven provinces to help identify those members of civil society and the unarmed political parties that could participate in the preparatory meeting in Gaborone. This resulted in the selection of 14 political parties, divided amongst pro-government and anti-government groups.[314] The tasks before the parties were roughly defined as: deciding the future of the country on the basis of consensus; the formation of a new national Army, comprised of the government forces, the RCD, and the MLC; and national reconciliation.

The participants chosen for the talks in Gabarone included 13 representatives from the DRC; 13 representatives of the MLC; 13 representatives of RCD-Goma; and six other persons represented by the various MLC and RCD factions led by Jean-Baptiste Tibasimi Mbogemu Atneyi, Ernest Wamba dia Wamba, and

311. Kofi Annan, "Tenth Report of the Secretary-General on the United Nations Organization Mission in the Democratic Republic of the Congo" (New York: UN Documents, February 15, 2002).

312. Phillipe Tremblay, 43.

313. MONUC, "Peacekeeping in the DRC: MONUC and the Road to peace; The Inter-Congolese Dialogue" (New York: UN Documents, October 2001) Monograph No. 66.

314. Ibid.

Nyamwisi. It also included 13 representatives from civil society. The unarmed political parties were represented by a delegation of their own. Included in the unarmed opposition were Etienne Tshisekedi's UDPS and Catherine Nzuzi wa Mbombo's MPR (Mobutu's former party). The Parti Démocratie et social chrétien (PDSC) was represented by Andre Boboliko, and also formed in May 2001 was the UFAD (Union des Forces Congolaises pour le respect integral de l'Accord de Lusaka et la tenue du Dialogue intercongolais), a broad umbrella front of the DRC's anti-government forces.[315]

At the Gabarone meeting, DRC foreign minister She Okitundu stated that, "Before we hold elections we will need a new constitution, and before we adopt the constitution we will hold a referendum. And of course before we hold a referendum we will need a new population census. With all this groundwork to be done, it will not be possible to hold elections for, say, three years."[316] That being the case, the team assigned to the oversight of the Inter-Congolese Dialogue envisioned the creation of four additional commissions. The first was to be a humanitarian/economic and social commission which was to come up with a plan for reconstruction of the Kivus. The second was an electoral commission (which would be funded by the EU). The third was a constitutional commission which would prepare a new constitution. And the fourth was a military commission to design a plan for demobilization and disarmament.[317]

This was, needless to say, a disappointment to the political opposition within the DRC. However, it was in keeping with the style of the new government, which although it had repealed Laurent Kabila's Decree Law No. 194 restricting the activities of political parties, was still arresting and detaining political opponents at this time.

On a more positive note, the DRC adopted a Congolese Charter for Human Rights that now abolished capital punishment, introduced democracy, and ensured equality for all citizens. Further, the DRC submitted a formal request to the UN Security Council for the creation of a UN International Tribunal for the DRC that could try perpetrators of human rights abuses, crimes against humanity, and violators of the Genocide Conventions within the DRC.

The DRC based its request on the model of the ICTR (International Criminal Tribunal of Rwanda) created in Arusha to try war crimes in Rwanda,

---

315. Ibid.
316. Ibid.
317. Ibid.

and would appear to have every right to expect a similar attempt at establishing justice at home. However, critics of the ICTR point out that the court has thus far sentenced only 6 individuals in connection with the Rwandan genocide of 1994. It has not brought to trial any of the masterminds behind the genocide and it was finally supplanted, in large part, by provincial and tribal courts that hope to provide local justice to the people of Rwanda in a sweeping and speedier fashion than the ICTR. Based on these observations, critics say that perhaps the empowerment of a court within the DRC with the participation of native Congolese judges would be best. Others advocate a mixed panel of judges including both foreigners and natives of the DRC. In any event, the international community must take steps to address human rights violations, crimes against humanity, and violations of the Genocide Conventions, beyond recommending that members of the ex-FAR/Interahamwe be turned over to the ICTR in Arusha. This is something on which all parties to the Lusaka Accord agree.

THE VIOLENCE CONTINUES

As Christian Scherrer notes, perhaps the only thing that had thus far saved the Kabila regime was that there was no significant linkage between the nonviolent political opposition and the various rebel movements. Instead, it seemed to be the strategy of the government to block the promised elections by sowing more discord among these groups and particularly by exporting the violence in the DRC to the neighboring countries of Rwanda, Uganda, and Burundi.[318] He writes, "this covert strategy became all the more important as Kabila's alliance with foreign states was continuously weakened by lack of funds (Zimbabwe), opposition at home (Zimbabwe and Namibia), humiliating defeats (Chad), war fatigue, and needs at home (Angola and Sudan)."[319]

But, 2002 was marked by a series of withdrawals. Burundi withdrew 700 troops as of October 11. And Rwanda, significantly, claimed to have withdrawn 23,760 troops by that same date. The governments of Rwanda and the DRC had signed a bilateral agreement on July 30, 2002, trading the dismantlement and disarmament of the Rwandan ex-FAR and Interahamwe (supported by the DRC) for the withdrawal of Rwandan Defense Forces. Accordingly, Kinshasa

---

318. Christian Scherrer, 264.
319. Ibid., 269.

also expelled the leadership of the Democratic Forces of the Liberation of Rwanda (FDLR), from the country, and also arrested one its key men. After Rwanda's withdrawal, Zimbabwe and Angola decided to complete the withdrawal of their own troops. Moreover, Uganda signed a bilateral security arrangement with the DRC on September 6, 2002. The agreement also provided for the establishment of a Pacification Commission for the particularly terrorized region of Ituri.[320]

The peacebuilding commission for Ituri (CoPI) is comprised of 177 delegates from the various communities affected by the fighting. The delegates were selected from among representatives of the Kinshasa government, civil society, rural militias, and the Ugandan government (which was still policing the area). The establishment of this body led to the election of an Interim Ituri Administration (AII), but its effectiveness is in question, with MONUC refusing to support the process.[321]

Violence also continued with fighting between the UPC and the RCD-ML around the area of Bunia, and the advance of the RCD-N towards Faradje, Wats, and Nia Nia (formerly controlled by the RCD-K/ML). The MLC reportedly reinforced the RCD-N with troops, equipment, and supplies, with the activities of all groups being driven by a desire to negotiate from a position of territorial strength in the ongoing Inter-Congolese Dialogue.

In the Hauts Plateaux areas, RPA and RCD-Goma operations were proceeding against a Banyamulenge group led by Patrick Masunzu, which had broken away from RCD-Goma. In reaction to the popularity of Masunzu, RCD-Goma had purged some of its members, and its attacks on the Hauts Plateaux led to the desertion of over 100 villages, with a concomitant increase of 20,000 families in the number of displaced.[322] The population in Kindu reported heavy violence between the RCD-Goma and the Mayi-Mayi in July, with both sides accused of arbitrary killing, rapes, and excessive use of force by security detachments. There was also an increase in the harassment of humanitarian staff. Orga-

---

320. Dr. Francois Gignon, "Testimony of Dr. Francois Grignon, Central Africa Project Director, International Crisis Group, Before a Hearing of the House of Representatives Committee on Foreign Relations — Africa Subcommittee" (Washington, DC: Committee on International Relations, April 3, 2002).

321. Phillipe Tremblay, 32.

322. Kofi Annan, "Twelfth Report of the Secretary-General on the United Nations Organization Mission in the Democratic Republic of the Congo." (New York: UN Documents, February 15, 2002).

nizations in Bunia and Dungu experienced threats of violence and looting, leading to the loss of nearly 14 tons of food.[323]

By 2002, MONUC was being asked to participate in the demobilization and disarmament of the irregular armed groups. Facing the issues of demobilization, disarmament, and the creation of durable solutions (what it calls the D-3 challenge), MONUC anticipated the creation of a 33-person Coordination Unit that would have expertise in "military, humanitarian and human rights issues, public information, civic programs, and international funding." The purpose of the draft D-3 plan is to "disarm, demobilize, repatriate, reintegrate (resettle) all armed groups in the DRC; hand over mass killers, perpetrators of crimes against humanity and other war criminals; and disarm all Congolese civilians who are illegally armed."[324] The latter include the ex-FAR/Interahamwe, Allied Democratic Forces, Lord's Resistance Army, Uganda National Rescue Front II, Former Uganda National Army, FDD, West Nile Bank Front, UNITA, ALiR, and others. At this stage, however, D-3 is based upon a voluntary process. As the official MONUC statement reports, the ideas is to conduct "an intensive media campaign...to induce combatants to report to assembly areas where they will be registered, disarmed, and moved to separate camps according to gender, age, and combat status. A screening process by the relevant international agencies will follow immediately to identify and apprehend those who are suspected of genocide, crimes against humanity, and war crimes. Suspects will be handed over to the International Court of Justice in Arusha. Those remaining will receive counseling to determine their future intentions, skills, aptitude, choice of country for resettlement or reintegration, preferred skills training and so on. All is supposed to occur within 30 days from assembly, to be completed within one year."[325]

Somewhat tartly, however, the report adds that "there is no guarantee that the international community will accede to all the tasks that the signatories to the Lusaka agreement demanded. It is already clear that MONUC does not wish to become involved in the screening of the Interahamwe for genocidaires and that it would rather pass this on to Rwanda."[326]

---

323. Ibid.
324. MONUC, "Peacekeeping in the DRC: MONUC and the Road to Peace: Facing the D3 Challenge" (New York: UN Documents, October 2001) Monograph No. 66.
325. Ibid.
326. Ibid.

THE SUN CITY AGREEMENT

As part of the Sun City (South Africa) plenary that occurred on April 17, 2002, the delegates adopted a commitment to the establishment of five civic institutions that would facilitate the democratic transition. These were: The Independent Electoral Commission (CEI); The National Human Rights Observatory (ONDH); The High Authority on the Media (HAM); The Truth and Reconciliation Commission (CVR); and The Ethics and Anti-Corruption Commission (CELAC).[327] Collectively, they are known by the acronym for their French name, ICAD.

The purpose of the CVR is to establish responsibility for the most heinous crimes with a view not to punishing the guilty parties but to requiring them to ask pardon from the victims and to ensure that they pay compensation. The CVR may examine political, economic, and social crimes dating as far back as those which were committed upon independence in 1960.[328] In order to be effective, Human Rights Watch has recommended that the DRC's general prosecutor create a mobile investigative unit responsible for collecting and preserving evidence in the DRC. It suggests that this unit should be composed of "international and Congolese specialists in law, forensic medicine, police investigative procedures, and sexual violence."[329] The head of the CVR is to be comprised of eight members, selected from the parties to the Inter-Congolese Dialogue. The paramount concerns regarding the selection process are that many of those who would participate in such a body stand themselves accused of war crimes. Then, too, there are others, such as the government, who would prefer to stand in the way of progress lest it lead to a collapse of the regime.

In particular, Congolese women were quick to insist upon their inclusion in the Sun City dialogue. They were pressing the issue of the Security Council's Resolution 1325, which called for states to take measures to ensure women's full participation in the process of peace-building and democratic transition. Women, therefore, held 40 of 307 seats at the Sun City dialogue, acting within a structure called the Congolese Women's Caucus. Although this fell short of the 30 percent threshold envisioned by the UN-sponsored Beijing Plan of action which set international targets for women's participation in democratic transi-

327. Phillipe Tremblay, 21.
328. Ibid., 58.
329. Ibid., 67.

tions, the final wording of the texts of the conference provided for ensuring "an appropriate level of representation of women at all levels of responsibility."[330]

Absent from the Sun City committee was the RCD-Goma. It and other armed groups went on to become part of the Alliance pour la Sauvegarde du Dialogue Inter-Congolais led by Etienne Tshisekedi. The RCD had flatly rejected a secret deal between Joseph Kabila and MLC leader Jean-Pierre Bemba, by which Kabila would remain president of a transitional government while Bemba would become prime minister. The RCD not only wanted to play its own part in any form of transitional government, it also wanted Kabila out of office. [331]

Also in April of 2002, the DRC chose to ratify the Rome Statute of the International Criminal Court (ICC). However, in order to be effective, the DRC must amend domestic legislation regarding the Act Respecting the Implementation of the Statute of the International Criminal Court Codifying Crimes Against Humanity and War Crimes.

Finally, the government signed the Gbadolite Agreement of December 31, 2002 between it and three rebel groups supported by Uganda (the MLC, RCD-N, and the RCD-ML). This obliged them to "stop fighting in the Isiro-Baf-wasende-Beni-Watsa quadrangle and to accept UN military observers, freedom of movement of the civilian population and humanitarian organizations."[332] While the treaty had limited effect in practice, it was still a step in the right direction.

---

330. Ibid., 25-26.
331. Kenneth Ingham, "Year in Review 2002: World Affairs, Democratic Republic of the Congo," Encyclopaedia Britannica, www.britannica.com.
332. Wikipedia.

CHAPTER 7. THE TRANSITIONAL GOVERNMENT

On December 17, 2002, the parties to the Inter-Congolese Dialogue finally signed a Global and All-Inclusive Agreement on the Transition in the DRC. In it, they agreed to lay down their arms and to build the transitional institutions that would lead to transparent elections and an improvement of human rights. Joseph Kabila was accepted as president and supreme commander of the armed forces, provided that he would accede to having four vice-presidents, including three from the main rebel groups (RCD-Goma and MLC) and the non-armed political opposition. RCD-Goma was given responsibility for security and defense, while the MLC was granted authority over the economy and finance.[333] The government component was to be responsible for reconstruction and development, whereas a social and cultural commission would be chaired by the political opposition. The government itself would be composed of 36 ministers and 25 deputy-ministers. The agreement also provided for a bicameral Parliament comprised of a National Assembly (which will have 500 members and whose president will be nominated by the MLC) and a Senate (which will have 150 members and whose president will be nominated by civil society).[334]

To ensure the security of the Transitional Government, it was agreed that the international community would deploy a neutral force, including bodyguards. The force was to be replaced by an integrated police force comprised of

---

333. Phillipe Tremblay, 19.
334. Kofi Annan, "Thirteenth Report of the Secretary-General on the United Nations Organization Mission in the Democratic Republic of the Congo" (New York: UN Documents, February 21, 2003).

the different parties to the Inter-Congolese Dialogue upon satisfactory training of the same by the international community.

A non-negotiable condition of the rebels for participation in the Transitional Government was that the president declare a state of amnesty for offences committed during the war. This he did, through the adoption of a decree law; however, the law does not provide for protection in the event of genocidal crimes, crimes against humanity, and other similar abuses. The latter will be tried through a tribunal that it is competent to hear such cases.[335]

THE GLOBAL-INCLUSIVE AGREEMENT

The following is part of the text that was adopted:

We, the various elements and entities involved in the Inter-Congolese Dialogue;

Aware of our responsibilities towards the Congolese people, Africa and the international community;

Considering the Agreement on a cease-fire in the Democratic Republic of the Congo signed in Lusaka on 10, 30 and 31 July, 1999;

Considering the relevant Resolutions of the UN Security Council concerning conflict in the Democratic Republic of the Congo;

Considering the Resolutions of the Inter-Congolese Dialogue which took place at Sun City (South Africa) from 25 February 2002 to 12 April 2002;

Calling on the following persons to bear witness: His Excellency Mr. Ketumile MASIRE, neutral facilitator in the Inter-Congolese Dialogue. His Excellency Mr. Kofi ANNAN, Secretary General of the United Nations Organisation, represented by his Excellency Mr. Moustapha NIASSE, Special Envoy of the Secretary General of the United Nations for the Inter-Congolese Dialogue. His Excellency Mr. Thabo MBEKI, President of the Republic of South Africa and current Chairman of the African Union;

Conclude this Global and Inclusive Agreement on Transition in the Democratic Republic of Congo, by agreeing as follows:

---

335. Phillipe Tremblay, 57.

I – Cessation of hostilities

The Parties to this Agreement and having armed forces, namely the Government of the DRC, the RCD, the MLC, the RDC-ML, the RCD-N, and the Mai-Mai renew their commitment, in accordance with the Lusaka Agreement, the Kampala Withdrawal Plan, the Harare Sub-Agreement and the relevant Security Council Resolutions, to cease hostilities and to seek a peaceful and equitable solution to the crisis that the country is facing.

The Parties to this Agreement and having armed forces agree to commit themselves to the process of creating a restructured, integrated national army in accordance with the Resolution adopted on 10 April 2002 by the Plenary of the Inter-Congolese Dialogue (DIC) at Sun City.

The various elements and entities involved in the DIC, Parties to this Agreement (the Parties), namely the Government of the DRC, the RCD, the MLC, the political opposition, civil society, the RDC-ML, the RCD-N, and the Mai-Mai, agree to combine their efforts in the implementation of the Security Council Resolutions for a withdrawal of all foreign troops from the territory of the DRC and the disarming of the armed groups and militia and to safeguard the sovereignty and territorial integrity of the DRC.

The Parties agree to combine their efforts in order to achieve national reconciliation. To this effect, they have decided to set up a government of national unity which will organize free and democratic elections after a period of transition the duration of which is fixed in this Agreement.

The Parties agree to take all the necessary measures to make the people and the leaders involved in the transition process fell secure both in Kinshasa and in the whole of the national territory. To this effect, measures will be taken to guarantee the security of the population, the institutions, the organizers and the main leaders of the different Parties to this Agreement and their armed forces.

II – Transition objectives

The principal transition objectives are:

- The reunification and reconstruction of the country, the re-establishment of peace and the restoration of territorial integrity and State authority in the whole of the national territory,

- National reconciliation,

- The creation of a restructured, integrated national army,

- The organization of free and transparent elections at all levels allowing a constitutional and democratic government to be put in place;

- The setting up of structures that will lead to a new political order.

III – Transition principles

To guarantee a peaceful transition, the Parties shall participate in the political administration of the country during the period of transition. The institutions that will be set up during the transition shall ensure appropriate representation of the eleven provinces of the country and of the different tendencies within the political and social forces. In particular, provision shall be made for appropriate representation of women at all levels of responsibility.

To ensure the stability of the transitional institutions, the President, the Vice-presidents and the Presidents of the National Assembly and the Senate shall remain in office during the whole transitional period, unless they resign, die, are impeached, or convicted for high treason, misappropriation of public funds, extortion or corruption.

The Parties shall reaffirm their support for the Universal Declaration of Human Rights, the International Pact on Civil and Political Rights of 1966, the International Pact on Economic and Socio-Cultural Rights of 1966, the African Charter on Human Rights and the Rights of Peoples of 1981, and duly ratified international conventions. From that standpoint, they shall undertake to strive during the transitional period for a system that will respect democratic values, human rights and fundamental liberties.

The transitional institutions shall be based on the principle of the separation of the executive legislative and judicial powers.

The transitional institutions shall be run on the basis of consensus, inclusiveness and the avoidance of conflict.

The division of responsibilities within transitional institutions and at different State levels shall be done on the basis of the principle of inclusiveness and equitable sharing between the various elements and entities involved in the Inter-Congolese Dialogue, in accordance with criteria such as ability, credibility and integrity and in a spirit of national reconciliation. Provision is made in the Annex to this Agreement for the modalities of the implementation of the principle of inclusiveness.

The allocation among the different Parties of posts within the transitional government and, in particular, within the government committees shall be as equitable as possible in terms of the number and the importance of the ministries and government posts. A balance should be sought between the committees themselves. The allocation of posts within each committee shall be done by the signatory Parties according to an order of priority guaranteeing a general balance between the Parties.

To achieve national reconciliation, amnesty shall be granted for acts of war, political and opinion breaches of the law, with the exception of war crimes, genocide and crimes against humanity. To this effect, the transitional national assembly shall adopt an amnesty law in accordance with universal principles and international law. On a temporary basis, and until the amnesty law is adopted and promulgated, amnesty shall be promulgated by presidential decree-law. The principle of amnesty shall be established in the transitional constitution.

IV – Duration of the transition

The period of transition shall come into effect from the investiture of the transitional government. The election of the new President shall mark the end of the transitional period. The election of the new President shall take place after the legislative elections. The elections shall be held within the 24 months following the beginning of the transitional period. Because of problems specifically linked to the organization of the elections, this period may be extended by 6 months, renewable once for a period of six months, if circumstances so require, on the recommendation of the Independent Electoral Commission and by a well-founded joint decision of the National Assembly and the Senate.

V – Transitional institutions

During the transitional period, a transitional Executive, a transitional Parliament consisting of a National Assembly and a Senate, a judiciary composed principally of the existing courts and tribunals, and institutions supporting democracy shall be formed under the conditions specified in the transitional constitution.

The transitional institutions shall be as follows:

    The President of the Republic
    The Government
    The National Assembly
    The Senate
    The courts and tribunals

In addition to the above institutions, the following institutions supporting democracy shall be set up:

The Independent Electoral Commission
The National Watchdog on Human Rights
The Media Authority
The Truth and Reconciliation Commission
The Committee on Ethics and the Fight against Corruption

The Executive Power

The President

The President of the Republic shall be the Head of State. He shall represent the nation. He shall see to it that the transitional constitution is observed. The President of the Republic shall be the supreme commander of the armed forces. He shall chair the Defence Council. He shall convene and chair Cabinet meetings every fortnight. He shall remain in office until the end of the transitional period.

The duties and powers of the President of the Republic shall be as follows:

b.1 He shall promulgate laws.

b.2 He shall appoint and dismiss ministers and deputy ministers, at the instigation of the elements and entities involved in the DIC

b.3 He shall accredit ambassadors and special envoys to foreign countries and international organizations. He shall grant accreditation to foreign ambassadors and special envoys.

b.4 In accordance with this Agreement and the Annexes thereto, he shall appoint:

- Senior public servants
- Army and police officers, after consultation with the Defence Council.
- Provincial governors and deputy governors
- The Governor and Deputy Governors of the Reserve Bank
- Ambassadors and special envoys
- Members of the Magistrates' Council
- State representatives in public enterprises and parastatals

b.5 On the advice of the Magistrates' Council, he shall appoint and dismiss judges and public prosecutors, after informing the Government accordingly.

b.6 He shall confer the ranks of national orders and decorations in accordance with the law.

b.7 He shall have the right to remit, commute or reduce penalties after informing the government accordingly.

b.8 He can declare war and a state of siege or emergency following a Cabinet decision after the agreement of both Chambers of Parliament.

The duties of the President of the Republic shall be terminated by resignation, death, impeachment, conviction for high treason, embezzlement, misappropriation of public funds, extortion or corruption. In the case of resignation, the element to which the President of the Republic belongs shall present his substitute to the National Assembly for confirmation within seven days. The Vice-President from the Government element shall provide the acting president. The conditions for the implementation of this provision shall be set out in the transitional constitution.

The Presidency

The Presidency shall comprise the President and four Vice-Presidents.

The President and the Vice-President shall provide the necessary and exemplary leadership in the interests of national unity in the DRC.

The President of the Republic, together with the Vice-Presidents, shall deal with all matters relating to the running of the government as well as the matters mentioned under points A/b/b4 (i) and (v).

The meetings between the President and the Vice–Presidents shall be held regularly, at least once a fortnight, and in all cases before each Cabinet meeting. The meetings between the President of the Republic and the Vice-Presidents can also be convened by the President at the request of a Vice-President. In the absence of the President of the Republic, the latter shall appoint, in rotation, the Vice-President who is to chair the meetings.

The Vice-Presidents

There shall be four vice-president posts. The Vice-Presidents shall come from the following elements: the Government, RCD, MCL and the political opposition. Each Vice-President shall be in charge of one of the following four government committees:
- The Political Committee (RCD)
- The Economic and Finance committee (MCL)

- The Committee for Reconstruction and Development (Government element)
- The Social and Cultural Committee (political opposition)

i. The duties of the Vice-Presidents shall be as follows:

i/1 They shall convene and chair the meetings of their Committee.

i/2 They shall present the reports of their Committee to the Cabinet.

i/3 They shall coordinate and supervise the implementation of Cabinet decisions relating to their respective Committees.

i/4 They shall make proposals to the President of the Republic regarding the ranks of national orders and decorations, in accordance of the law.

j The duties of the Vice-President shall be terminated in the case of his resignation, death, impeachment, conviction for high treason, or in the case of misappropriation of public funds, extortion or corruption. If his duties cease, the element from which the Vice-President came shall present his substitute to the National Assembly for confirmation. The substitute as well as the conditions for the implementation of this provision shall be specified in the transitional constitution.

The Government

The government shall consist of the President of the Republic, the vice-presidents, the ministers and deputy ministers. The ministerial portfolios shall be allocated among the elements and entities involved in the Inter-Congolese Dialogue under the conditions and according to the criteria set out in Annex I to this Agreement.

The government shall determine and conduct the policy of the nation in accordance with the Resolutions of the Inter-Congolese Dialogue.

The government shall have full responsibility for the conduct of public affairs and shall be accountable to the National Assembly under the conditions set out in the transitional constitution. However, during the whole transitional period, the National Assembly may not vote in favour of a motion of censure of the government as a whole.

Government or Cabinet meetings shall be chaired by the President of the Republic or in his absence, or if he should so decide, by one of the Vice-Presidents, in rotation.

The government shall be consulted by the President of the Republic on the matters mentioned under points A/b/b4 (i) and (v) above.

While in office, the members of government may not by themselves nor through a third party buy or rent anything belonging to the State. They shall be obliged, from the day of taking office and on expiry thereof to declare all their belongings in writing and on their word to the National Assembly.

The term of office of ministers and deputy ministers shall be terminated in the case of their resignation, dismissal, death, impeachment, conviction for high treason, or in the case of misappropriation of public funds, extortion or corruption. Where a vacancy arises, the element or entity of the DIC from which the minister or deputy minister concerned comes shall present his successor to the President of the Republic. The conditions for the implementation of this provision shall be specified in the transitional constitution.

A general secretariat of the government shall assist the President and the Vice-Presidents in the coordination of government action. It shall prepare the meetings, the work and all the matters to be discussed between the President and the Vice-Presidents and at Cabinet level.

The transitional Executive shall work together, in the spirit of a government of national unity and on the basis of a common government programme founded on the Resolutions adopted within the DRC.

– The Legislative Power

The transitional Parliament shall consist of two Chambers: the National Assembly and the Senate.

The National Assembly shall be the legislative body during the transitional period. It shall exercise the powers and functions set out in the transitional constitution which forms an integral part of this Agreement.

The National Assembly shall consist of 500 members. The members of the National Assembly shall be called deputies. The minimum age for a deputy shall be 25 years by the date of appointment. The deputies shall be entitled to an equitable monthly salary that will allow them to be independent and to leave honorably at the end of their term of office.

The deputies shall be appointed by their elements and entities within the DIC under the conditions set out in the Annex to this Agreement. All the elements and entities shall ensure a balanced provincial representation within their group.

The Bureau of the National Assembly shall consist of a chairman, three deputy chairmen, a rapporteur and three assistant rapporteurs. Each of them shall come from a different element or entity.

The Senate shall play the role of a mediator in a case of conflict between the institutions. The Senate shall prepare the draft of a post-transition constitution. It shall have a legislative function together with the National Assembly in al matters concerning citizenship, decentralization, the electoral process an the institutions supporting democracy.

The Senate shall consist of 120 members. The members of the Senate shall be called Senators. The minimum age for a senator shall be 40 years by the date of appointment. The senators shall be entitled to an equitable monthly salary that will allow them to be independent and to leave honourably at the end of their term of office.

The Senators shall be appointed by their elements and entities within the DIC under the conditions set out in the Annex to this Agreement. The Senate shall be constituted in such a way as to be representative of all the provinces.

The Bureau of the Senate shall consist of a chairman, three deputy chairmen, a rapporteur and three assistant rapporteurs, as provided for in this Agreement. Each of them shall come from a different element or entity.

The duties of the Presidents of the National Assembly and the Senate shall be terminated in the case of their resignation, death, impeachment, conviction for high treason, or in the case of misappropriation of public funds, extortion or corruption.

– The Judicial Power

The Parties reaffirm the need for an independent judiciary. The Magistrates' Council shall constitute the disciplinary jurisdiction for judges. It shall keep an eye on the career of judges and on safeguarding their independence.

The organization of the judiciary shall be set out in the transitional constitution and in a law.

The first president of the Supreme Court of Justice, the public prosecutor and the auditor general of the armed forces shall be appointed as soon as possible after the signing of this Global and Inclusive Agreement, with due regard for a national balance, according to a mechanism to be determined by the Parties.

– The Institutions supporting democracy

The following institutions supporting democracy shall be created:
- The Independent Electoral Commission
- The Media Authority
- The Truth and Reconciliation Commission

- The National Watchdog on Human Rights
- The Committee on Ethics and the Fight against Corruption

The organization, functioning and powers of the institutions supporting democracy shall be established by law.

The duties of the presidents of institutions supporting democracy shall go to the civil society component. The presidents of institutions supporting democracy shall have the status of minister. The institutions supporting democracy shall function independently of the transitional government. The duties of the presidents of institutions supporting democracy shall be terminated in the case of their resignation, death, impeachment, conviction for high treason, or in the case of misappropriation of public funds, extortion or corruption. Where a term of office is terminated, the element to which the president of one of the institutions belongs shall present its substitute to the National Assembly for confirmation within seven days.

VI – The Army

A meeting of the staff of the FAC, RCD, MLC, RCD-N, RCD-ML and Mai-Mai shall be convened before the setting up of the transitional government. It shall develop the military mechanism entrusted with the training of the other staff up to the level of military regions.

A Defence Council shall be set up. This Council shall be chaired by the President of the Republic and, in his absence, by the Vice-President whose responsibilities include Defence.

The Defence Council shall be composed as follows:

The President of the Republic
The four Vice-Presidents
The Minister of Defence
The Minister of the Interior, Decentralisation and Security
The Minister of Foreign Affairs
The Army Chief of Staff (his deputies may also be invited)
The Chiefs of Staff of the Air Force, Army and Navy

The Defence Council shall give its assent to a declaration of a state of siege, a declaration of a state of emergency or a declaration of war.

The Army and National Defence Law shall establish the responsibilities and the functioning of the Defence Council.

The Defence Council shall give advice particularly on the following matters:

> The setting up of a restructured and integrated national army
> The disarming of armed groups
> Supervising the withdrawal of foreign troops
> The drafting of defence policy

The conditions for the implementation of the provisions regarding the army shall be established by law.

VII – Final provisions

The transitional constitution shall be drafted on the basis of this inclusive Agreement on transition in the DRC and shall form an integral part thereof.

The Parties shall accept as obligatory the appended Annexes that constitute an integral part of this Agreement.

The Parties shall agree to set up a mechanism for the implementation of this Agreement.

This Global and Inclusive Agreement shall come into force on the date of its adoption by the DIC. The transitional constitution that will be adopted by the DIC shall come into force on the date of its promulgation by the President of the Republic.

The Parties shall undertake to implement this Agreement in good faith, to observe its provisions and to participate in all the institutions, structures and committees that will be set up in accordance with its provisions. The Parties shall undertake to do their utmost to see that this Agreement is observed and implemented.

Annex I: The Division of Responsibilities

The Government

The participation of the elements and entities of the DIC in the transitional government shall be based on the manner of their participation in the DIC at Sun City.

The transitional government shall be composed of the following Ministries.

 Interior, Decentralisation and Security
 Foreign Affairs and International Cooperation
 National Defence, Demobilisation and War Veterans
 Women's and Family Affairs
 Justice
 Human Rights
 The Press and Information
 Planning
 Budget
 Finance
 Economic Affairs
 Industry of Small and Medium-sized Enterprises
 Mining
 Energy
 Foreign Trade
 Portfolio Matters
 Public Service
 Agriculture
 Rural Development
 Posts and Telecommunications
 Scientific Research
 Public Works and Infrastructure
 Transport
 Culture and Arts
 Environment
 Tourism
 Land Affairs
 Town Planning
 Health
 Higher and University Education
 Primary and Secondary Education
 Labour and Social Welfare
 Social Affairs
 Youth and Sport
 Solidarity and Humanitarian Affairs

The transitional government shall also comprise the deputy ministers responsible for the following portfolios:

Foreign Affairs
Interior
Integration of the Army
International Cooperation
Defence
War Veterans and Demobilisation
Security and Public Order
Justice
The Press and Information
Planning
Finance
Budget
Portfolio Matters
Mining
Energy
Trade
Agriculture
Public Works and Infrastructure
Public Service
Transport
Health
Higher and University Education
Primary and Secondary Education and Vocational Training
Social Affairs
Labour and Social Welfare

Seven ministries and four deputy minister posts shall be allocated to each of the following elements: the Government, RCD, MLC, and the political opposition.

Two ministries and three deputy minister posts shall be allocated to the civil society component (in addition to the Presidency and five institutions supporting democracy).

Two ministries and two deputy minister posts shall be allocated to each of the following entities: RCD-ML, RCD-N and Mai-Mai.

The National Assembly

The participation of the elements and entities of the DIC in the National Assembly shall be based on the manner of their participation in the DIC at Sun City. The Assembly shall be composed as follows:

Elements/Entities	Number of Deputies
RCD	94
MLC	94
Government	94
Political Opposition	94
Civil Society	94
RCD-ML	15
RCD-N	5
Mai-Mai	10
Total	500

The Bureau of the National Assembly shall be composed as follows:

- Chairman:MLC
- First deputy chairman:Government
- Second deputy chairman:RCD
- Third deputy chairman:Political opposition
- Rapporteur:Mai-Mai
- First assistant rapporteur:Civil society
- Second assistant rapporteur:RCD-N
- Third assistant rapporteur:RCD-ML

The Senate

The participation of the elements and entities of the DIC in the Senate shall be based on the manner of their participation in the DIC at Sun City. The Senate shall be composed as follows:

Elements/Entities	Number of Senators
RCD	22
MLC	22
Government	22
Political opposition	22
Civil society	22
RCD-ML	4
RCD-N	2
Mai-Mai	4
Total	120

The Bureau of the Senate shall be composed as follows:
- Chairman:Civil society
- First deputy chairman:RCD
- Second deputy chairman:Political Opposition
- Third deputy chairman:Government
- Rapporteur:RCD-ML
- First assistant rapporteur:RCD-N
- Second assistant rapporteur:MLC
- Third assistant rapporteur:Mai-Mai

Provincial Administration

The governors and deputy governors in office shall remain there until new governors and deputy governors are appointed by the government of national unity.

Diplomacy

The transitional government shall appoint ambassadors during the first six months, taking into account proportional representation of political tendencies within the government.

Career ambassadors shall be borne in mind when appointments are made.

ANNEX II: PUBLIC ENTERPRISES

The government of national unity shall appoint the administrators of public enterprises and parastatals, taking into account criteria such as morals, competence and experience. In the meantime, the current administrators shall remain in office.

ANNEX III: THE COMMITTEE FOR FOLLOW-UP OF THE AGREEMENT

A committee shall be set up for follow-up of the implementation of this Agreement, hereinafter called the Committee for Follow-up of the Agreement.

The Committee for Follow-up of the Agreement shall be chaired by the President of the Democratic Republic of Congo, His Excellency Major-General Joseph Kabila.

The Committee for Follow-up of the Agreement shall consist of two high-ranking representatives per element and one high-ranking representative per entity, not including the chairman of the Committee himself.

The Committee for Follow-up of the Agreement shall have the following duties:

To ensure the positive implementation of the provisions of this Agreement.

To see to the correct interpretation of this Agreement.

To reconcile points of view and to assist in resolving any disagreements that may arise between the signatories.

The Committee for Follow-up of the Agreement shall be set up as from the entry into force of this Agreement. Its mission shall end after the submission of its report to the transitional government, at the latest a month after the installation of the said government.

ANNEX IV: INTERNATIONAL GUARANTEE

Provision shall be made for an international committee to guarantee the proper implementation of this Agreement and to support the programme for transition in the DRC, in accordance with these provisions.

The international committee shall give active support to ensure the security of the transitional institutions resulting from the DIC and the positive implementation of the provisions of Chapter 8.2.2 of Annex A of the Lusaka Agreement, particularly in regard to the neutralization and repatriation of the armed groups operating within the territory of the DRC.

The international committee shall arbitrate and make a decision in any disagreement that may arise between the Parties to this Agreement.

The international committee shall assist the Committee for Follow-up of the Agreement in fulfilling its mandate.

ANNEX V: SECURITY ISSUES

The security of the political leaders in Kinshasa shall be ensured as follows:

Each political leader shall have 5 to 15 bodyguards to ensure his personal safety.

No additional Congolese armed force may be brought into Kinshasa so as to prevent any possibility of armed confrontation.

The meeting of the staffs of the FAC, RCD, MLC, RCD-N, RCD-ML and Mai-Mai may propose additional security measures for certain leaders according to requirements.

The following interim security measures shall be taken:

An integrated police force shall be responsible for ensuring the safety of the government and the population.

The international community shall give active support to ensuring the security of the transitional institutions.

Signed in Pretoria on 16 December 2002
Here ends the Global and Inclusive Agreement.

THE INTERNATIONAL COMMITTEE ACCOMPANYING THE TRANSITION

CIAT, an International Committee Accompanying the Transition, was established under Annex IV of the Global and Inclusive Agreement. Belonging to this committee are ambassadors of the permanent Security Council member countries and those of other countries and regional organizations that have a stake in the peace process, such as South Africa, Mozambique, Zambia, Gabon, Angola, Belgium, Canada, the African Union, and the European Union. CIAT is headed by William L. Swing (an American) who is the special representative of the UN Secretary-General to the Congo.[336]

At the urging of these countries, the IMF and World Bank International Development Association (IDA) are granting the DRC debt relief worth some US $20 billion under the Heavily Indebted Poor Countries (HIPC) Initiative. As a result, the DRC's total external debt will be reduced by approximately 90 percent.[337]

Speaking at a hearing of the Subcommittee on Domestic and International Monetary Policy regarding the debt cancellation, US Representative Barney Frank (D-MA) said, "The moral argument for canceling the debt, the debt would have to be repaid by very poor people who got very little benefit when it was

---

336. Ibid.
337. Diamond Intelligence Briefs, "DRC granted US$10 billion in debt relief," *Diamond Intelligence Briefs*, August 17, 2003.

incurred. There is no point in cracking down on debt collection when it comes from the people who were not the beneficiaries of the indebtedness. That is why we are not talking about an individual who borrowed money and forgiving that individual. We are talking about poor people who have been victimized, and debt cancellation is a way of recognizing that."[338]

In the case of the DRC, it was also suggested that the country's debt was "odious," which is to say that it was incurred for illegitimate reasons by an illegitimate ruler (Mobutu). When borrowed for nefarious purposes, the concept of odious debt gains particular legitimacy and warrants debt forgiveness. Clearly, then, the international community does not see President Joseph Kabila as following in Mobutu's footsteps.

By early 2003, Joseph Kabila abolished the Court of Military Order (at least in the western part of the country), replacing it with a system of military courts that could not impose the death penalty. Still in existence, however, is the Cour de Sûreté de l'Etat, which tries political offences and continues to judge opponents, journalists, and other persons responsible for "disrupting public order,"[339] without due process.

On March 6, 2003, the parties finalized a Constitution of transition and agreed on a plan for the integration of all armed forces into a reformed national army. The new Forces Armées de la République Démocratique du Congo (FARDC) will include all belligerents, such as the Mayi-Mayi, in addition to the main rebel groups. The World Bank and other donors agreed to make significant financial contributions to the process of disarmament and reintegration, but the aid has been slow in coming and the process itself will by no means be easy to achieve. As Phillipe Tremblay notes, "Since those opposed to the peace process have no representatives in the transitional institutions, disarmament for them is an irreplaceable loss of political influence and the renunciation of racketeering as the means of subsistence. It will be surprising if they go along without a fight."[340] Also, while the Transitional Government established an interministerial commission to coordinate and execute the program and the World Bank conditioned a payment of US $1.3 billion for it upon the appointment of a national coordinator, such a figure had yet to emerge as late as 2004.[341]

---

338. Washington Transcript Service, "Hearing before the Subcommittee on Domestic and International Monetary Policy," http://www.highbeam.com/library/doc3asp?DOCID=1P1:109828576 &num=103&ctrlINfo.

339. Phillipe Tremblay., 56.

340. Ibid., 39.

In addition, a bill was drafted in July 2003 by the Congolese Standing Commission on Law Reform to address the implementation of the ICC's Statute of the International Criminal Court Codifying Crimes Against Humanity and War Crimes. However, even the ICC prosecutor has indicated that the Court's eventual role is tied to the political transition. "If the Security Council fears that the ICC's actions are likely to jeopardize normalization, it could call for their suspension."[342] The ICC did indicate that it intended to examine the Congolese case. But this does not mean that the ICC will be empowered to judge those offences which occurred prior to its inception, before July 1, 2002. Since most of the crimes in the DRC were committed before that date, it will be the role of the CVR (Truth and Reconciliation Commission) to address earlier offenses.

THE TRANSITIONAL CONSTITUTION

The Preamble to the transitional constitution opens with some very tall orders for achievements that have thus far eluded the country under conditions of dictatorship. These are:

- To uphold the values of equality, justice, freedom, democratic tolerance, and social solidarity
- To build a lasting State of Law based on political pluralism
- To effect the separation of powers between the executive, legislative and judicial branches
- To subordinate the control of the governors to those who are to be governed
- To guarantee the fundamental rights and freedoms of Congolese citizens and to defend those of women and children, and
- To create a national army, restructured and integrated

From there, it quickly proceeds to establish the sacred duty and obligation of all Congolese to protect the country from insurrection. To be defended by its citizens are the country's territorial integrity and the seat of the government. There is emphasis on this provision in Articles 3 and 6, thus attesting to the immediacy of the problem of continued insurrection and military instability that is, even now, plaguing the country.

---

341. Ibid.
342. Ibid., 60-61.

As of 2003, the US State Department reported the following proliferation of rebel groups and activities:

> Rebel factions backed by the governments of Rwanda and Uganda, ethnic militias, and other armed groups continued to operate in more than half of the country during the year. There were continued, unconfirmed reports that Rwanda Defense Force (RDF) military advisors remained integrated with the Congolese Rally for Democracy (RCD/G) and Union of Congolese Patriots (UPC) forces. Approximately 5,000 Uganda People's Defense Forces (UPDF) troops remained in Ituri until early May. The largest rebel groups were the Rwandan-backed RCD/G, the Movement for the Liberation of Congo (MLC), and the Congolese Rally for Democracy based in Beni-Butembo (RCD/ML). The RCD/National (RCD/N), which was backed by the MLC, continued to operate.[343]
>
> In the Ituri district of Province Orientale, numerous tribally-based armed groups continued to fight for control of territory and resources during the year: The Lendu and Ngiti-dominated Front for the National Integration/Patriotic Force of Resistance in Ituri (FNI/FRPI), led by Floribert Njabu; the Hema-dominated UPC, led by Tomas Lubanga and supported by the governments of Uganda and Rwanda; the Hema-dominated Party for the safeguarding of the Congo (PUSIC), which split from the UPC early in the year and was led by Chief Kawa Mandra; the mixed People's Army of Congo (FAPC), led by General Jerome Bakonde; and the Alur and Lugbara-dominated Popular Force for Democracy in Congo (FPDC) led by Thomas Unen Chen. In addition, there were numerous loosely affiliated Lendu militia groups.[344]
>
> In North and South Kivu, a number of Hutu militia and Mai Mai groups operated. In South Kivu, there were also incursions by two Hutu rebel groups from Burundi, the Palipehutu/National Liberation Force (FNL) and the National Council for the Defense of Democracy/Forces for the Defense of Democracy (CNDD/FDD).[345]

Thus, it is not surprising that the foremost concern of the transitional constitution was the defense of the national territory.

In the transitional constitution, the country is described as a unitary decentralized State, consisting of the capital of Kinshasa and ten other provinces: Bandundu, Lower-Congo, Equator, West-Kasia, East-Kasai, Katanga, Maniema, North-Kivu, West Province, and South-Kivu. The division of competences between the capital and the provinces are to be determined by legislation within the first session of the National Assembly and the Senate.

---

343. US State Department, "Congo, Democratic Republic of the: Country Reports on Human Rights Practices – 2003," http://www.state.gov/g/drl/rls/hrrpt/2003/27721.htm.
344. Ibid.
345. Ibid.

Notably, the constitution declares that the soil and the subsoil are the property of the State. The State, in turn, is to assure that concessions are granted as the means to provide for the people. This attests to the presence of lands for communal farming, a process in which the participants are mainly women. Women survive in the Congo by farming for their communities, although many are engaged in it at bare subsistence levels. Although the constitution is seen to provide for the current practices in the country, it will be interesting to see what happens to communal lands once IMF and World Bank programs for an efficiency orientation are implemented. The typical result of Structural Adjustment Programmes is that communal lands are eliminated, as the "sacred cows" that come under attack in a liberalized economy, especially if the country wishes to attract foreign direct investment (FDI).

In opposition to its history of dictatorship, the constitution declares that no party or parties shall have the right to take power unto itself. The people shall control the government through universal suffrage. The conditions for elections and referendums are established, with the right to politically organize enshrined in Article 11. Article 12 provides that the government may subsidize political parties. And Article 13 protects the right of a democratic transition. The outcome of elections is to be generally respected.

Addressing the nationality question, particularly with regard to the Banya-mulenge (Zairian Tutsis) who were denied citizenship under Mobutu and Laurent Kabila, the constitution proclaims that "all ethnic groups and nationalities, which make up the people and territory of what has become the Congo (currently the Democratic Republic of the Congo) upon independence, shall enjoy equal rights and protection under the law as citizens."[346] Thus, the right of citizenship extends retroactive to the date of 1960.

Forbidden under the law are torture and other inhumane and degrading forms of cruelty. Slavery, such as that which takes place in the mines under the control of the rebel groups, is outlawed. Discrimination on the basis of religion, sex, family origin, social condition, residence, opinions or political convictions, or inclusion in an ethnic or tribal group is equally forbidden in matters of education and access to public functions.

In contrast to the conditions that developed under dictatorship where people could be stopped, arrested, and detained without charge and without

---

346. Oceana Law, "The Constitution of the Transition of the Democratic Republic of the Congo," http://www.oceanalaw.com/NXT/gateway.dll/CCW/current/congo%.

access to family or counsel, the constitution reverses this. Everyone has the right to be informed within 24 hours of the charges levied against him, and custody by the police cannot exceed 24 hours. Upon the expiration of that period, the person charged must be placed before a competent judicial authority. When placed in detention, the person has the right to proper care, including healthy and adequate food. He is entitled to treatment that "preserves his life, his physical and mental health as well as his dignity."[347]

However, a report issued by the US State Department in 2003 was particularly scathing on this account. It noted that the conditions of detainment were wholly inhumane and utterly unsustainable if the lives of the detainees were to be preserved. The report noted that:

> The conditions in most of the large, central prisons were harsh, and at times life threatening. The penal system continued to suffer from severe shortages of funds and trained personnel; however the Government continued to make efforts to respond to NGO complaints about prison conditions, particularly at Makala. Health care and medical attention remained inadequate, and widespread infectious diseases were a problem; however, a prison doctor was available. There continued to be fewer reported cases of infectious disease. The government-provided food remained inadequate, and the Government did not provide any food to prisoners at Makala for several weeks during September. Prisoners were dependent on the personal resources of family or friends, and families were allowed to bring food and other necessities to prisoners during regular visiting hours 3 days a week. Local NGOs reported that in a few cases, family members were forced to pay bribes to bring food to prisoners. Makala remained overcrowded...Conditions in small detention facilities (legal and illegal) also remained harsh and life threatening and resulted in an undetermined number of deaths, particularly from communicable diseases such as tuberculosis. These facilities were generally intended for short-term pre-trial detentions; however, in practice they were often used for lengthy detentions. Authorities often arbitrarily beat or tortured detainees. There usually were no toilets, mattresses, or medical care and inmates often received insufficient amounts of light, air, and water. Such prisons generally operated without a budget and with minimal government regulation or oversight.[348]

As it pertained to prison facilities outside the reach of the government, such as those being operated by the country's rebel groups, the report is even more discouraging.

> Prison conditions in areas outside of government control were extremely harsh and life threatening. Most detention facilities were not designed for detaining persons, and detainees often were kept in overcrowded rooms with little or no light or ventilation. For example, the RCD/Goma managed underground prisons in Kavumu and Chibingu outside Bukavu, South Kivu, and the UPC maintained several underground prisons in and around Bunia. They ranged in size from approximately 2 feet wide by 4 feet by 2 feet deep for 1 person to 15 feet by 15 feet by 5 feet deep for 15 to

---

347. Ibid.
348. US State Department

20 persons. Detainees typically slept on cement or dirt floors without beddin g and had no access to sanitation, potable water, toilets, or adequate medical care. Tuberculosis, red diarrhea, and other infectious diseases were widespread. Little or no food was provided to detainees, and guards demanded bribes to allow family members of friends to bring food to prisoners. Prisoners frequently were subjected to torture, beatings, and other abuse with no medical attention. Unlike in previous years, there were no reports that rebel forces released prisoners to their families just in time to die.[349]

Finally, the report observes that the practice of detaining people without informing them of the charges, and refusing to allow them contact with counsel or family continued within state security forces. Hence, the transitional constitution may be seen as having far reaching goals, but little was being done on the ground to ensure their implementation, at least in the security sector.

The transitional constitution provides for freedom of religion and of expression. It also upholds the right of citizens to acquire information. Particularly guaranteed is the "objectivity, impartiality, and plurality of opinions" within the State run media.

All Congolese have the right to peaceful demonstration, but can not be compelled to participate. Petitions can also be submitted to public authorities without discrimination against their authors.

Article 33 provides that no Congolese can be forcibly exiled for political, ethnic, or any other reasons. They may also not be deported.

Under Article 35, the right of sanctuary is recognized. It is extended to foreigners who may have been persecuted in their own countries for reason of their opinions, beliefs, allegiance to a racial, tribal, ethnic, linguistic group or their action in favor of democracy and the defense of human rights. Of course, it is forbidden for any person seeking sanctuary to conduct subversive activity toward his country of origin within the national territory.

Articles 36 and 37 prohibit nationalization of foreign-owned properties. Such actions may only take place where the law provides for the establishment of public utilities, upon condition that appropriate compensation is issued.

Articles 41 and 42 uphold the right to unionize, and the right to strike is recognized.

Every child has the right to know the names of his mother and father, and all children shall be protected by the State as part of the sacred family. The State upholds the right to work and to have unemployment security in order to provide for the family. It also shall take action against abuses of the children,

---

349. Ibid.

particularly those which involve sexual misconduct, such as forced prostitution, procurement, and any form of harassment.

Although education is compulsory, parents have the right to choose the type of education that their children receive from public or private institutes. In that sense, both parochial and public schools have the support of the national government. The State shall intervene in education so as to promote the eradication of illiteracy and to teach the general populace the text of the constitution and national agreements pertaining to the defense of human rights.

Under Article 51, all discrimination toward women shall be eliminated. The State shall take measures to ensure women's cultural, economic, and social development, and also to fight against violence. Women have the right to "significant" representation in political institutions.

Senior citizens, handicapped people and invalids also have the right to national protection. The state shall take measures to ensure that their physical, intellectual, and moral needs are met.

All Congolese have the right to benefit from the country's national wealth. The State is responsible to oversee its distribution and to encourage participation in economic advancement.

The political institutions of the government of transition are the President of the Republic, the Government, the National Assembly, the Senate, and the Courts and Tribunals.

The duties of the President shall end upon his resignation, death, or conviction for high treason, the embezzlement of public funds, misappropriation, or corruption.

The President presides over the High Council of Defense and is the Supreme Commander of the armed forces. He appoints or removes army and police officers in consultation with the High Council of Defense. The President may declare a state of emergency after consulting with the Council of Ministers, the High Council of Defense, the National Assembly, and the Senate.

The President appoints all foreign ambassadors. He may also name the State's senior civil servants, the province governors and vice-governors, the Central Bank governor and vice-governor, the member of the High Council of the Judiciary, and the State's representatives to public and semi-public establishments. The President may appoint or dismiss judges and public prosecutors.

The President has the right to pardon offenses, and commute or reduce sentences.

The Presidency is comprised of the President and four Vice-Presidents. The Vice-Presidents shall be chosen from the Congolese Rally for Democracy (RCD), the Movement for the Liberation of the Congo (MLC), the nonmilitary political opposition, and the Government. The RCD shall have responsibility for the Political, Defense and Security Commission. The MLC shall have responsibility for the Economic and Financial Commission. The Government shall have responsibility for the Reconstruction and Development Commission. And the nonmilitary political opposition shall be in charge of the Social and Cultural Commission.

The Government is comprised of the President, Vice-Presidents, Ministers, and Vice-Ministers. The President appoints the Ministers and Vice-Ministers.

Vice-Presidents, Ministers, and Vice-Ministers may be terminated upon resignation, death, conviction for embezzlement of public funds, misappropriation, or corruption. Ministers and Vice-Ministers may also be dismissed.

Articles 97 through 103 concern the establishment of the National Assembly. The National Assembly is comprised of 500 members. It votes laws; controls the Government, public corporations, establishments, and services; controls the implementation of the Resolutions of the inter-Congolese Dialogue; and adopts the project of the Constitution to be submitted to referendum.[350]

The Senate, dealt with in Articles 104 through 109, shall be comprised of 120 members. Together with the National Assembly, it examines those matters concerning: citizenship, decentralization, public finances, the electoral process, and the institutions supporting democracy.[351]

In the event of a disagreement between the Senate and the National Assembly, a Joint Committee shall be established to produce a mutually agreeable text.

Both the Senate and the National Assembly are governed by their internal regulations. Annually, there are two ordinary sessions of the Senate and the National Assembly. Each session is limited to three months time. However, special sessions may be called, whose duration shall last until the agenda has been exhausted. A majority of members must be present for each session of the Senate and National Assembly.

---

350. Oceana Law
351. Ibid.

The Government may request from the National Assembly the right to rule on certain matters by decree.

Although the President has the right to declare a state of siege or emergency, the period prescribed in the Constitution for said state to exist is limited to 30 days. It may thereafter be extended for successive periods of 15 days by the National Assembly and the Senate. The National Assembly and the Senate may declare an end to the state of emergency at any time. Measures which are taken by the President during a state of emergency shall also be submitted to the Supreme Court of Justice for a ruling as to whether they undermine the Constitution.

Article 147 establishes the independent power of the judiciary. It is exercised by the Supreme Court of Justice, the Appeal courts, the civil and military courts and tribunals, and the office of the public prosecutor. The Supreme Court of Justice has jurisdiction over the constitutionality of laws and acts with the force of law, as well as interpretations of the Constitution. It is also the judge of disputes over presidential and legislative elections, as well as referendums. In the event that a ruling or decision has no access to the Court of Appeals, the Supreme Court of Justice shall have jurisdiction.

The institutions that were established by the Inter-Congolese Dialogue in support of democracy are: the Independent Electoral Commission, the National Observatory of Human Rights, the High Authority on Media, the Truth and Reconciliation Commission, and the Commission on Ethics and the Fight Against Corruption. The terms of their members may be ended upon resignation, incapacitation, death, conviction of high treason, embezzlement of public funds, misappropriation, or corruption. The institutions supporting democracy are independent of the Government institutions and have juridical personality.

The Court of Audit controls the management of resources of all public corporations and entities. It reports to the National Assembly. Members of the Court of Audit shall be appointed or replaced by the President.

According to Article 168 of the Constitution, the Central Bank of the Congo enjoys management autonomy and shall be overseen by the Minister of Finance. The Central Bank is the Governments financial and economic advisor.

Finally, the National Police can not be diverted to personal use. Its purpose is to maintain public security and establish law and order. It is an apolitical institution placed under the authority of the Minister of Interior. The selection of the National Police shall take into account equality between the provinces. No one may be recruited into its service who is not 18 years of age.

The armed forces of the Congo include the naval, air, and land forces. They are national, apolitical, and republican. They are entrusted with protecting the country from international aggression and also for ensuring the country's economic, social, and cultural development. The armed forces are subordinate to civilian authority in the form of the High Commander of the Armed Forces. It is high treason to maintain or organize any other military or paramilitary force.

The High Council of Defense includes the President, the four Vice-Presidents, the Minister of Defense, and the Minister of the Interior, Decentralization and Security. It is chaired by the President.

The President is responsible for the ratification of all international agreements and treaties. If the Supreme Court of Justice decides that a treaty or agreement is in conflict with the Constitution, that treaty or agreement may only be ratified after revision of the Constitution. The President may conclude treaties or partnerships that entail a partial surrender of sovereignty for purposes of supporting the African Union.

The period of the Transition shall last for twenty-four months. During this time, the President, the four Vice-Presidents, and the Presidents of the Senate and the National Assembly shall rule without interruption.

This concludes our cursory study of the Transitional Constitution.

MONUC PHASE III

The focus of MONUC Phase III is the "orderly withdrawal of foreign forces; national dialogue and reconciliation; reestablishment of state administration over the territory of the DRC; disarmament of the armed groups; formation of a national army; and normalization of the security situation along the common borders between the DRC and its neighbors."[352]

Indeed, steps had been taken by enacting a transitional government to address many of these points; however, the biggest stumbling block to progress was still violence on the ground. The MLC and the RCD-K/ML continued to fight in the northeast, with eyewitnesses reporting that the MLC and the RCD engaged in looting, gratuitous killing, and violence against women including rape. There were summary executions, instances of mutilation, and even some

---

352. MONUC, "Peacekeeping in the DRC: MONUC and the Road to Peace: Facing the D3 Challenge."

reports of cannibalism wherein Pygmies were the victims. One observer said, "It is affirmed that Movement for the Liberation of the Congo warriors forced family members to eat their own relatives. A wife said that she was made to eat the flesh of her husband."[353] Also reported was the disappearance of some 96 people, the majority of whom were children.

The RCD-K/ML, in conjunction with Lendu combatants, took Irumu and Komanda, and strengthened their positions around Mahagi and Rethy during November. On October 13, the combined forces of Banyamulenge leader Commander Masunzu and Mayi-Mayi took Uvira. By the latter half of December 2002, UDPF (Ugandan) troops were brought back to Bunia in strength. Finally, there were violent clashes in Ankoro between the FAC and Mayi-Mayi, as a result of which there were 48 civilian deaths and 4,000 homes were burned.[354]

A report of the US State Department regarding joint campaign that was conducted by the RCD/N and MLC to capture Mambasa, North Kivu, which took place between October 2002 and December 2002, was even more explicit about the atrocities committed. It reads:

> The campaign "erase the blackboard" was led by Colonel Freddy Ngalimo (Grand Mopao), who reportedly described the operation as a "vaccination operation" involving the looting of each house and the raping of every female. During the military operation along the Beni-Mambasa axis, the soldiers systematically looted, raped, and executed the populations of entire villages. The UN confirmed 117 cases of arbitrary execution and 65 rapes, and local Red Cross officials reported that 185 victims were buried between October and December 2002. Many were executed in Mambasa, where two corpses were exposed to the population as a warning. Several of the victims were subjected to mutilation and in some cases were forced to eat their own flesh. Nande and Pygmy populations were targeted for mutilation and cannibalism, and in some cases, sexual organs were removed and hung around the necks of the soldiers as amulets. In one case, the body of an executed Pygmy was mutilated, with the heart taken out and sucked by the soldiers before the family members.[355]

While the UN Secretary-General's report for this period indicates that the training of an integrated police force was bearing fruit slowly, the total number of police officers trained thus far having amounted to only 161. The training of a second group of 197 was to begin on February 3, 2003.[356] However, since the

---

353. Gill Donovan, "Cannibalism shows depths of war's evil, bishop says," *National Catholic Reporter*, February 14, 2003.
354. Kofi Annan, "Thirteenth Report of the Secretary-General on the United Nations Organization Mission in the Democratic Republic of the Congo."
355. US State Department
356. Ibid.

establishment of the Lubero disarmament, demobilization, repatriation, reset-tlement, and reintegration (DDRRR) center in December 2002, MONUC had conducted intensive discussions with representatives of Rwandans. It estimated that some 3,000 to 4,000 combatants and several thousand of their dependents were prepared to disengage, but that, due to hard-line sentiments within the leadership of the Rwandans, this was unlikely to occur.[357]

According to the Secretary-General's report of May 2003, the impact of the war on Ituri's 4.6 million inhabitants was purely "catastrophic." He notes:

> Between 500,00 and 600,000 internally displaced persons in addition to nearly 100,00 refugees from Uganda and the Sudan are dispersed throughout the area. Since the onslaught of violence in June 1999, the death toll has been more than 60,000 and countless others have been left maimed or severely mutilated. Of the estimated 400 health centers, 212 have closed and not a single surgeon is present. It is estimated that 200 schools have been destroyed.[358]

Within Bunia, which had been recaptured by the UPDF on March 6, a ceasefire led to the convening of the Ituri Pacification Commission, representing Ituri's main communities and groups. Subsequently, the UPDF began with-drawing from Ituri on April 25, with the removal of some 2,000 troops. Immedi-ately following this, the town of Bunia was set upon by Hema and Lendu militia who fought for control of the region. Approximately 420 civilians were killed as a result of being caught in the crossfire.

By Resolution 1484, the UN Security Council approved the deployment to Bunia of an Interim Emergency Multinational Force (IEMF) on May 30, 2003. The French-led force was comprised of troops from France, Austria, Belgium, Brazil, Canada, Cyprus, Germany, Greece, Hungary, Ireland, Italy, the Nether-lands, Portugal, South Africa, Spain, Sweden, and the United Kingdom of Great Britain and Northern Ireland, with 500 support staff in Entebbe. It was grad-ually replaced, in mid-August 2003, by the MONUC Ituri brigade, which was authorized by Resolution 1493 to include up to 4,800 troops.[359]

In November, following their deployment to Tchomia to break up a battle over the town between the UPC and the PUSIC (Parti pour l'unité, la solidarité

---

357. Kofi Annan, "Second Special Report of the Secretary-General on the United Nations Organization Mission in the Democratic Republic of the Congo" (New York: UN Documents, May 27, 2003).

358. Ibid.

359. Kofi Annan, "Fourteenth Report of the Secretary-General on the United Nations Organization Mission in the Democratic Republic of the Congo" (New York: UN Documents, November 17, 2003).

et l'integrité du Congo), UPC elements in Bunia struck back at MONUC by withdrawing cooperation from the Ituri Interim Administration and by firing on UN checkpoints. In retaliation, MONUC seized weapons and detained a number of fighters.

On July 28, 2003, the Security Council authorized Resolution 1493, giving MONUC a more robust mandate and authorizing an increase in troops to 10,800. Henceforth, the Council authorized MONUC to take the necessary measures in the areas of deployment of its armed units to "protect civilians and humanitarian workers under imminent threat of physical violence; protect UN personnel and facilities and to ensure its freedom of movement, in particular those engaged in missions of observation, verification or demobilization, disarmament, repatriation, reintegration or resettlement; and contribute to the improvement of security conditions in which humanitarian assistance is provided."[360] It also imposed an arms embargo on the Kivus and Ituri and requested that MONUC monitor the arms flow in the region.[361] The EU adopted similar measures, maintaining an arms embargo. However, there are no embargoes on the foreign governments that remain engaged in the Congo, with this posing a significant problem.[362]

Between July 18 and 24, the new ministers and vice-ministers of the agreed on Transitional Government were officially sworn in. Abdoulaye Yerodia Ndombasi and Azarias Ruberwa (RCD-Goma), Jean-Pierre Bemba (MLC), and Arthur Z'Ahidi Ngoma (political opposition) were sworn in as vice-presidents. The 500-member National Assembly and the 150-member Senate were inaugurated on August 22, with Oliver Kamitatu (MLC) leading the former and Marini Bodho (civil society) leading the latter. The National Assembly held its first session on October 6.[363]

There was a coup attempt in March of 2004, carried out by attackers believed to be loyal to Mobutu. Their attacks began before dawn, lasting through four hours of gunfire, and targeting an army camp in the vicinity of Kabila's

---

360. M2 Presswire, "Security Council extends Democratic Republic of Congo mission until 30 July 2004, raises troop level to 10,800; unanimously adopts Resolution 1493 (2003); Institutes 12-month arms embargo on North and South Kivu, Ituri," *M2 Presswire,* July 29, 2003.

361. Kofi Annan, "Fourteenth Report of the Secretary-General on the United Nations Organization Mission in the Democratic Republic of the Congo."

362. Oxfam, "A Forgotten War — A Forgotten Emergency: The Democratic Republic of Congo," www.oxfam.org.uk.

363. Kofi Annan, "Fourteenth Report of the Secretary-General on the United Nations Organization Mission in the Democratic Republic of the Congo."

offices, a military airport, a naval shipyard on the Congo River, and the national radio and television headquarters. Congolese forces apprehended 12 assailants, while an untold number of fighters disappeared into the crowds. According to one Army officer, the attackers had come from French Brazzaville overnight.[364]

THE FALL OF BUKAVU

By now, the MONUC brigade was deployed to eight locations in Ituri, including Bunia, Iga-Barriere, Fataki, Kpandroma, Mahagi, Kanyi-Tchomia, Marabo, and Bogor. However, General Laurent Nkunda, a renegade ex-RCD-Goma officer who had refused to go to Kinshasa to be sworn into the new FARDC, began moving toward Bukavu from North Kivu under the pretext of preventing a genocide against the Banyamulenge. Although MONUC tried to create a buffer zone around the area of Bukavu and even reinforced it with troops, Nkunda overtook the town on June 1. Kabila's troops fled before the onslaught and MONUC was unable to protect some 4,000 internally displaced persons who were placed at imminent risk. The result was that MONUC was blamed by the Transitional Government for not pursuing its Chapter VII mandate, which empowered it to protect civilians from the threat of physical harm. There were violent demonstrations against the fall of Bukavu in the cities of Kinshasa, Lumbumbashi, Kalemi, Mbandaka, Kisangani, Beni, and Kindu, causing over $1 million worth of destruction. UN premises, humanitarian agencies, and NGOs were looted, and UN personnel were harassed and physically assaulted.[365] Battling the crowds, peacekeepers in Kinshasa fired directly into their midst, killing three of the rioters. In all, reports indicated that 12 people died and 88 were injured.[366]

On June 11, some 40 presidential guards who accused the Transitional Government of incompetence attempted a coup d'état. The group's leader was Major Eric Lenge, a trusted aide frequently photographed behind Kabila at official functions. Lenge launched the coup by commandeering state broadcast centers where

---

364. AP Worldstream, "Congo government forces quash apparent coup attempt," *AP Worldstream,* March 28, 2004.
365. Kofi Annan, "Third Special Report of the Secretary-General on the United Nations Organization Mission in the Democratic Republic of the Congo" (New York: UN Documents, August 16, 2004).
366. Rodrique Ngowi, "Renegades battle government forces in eastern Congo, UN evacuates some staff," *AP Worldstream,* June 7, 2004.

he announced that he was neutralizing the Transition Government.[367] Although Lenge escaped, Kabila suspended the commander of the presidential guard and the chief of the Maison militaire du Chef de l'Etat. He also replaced the Chief of Staff of the Army. In their own form of protest against the Government, eight RCD-Goma members of the National Assembly unilaterally suspended their membership and called on the other RCD-Goma members to follow.

Throughout 2004, sporadic violence continued. In early December, MONUC took over Ndrele and Mahagi from FAPC militias which had been abusing local civilians and preventing children from disarming. AP Worldstream reported in November that a full forty percent of the DRC's combatants are, in fact, children, with at least ten percent being under the age of fifteen. This is particularly prevalent among the Mayi-Mayi, of whom half are underage.[368]

Later in the month, a small rebel group invaded Kwila and its population fled from fear of reprisals by the FARDC. FARDC was responsible for the killing of over 70 persons. Security between the borders of Rwanda and the DRC also deteriorated seriously in November and December due to cross-border raids by the FDLR. In all, it was estimated that between 8,000 and 10,000 soldiers allied with armed opposition forces from neighboring countries remained on Congolese soil. These rebel groups are more like criminal gangs than parties, relying on terror and violence for sustenance.[369] In the Kivus, between 20,000 and 150,000 people were fleeing an advance of government troops against breakaway national army soldiers.

In Resolution 1565 (2004) the Security Council authorized an increase in the strength of MONUC of 5,900 personnel, which was 7,200 fewer than the Secretary-General requested. Violence was worst in Ituri and the Kivus, despite the presence of MONUC in Bunia and surrounding towns. In his report of December 2004, the Secretary-General noted that women were particularly vulnerable to abuses, and that sex slavery was rampant. Particularly targeted in the Kivus were Maniema, Katanga, and Oriental province. He also reported abuses by the Presidential Guard in Kindu, Kisangani, Lumbumbashi and Kinshasa.[370]

At this time, Amnesty International reported that 40,000 cases of rape had been reported over the previous six years. It claimed that all the armed parties

---

367. Daniel Balint-Kurti, "'Gunfire as Congo's government puts down coup attempt in the capital," *AP Worldstream,* June 12, 2004.
368. Aloys Niyoyita, "Child soldiers: 40 percent of Congo's troops are boys, private groups say," *AP Worldstream,* November 17, 2004.
369. Phillipe Tremblay, 41.

are guilty of rape, with their particular medical concern being the abnormally high rate of women suffering from vaginal fistulae (resulting from gang rape). But even Amnesty International cannot claim to possess complete figures. Due to the conditions of Congolese society, in which a woman is blamed for rape and ostracized by her community, it is likely that thousands, perhaps even tens of thousands, more have not reported their rapes.

Apart from the physical and psychological trauma that rape engenders, it also results in the continued spread of diseases. In the Democratic Republic of Congo, there are 10 times as many people living with HIV/AIDS as the number of people who died from AIDS in 2003.[371]

Women represent 80 percent of the agricultural workforce, and the threat of rape forces them out of the fields. This compromises the food security of entire Congolese communities who cannot otherwise provide for themselves.

By 2005, the EU had announced its own initiative to provide a police mission in Kinshasa. According to reports, a 30-strong team would help monitor, mentor, and train local police over a year-long period with a view toward creating an integrated police force. A draft operation for the plan, which they hoped to go forward with in February, was to be presented to a meeting of the EU foreign ministers on January 31.[372]

Also in January, the Transitional Government announced that it would delay the upcoming elections which had been scheduled for June 2005. In Kinshasa, crowds rioted over the issue, forcing security forces to fire bullets and tear gas. Residents joined students in setting fire to tires in the neighborhood near the airport. One man interviewed at the scene explained, "The people are saying we need elections. They don't want elections to be delayed, and the economy is bad and everyday our money becomes more worthless. The people are protesting these things."[373] Government representatives said that elections could be postponed until October or November, and blamed the state of the economy on eleven government ministers whom Kabila had just sacked. In January, the

370. Kofi Annan, "Sixteenth Report of the Secretary-General on the United Nations Organization Mission in the Democratic Republic of the Congo" (New York: UN Documents, December 31, 2004).
371. New York Times Upfront, "AIDS ravages Africa, *New York Times Upfront,* May 9, 2005.
372. European Report, "EU/Congo: Police Mission Set to be Up and Running in Mid-February," *European Report,* January 22, 2005.
373. AP Worldstream, "Congo security forces deploy in capital to quell protestors angry over election delay," *AP Worldstream,* January 11, 2005.

European Union had pledged some 80 million euros to funding the elections in June. It was the single largest donation that the EU had ever dedicated to a political election process.[374]

Visiting Kinshasa in June, 2005, European Commission (EC) President Jose Manuel Barroso warned that June 30, 2006 would be the final deadline for the transitional government to hold elections. He held talks with President Joseph Kabila, after which he addressed the parliament, warning that "Those who work against this objective [elections], by fraud, by the instigation of violence or ethnic hatred, will be rejected by the international community." He expressed the fear that, "If, by the end of the transition, the Congo has not become a reliable partner for the rest of the world, I worry deeply that it will lose, for a long time, the high place it enjoys today on the international agenda. This is what happened to Somalia a few years ago..."[375]

Regarding the delay of elections, UN Secretary-General Kofi Annan released the following statement in his special report to the Security Council:

> They will involve a number of formidable challenges: the logistical task of reaching all eligible voters in a country the size of Europe with virtually no roads, a population without identity cards and no census since 1984; insecurity from armed groups in some areas and political tensions in others; and the pressure of the public's high expectations for change. The electoral process will also be affected by a number of key issues on the transitional agenda of which progress remains significantly delayed, in particular integration and reform of the army and police, the legislative agenda, the extension of State administration, and the financial management of the country.[376]

Based upon the findings of a United Nations mission to assess electoral preparations that was launched in April, 2005, Annan noted with satisfaction that the legislative framework for holding elections was basically in place including the laws on nationality and voter registration, and the adoption of a new draft Constitution on 13 May, 2005. But still to be adopted were the amnesty, referendum, and electoral laws. He stated that the forthcoming electoral law was of paramount importance, since it would be necessary to assure the people that the elections would be both free and fully transparent.

As for the progress of the Independent Electoral Commission (IEC), Annan found that it had established its base in Kinshasa, 11 provincial offices,

374. The Voice, "Election in Congo Gets Euro Boost," The Voice, January 9, 2005.
375. Xinhua News Agency, "EC President sets deadline for Cogno's interim government," Xinhua News Agency, June 28, 2005.
376. Kofi Annan, "Special report of the Secretary-General on elections in the Democratic Republic of Congo," May 26, 2005.

and most of the planned 64 liaison offices which were designed to cover the 145 territories and 25 cities that comprise the local administration. A test of registration equipment was conducted from April 25 to May 1, and the first batch of voter registration machines was expected to arrive in June.

Although donors had approved an estimated election budget of $285 million in June, 2004, Annan observed that only $181 million of the budget had actually been pledged, and the current funds available amounted to only $88 million. Of the $20 million committed by the government of the DRC, only $2 million had thus far been dispersed.[377] This had resulted in a cash-flow problem, which Annan hoped would be overcome if the government was to proceed with purchasing voter materials.

Annan also made some very critical comments regarding the lack of fiscal responsibility and corruption on the part of the transitional government officials, noting that "Major donors have reported increasing signs of financial mismanagement, corruption and a lack of transparency in the collection of revenues and Government expenditures. It has been noted that these trends could be related to the manipulation of revenues by officials who would not expect to return to the administration after the elections, as well as by those seeking to influence the campaign process. Donors have expressed concern that, while they provide support for half the national budget, the Government is still not covering basic services, including the salaries of civil servants. Serious concern has arisen over the prospect that, with the depreciation of the Congolese franc and increasing rates of inflation, the frustration of the Congolese people, including underpaid military and police personnel, could be easily manipulated by political spoilers."[378]

Annan was especially worried about the abuse of State resources, recommending that the UN should sponsor the establishment of a "Group of Friends of Good Governance," which should include the World Bank, the International Monetary Fund, and the UNDP (United Nations Development Programme). (It is worth noting here that the IMF had approved a loan of approximately $848.6 million for the DRC under the Poverty Reduction and Growth Facility arrangement in 2002.[379] Thus, it has a vested stake in determining how that funding is applied.) In any event, the "Group of Friends of Good Governance"

---

377. Ibid.
378. Ibid.
379. M2 Presswire, "IMF Executive Board extends the Democratic Republic of the Congo's three-year PRGF arrangement, *M2 Presswire*, June 29, 2005.

would be responsible for supporting the transparent management of State resources, including revenue from the mining sector. Otherwise, he bemoaned the potential for the State to continue in its mismanagement, particularly with a view toward extorting participation of the military and the police in manipulation of the pre-election efforts. He feared that they would be forcefully used by the State to cow the opposition and to prevent people from forming free associations. Another way that he saw to avoid this was to re-deploy the UN forces to the centers of national discourse. He recommended that the UN augment the current MONUC force of 16,700 troops with an additional three battalions, broken down into 160 personnel for a brigade headquarters and three infantry battalions at 850 personnel each. With the inclusion of additional personnel for observation helicopters, hospital services, and an engineering company, he recommended that the total of UN forces should be brought to 19,290.[380]

On a separate note, the African Union decided to deploy an African force to beef up MONUC's efforts. Rwandan President Paul Kagame said that the time had come to disarm the ex-FAR/Interahamwe once and for all. DRC Foreign Minister Charles Murigande welcomed the AU's initiative.[381] It couldn't have come at a better time.

Toward the end of January, over 2,000 people fled the village of Tche, about forty miles north of Bunia. They sought refuge near UN peacekeepers after Lendu fighters scourged their village, looting and burning homes, and murdering in the night. Those who fled claimed that the militia had also kidnapped 34 women and young girls.[382]

Believing that the flow of weapons to the Congo remains part of the problem, UN Secretary-General Kofi Annan asked the UN Security Council to adopt a new policy of "shaming and blaming" those who continue to evade the embargoes. He said, "Considering the close links between the illegal trade in small arms and trafficking in women and children, the Council may wish to assist in bringing those responsible for such crimes before the ICC for prosecution."[383] Although the illegal flow of weapons is primarily confined to small

---

380. Ibid.

381. Xinhua News Agency, "Rwanda wants all Congo-based rebels disarmed in 2005," *Xinhua News Agency*, January 26, 2005.

382. Bryan Mealer, "UN: Thousands flee homes after weeks of attacks in eastern Congo," *AP Worldstream*, January 31, 2005.

383. Inter Press Service English News Wire, "UN: Annan says "Name and Shame" Violators of Arms Embargoes," *Inter Press Service English News Wire*, February 18, 2005.

arms including handguns, assault rifles, machine guns, mortars, rocket launchers, and anti-personnel mines, the resistance by governments to a global tracking system has meant that it is nearly impossible to stop the fighting.

But it appears now that the UN has also been part of the problem. Beginning in February, allegations began to surface that MONUC soldiers were engaged in prostitution and rape. Both military and civilian personnel traded money, food, or jobs for sex, and sometimes the acts were forced. Many women complained of being made pregnant without consent.[384] One man, Didier Bourguet (age 41), has given detailed accounts to French prosecutors of how he had intercourse with girls aged between 12 and 16. He sometimes paid a few dollars for these favors, and videotaped the encounters. The UN is investigating 150 allegations against 50 of the 11,000 peacekeepers in the Congo. And now that the cat is out of the bag, they are bracing for reports of similar abuse in peace-keeping contingents stationed in Burundi, Sierra Leone, Ivory Coast, and Haiti. Assistant Secretary-General for Peacekeeping Operations Jane Hull said, "We think this will look worse before it begins to look better."[385]

This, combined with complaints that the UN has not done enough under its Chapter VII mandate to protect people at risk, makes many people wonder what exactly the UN is supposed to be doing in the Congo. While it remains a sad truth that the force is simply not large enough to cover enough of the region, it also remains clear that the UN will not engage. It will not serve as an interposition force, nor act to disarm the rebels by force, which is what is most needed in the Congo.

This becomes clearer and clearer with each passing day. Recently, over 88,000 people were forced to flee their homes in the territory of Djugu. Humanitarian agencies suspended assistance to over 54,000 of these people in the Kakwa, Tche and Gina areas due to security concerns. Children as young as eight and women were among the militia who attacked several villages in Ituri, forcing another 70,000 to flee. The militias take people hostage to use as sex slaves and to ferry gold and other goods. Now there are even slavery raids. Adrian Blomfield reports that tribal raiders are preying on the villages of eastern Congo and carrying off their inhabitants to be forced into slavery through beatings and amputations. Those who are fat or elderly or deemed unsuited for

---

384. University Wire, "Editorial: UN officials' behavior horrific, intolerable," *University Wire*, February 16, 2005.

385. David Usborne, "UN to tackle claims of Congo sex abuse," *The Independent*, March 2, 2005.

work are quite simply killed. Those who remain are beaten with rubber whips and subjected to having their hands hacked off for disobedience, just as it was in the days of King Leopold II.[386] If anything, the rebels have been emboldened by the UN's refusal to act.

On February 25, the rebels also struck the United Nations directly. A group called the Front des Nationalistes et Intégrationnistes (FNI) attacked a Bangladeshi contingent in Ituri, killing nine peacekeepers. In response, the UN deployed a force of 800 peacekeepers to track down the FNI. It resulted in a pitched battle wherein the UN killed 60 rebel soldiers. The Security Council applauded the tough stance of MONUC and felt encouraged by its progress.

But why does the UN only take action when it is the lives of the peace-keepers at issue? Do the lives of the Congolese mean less? How can the world have stood by for more than six years while nearly 4 million people died?

Those who feel that the world has done something positive for the Congo by deploying MONUC to the region have not faced the facts. The truth is that people continued to die between 2003 and 2004 at the rate of 1,000 people per day.[387] That is 31,000 per month; and nearly 4 million are dead. Almost half the victims were children under 5. The vast majority died from disease and malnu-trition, which could have been at least in part prevented had donor response been high. But, the fact is that it was not. In 1999, for example, donor govern-ments gave just $8 per person in the DRC, while providing $207 per person in response to the appeal for former Yugoslavia. The UN consolidated appeal showed a shortfall of nearly 40 percent.[388] Comparing the war with Iraq in the year 2004, the International Rescue Committee noted that the results were even worse. Whereas Iraq received aid worth $138 per person, the Congo received $3 per person.[389] This also shows that the amount of aid the Congo received has been more than halved since 1999.

Instead of rising to meet the crisis, it appears that the world's donor gov-ernments have all but lost interest.

---

386. Adrian Blomfield, "Tribal slave raids bring new wave of terror to Congo," *Daily Tele-graph*, March 9, 2005.
387. US Newswire, "IRC Study Revelas 31,000 Die Monthly in Congo Conflict, 3.8 Million Died in Past Six Years, When Will the World Pay Attention? Asks the IRC," *US News-wire*, December 9, 2004.
388. Oxfam.
389. Wikipedia.

Why is it so difficult to increase aid now, when the world spent millions of dollars to arm Africa in the first place? The United States alone spent more than $125 million in direct government-to-government weapons deliveries, commercial sales, and International Military Education and Training (IMET) to the states directly involved.[390] William Hartung and Bridget Moix point out that, "the US falls dead last among industrialized nations in providing non-military foreign aid to the developing world. In 1997, the US devoted only 0.09 percent of GNP to international development assistance."[391]

As Hartung and Moix advise:

> The administration and Congress should restore the previous level of $800 million in development assistance to Africa...This level of funding should serve as the floor — not the ceiling — for future aid packages. The US should further strive to raise African development funding to $2 billion...and consult directly with nongovernmental institutions to ensure that funds are dispersed and used appropriately. The negligible amount of aid provided each year for African development can only be called disgraceful in comparison to the billion spent each year on the US arms trade.[392]

What is more, the US should contribute troops to the operation in the DRC.

CONCLUSION

The Congolese have led a miserable existence for generations on generations, with no brighter end in sight. While there is the native rebel component to this last six years of war, it is no less true that the violence and predation are funded and fuelled by neighboring countries and those who desire access to the Congo's mineral wealth. Quite simply, Leopold's treachery and Mobutu's violent kleptocracy have been replaced by what many people are calling "Africa's Scramble for Africa," a scramble in which foreign pecuniary interests have been only too happy to participate. And the government sponsors of the latter have been responsible for the policy of arming Africa since the start of the Cold War.

These twin factors — arms deals with African countries and reliance on Congolese resources like the gems now commonly called "blood diamonds" —

---

390. William d. Hartung and Bridget Moix, "Deadly Legacy: US Arms to Africa and the Congo War," (New York: Arms Trade Resource Center, January 2000.
391. Ibid.
392. Ibid.

contribute to produce a scenario in which escape from war and bloodshed appears most unlikely until such time as world governments who have interests in the Congo are willing to act, and act decisively, to bring the conflict to a conclusion. Why the world did not provide a sufficient peacekeeping body when the Congo and the rebel parties signed the Lusaka Accord remains an open question. In Yugoslavia, a 20,000-man force was provided once a peace agreement was signed. This, in addition to the fact that Yugoslavia received far more in humanitarian aid, would appear to indicate that the people of the developed countries care less about what happens in Africa than in other parts of the world.

The genocide of Rwanda, which was responsible for the penetration of the DRC by the ex-FAR and Interahamwe, was likewise allowed to happen because the world was indifferent to it. Having been burned by the failed intervention in Somalia, a humanitarian aid mission gone wrong, the US, in particular, opposed providing military solutions for needy African countries. Although Richard Holbrooke, the US representative to the United Nations proclaimed that the month of his chairmanship of the Security Council was to be the "month of Africa," renewed focus on the region did not serve to end the conflict. The DRC was allowed to languish, with the overriding concern being that MONUC's Chapter VII mandate should not be employed for active combat.

While no one doubts that the security of UN personnel is of paramount concern, it remains very much the case that force is only employed when the UN force is in danger. Then, what takes place is retribution. Barring a desire to intervene between the parties, the least that the UN could do is improve the humanitarian situation. Proposals for a forceful humanitarian mission[393] (which have been dubbed "HUMPROFOR," for "Humanitarian Protection Force") have been presented as the means to resolve the difficulties facing vulnerable aid agencies. Such a force has yet to materialize, though the suggestion was years in the making. HUMPROFOR presumably would employ ex-military personnel who have had extensive combat training and who would be compensated richly for the risks involved in aid administration under active combat conditions. It would be coordinated by the military and would replace those aid agencies that are ordinarily defenseless.

---

393. Jeanne Haskin, *Bosnia and Beyond: Recognizing and Halting Genocide.* NY: Algora Publishing, forthcoming (spring 2006).

If there was one encouraging fact concerning the war in the DRC, it was that none of the main rebel factions has demanded independence, choosing not to pursue goals of separatism but rather goals of inclusion. In that sense, the DRC's struggle is to throw off the yoke of oppression. The fear that the DRC would dissolve without the likes of someone like Mobutu has failed to be justified, thus undermining the theory that a "strong man" is needed. What the DRC needs is help to expel the ex-FAR/Interahamwe, along with the other foreign insurgents who continue to operate on its soil. Also needed is reeducation for the Army, whose dissident elements continue to pose a problem. Just as retired military advisors were provided by the US for the confrontation in Yugoslavia once Croatia and Bosnia made peace, so can the United States provide the DRC with professional help. The EU has taken steps to implement a police training program, but that is not enough.

Finally, elections must take place if anything is to change. The government in power should be monitored and aided, with funding provided to the commissions that are necessary for progress. The Truth and Reconciliation Commission, the Commission on Anti-corruption, the Electoral commission, and the High Authority on the Media are all needed by the country to redress the wrongs of the past and to avoid abuse in the future. World governments, therefore, need to take a serious look at providing the necessary funding and pressure to make these bodies effective. Individuals can encourage this by writing to political representatives at the state and federal levels.

Progress finally has been made. Should the world allow this historic chance for freedom to bypass the Congolese, history will stand in judgment.

Epilogue

While preparing this book, the author has corresponded with people in the Congo regarding the state of the country and its prospects for peaceful change. Quite a scare was building. It appeared that people at the grass-roots level had had enough of waiting for their government to change. They were originally promised elections to coincide with the anniversary of the Congo's independence, and, when these were postponed, many were wondering whether they should take matters into their own hands. Plans were being made to march against the government, to take to the streets in numbers, and to voice their opposition to the delays of the transitional regime through violence if need be. In that vein, tools for self-defense (particularly machetes) were being purchased at an alarming rate in anticipation of a government crack-down.

For the most part, the government sought to counter the opposition in advance of June 30 by closing down those television and radio stations that were broadcasting news of people buying machetes and preparing to march in protest. But, as we shall see, it also took pains to warn the students that they would be expelled and punished if they joined the opposition.

ACTION AGAINST SECESSIONISTS AND STUDENTS

With Katanga, Kasai, and the Kivus receiving arms shipments in preparation for the planned uprising, a very real feeling had grown up that they would fight for rights of autonomy, if not outright secession. Here is the context of a letter that I received regarding the same, which accuses the party of Etienne Tshisekedi of fomenting their troubles:

> It confirms itself more and more that the UDPS has been the basis of instigating and coordinating the former SECESSIONIST action of Katanga, Kasai and Kivu. The party has organized the flight of weapons into our different military quarters...For that giant BOOOM which will explode on 30 June 2005. On 30 June 2005, the people *illicitly, illegally, and illegitimately* will take it upon themselves to make the changes that will *finish the transition* [author's emphasis].

In early 2005, there was already talk of secession in mineral-rich Katanga, resurrecting a very old problem that dates back to the first days of independence. In connection with this threat, the government claims that it has arrested 35 people, one of them being the son of Moise Tshombe (the leader of Katangese secession back in 1960). Other sources, such as human rights groups, have claimed the number arrested was nearer to 100. ASADHO/Katanga, the African Association of Defense of Human Rights representing Katanga (a group funded by the US Embassy in Kinshasa), has issued a statement condemning the arbitrary arrest and detainment under exceedingly inhumane conditions of 26 people, thus far listed as follows:

Colonel Ipanga, Commandant FARDC, Battalion Kipushi

Colonel Ferdinand Mahina Bichilo, Commandant FARDC, Camp Vangu

Colonel Ndala Nguza, Commandant FARDC, Likasi

Colonel Mbumb Musang, Commandant FARDC, Kolwezi

Colonel Muland Daniel, Commandant FARDC, Kolwezi

Colonel Mwan'angola Damas, Commandant FARDC, Dilolo

Colonel Mukaz Ditend Honore, Commandant FARDC, Sandoa

Colonel Kabinad Yav, Commandant FARDC, Equateur

Colonel Yav A Yav, Commandant FARDC, Equateur

Major Masoj, Commandant FARDC, Dilolo

Major Kadimbili, Commandant FARDC, Equateur

Major Kamboyi, Commandant FARDC, Equateur

Captain Itala, Commandant FARDC, Kimbembe

Captain Nkemba, Commandant FARDC, Equateur

Mr. Andre Tshombe, son of Moise Tshombe, President of CONACO

Mr. Josue Tshingej Tshikomb

Mr. Robert Mutombo

Mrs. Mujinga Masuka

Miss Kamwang Mjuing

Miss Ma Wit Kasang

Mr. Felix Ulombe Kaputo

Mr. Serge Tshibangu

Mr. Jean Tshikwata

Mr. Franck Mutombo Tshinaweji

Mr. Domingo Monaji

Mr. Mukwiza Masoka

Their protest alleges that the detainees have yet to be placed before a magistrate, though the law provides that they must be legally charged within two weeks of their detainment, and that the detainees are being held in exceedingly close confinement. They are allegedly being subjected to torture and have been denied medical treatment.

In general, reports of the conditions of life in prison are dismal. Pictures taken of those who have been imprisoned for many months show that the men are absolutely skeletal. Their bones stand out in sharp relief against their shrunken musculature. One report comments that there is not even a line item regarding the purchase of food for the prisoners in the whole of the national budget.

ASADHO/Katanga has issued a further press release concerning threats that were issued to the students at universities, particularly that which is situated at Lumbumbashi. According to its statement of May 16, the students at Lumbumbashi were explicitly warned by administrators that they would be expelled from the university should they become involved in fomenting discord pending the date of June 30. The students' families, alarmed by reports that a commando unit of the military police would be circulating through the university on May 16 and 17, were evacuating their sons and daughters in droves. The statement of ASADHO calls on the government in Kinshasa to secure the universities, to desist in threatening those students specifically who have had any links to the UDPS (the party of Etienne Tshisekedi), and to make it possible for students to remain on the campuses without fearing for their safety.

In his attempts to investigate the rumors surrounding military harassment at the campuses, the president of ASADHO/Katanga claims that he was pursued by three men in a truck and fired upon before he escaped to the safety of the nearest UN base.

Dr. Tshisekedi's response to the troubles, and that of the UDPS, was to urge the Congolese and foreign governments everywhere to endorse his petition asking that he be appointed president of the country no later than June 15, 2005 in order to stave off, and hopefully prevent, the uprising as well as the threats of secession. Dr. Tshisekedi's claim was that this would be consistent with the spirit of the Sovereign National Conference (CNS) and the intent with which he signed the Sun City Agreement to become a participant in the Congo's transitional government. Part of his plea to the Congolese people, which accompanies his petition, is translated here:

> Conscious of the danger of the disorder, chaos, and implosion that are the pure perpetrators of the killings of the Congolese, we must all apply ourselves to looking for solutions for the country...We must express our adhesion to the schema of the CNS and demand the application of the resolutions of the CNS which are our common heritage. Demand the replacement of the formula of 1+4 by a formula of a President and of a First Minister by June 30, 2005. Mister Etienne Tshisekedi has asked in the spirit of the works of the CNS to take his responsibilities to drive the country toward free elections and transparent democracy. In this framework, Mister Tshisekedi assumes and authorizes himself the President of the Republic. Recommend now to President Tshisekedi to set up a government of national unity by June 15, 2005 at the latest. Let us ask MONUC, CIAT, and all friends of the DRC to help us put in place the army and the police to guarantee the security of the population and the good functioning of the institutions coming from the new formula...This is an institutional putsch that is recommended for President Tshisekedi to set up a government of national unity here on June 15, 2005 at the latest.

One of my Congolese correspondents commented in response to this open letter that the country did not need an institutional putsch but rather free elections. To allow Dr. Tshisekedi to assume the presidency by petition would, in the eyes of this person, be the same as allowing another dictator to rule the Congo.

Yet, in the eyes of many others, Dr. Tshisekedi has suffered greatly to bring significant change to the country. They see his assumption of the presidency as the key to preventing further violence and destruction.

A report released by *Les Points*, a Congolese publication, regarding voter tendencies surveyed between 2004 and 2005 indicates that Dr. Tshisekedi has garnered a majority of support amongst the 1200 potential voters who responded. The following are reproductions of some of their tables, showing the distribution of ages and provinces of origin, as well as answers to some of the tough questions that are facing the populace today in connection with the elections.

According to this poll, the majority of those surveyed blamed government policies for the delay in the elections and felt that the government had likewise failed to respond appropriately to those who felt that the day of June 30 should mark the end of the system of 1+4, whereby President Kabila rules in conjunction with four Vice Presidents.

Gender of Respondents

Gender	Number of Respondents	%
Masculine	820	76.19
Feminine	380	21.9
N/A	20	1.9
Total	1,200	100

Age of Respondents

Age	Number of Respondents	%
18-25	430	35.8
26-35	420	35
35-X's	330	27.5
N/A	20	1.6
Total	1,200	100

Education Level of Respondents

Level Education	Number of Respondents	%
Primary	42	3.5
Secondary	302	25.1
University	780	65
N/A	76	6.3
Total	1200	100

Geographic Base of Respondents

Province of origin	Number of Respondents	%
Low Congo	173	14.4
Bandundu	166	13.8

Equateur	100	8.3
Kasai Occ	124	10.3
Kasai Now	118	9.8
KATANGA	85	7.8
KINSHASA	40	3.3
Manieme	98	8.1
North Kivu	82	6.8
Eastern Prov	45	3.75
South Kivu	71	5.9
N/A	98	8.16
Total	1,200	100

Probable Vote of Respondents

Candidate	Perdentage of Votes	As of Oct 04	As of Dec 04	As of Jan 05	As of Feb 05	As of Mar 05	As of May 05	
Etienne Tshisekedi	42.7	44.9	32.2	31.2	32.8	30	38.6	+8.6
Eugene Diomi	15.6	13.8	22.2	29.1	29.3	19.3	22.6	+3.4
Joseph Kabila	13	12.1	16.2	5.2	8.6	9.6	7.6	-2
John Pierre Bemba	7.7	7.0	2.7	3.2	8.1	8	3.1	-4.9
Antoine Gizenga	4.7	2.7	3.9	9.2	4.33	3	2.75	0.25
Gabriel Mokia	-	-	-	-	3.58	2.7	1.8	-0.9
Arthur Zhaidi	1.4	1.6	2.0	-	0.4	1	0.8	-0.2
Laurent Monsengo	2	-	0.8	6.0	4.33	4.6	8.5	3.9
Azarias Ruberwa	1.2	1.2	0.5	-	0.3	0.7	1.8	+1.8
Christophe Lutundula	-	-	1.0	1.1	-	-	1.5	

Q6. In your view, what is the main reason why the June 30, 2005 election is being postponed?

Government policies	767	63.8%
Lack of cohesion among the president's entourage	166	13.8%
Lack of logistical and financial means	138	11.5%
Lack of national defense services	12	1%
Lack of an adequate response or proposal	51	4.25%
N/A	66	5.5%
Total	1200	100%

Q7. The head of state addressed the population on Monday, May 16, 2005. Do you think that his message:

	No. of respondents	Percentage of total
Fails to meet the expectation of the opposition that calls for cancellation of the 1+4 formula outright and establishment of a new political order?	481	40%
Is objective as to the progress of the transition?	231	19.25%
Will be able to appease the opposition before June 30, 2005?	202	16.8%
Has the potential to destabilize the Presidency?	198	16.5%
Is demagogical?	76	7.7%
None of the above	12	1%
Total	1,200	100%

THE POLITICAL MOVEMENT IN BRUSSELS

People in exile from the Congo had also joined together in Brussels for a conference regarding elections. The conference took place between May 13 and May 16, 2005, and included Congolese living abroad as well as representatives of churches, pressure groups, artistic communities, and associative interests. In a declaration released on May 16, the Conference declared that, "conscious of the total degradation of political and social life in the Democratic Republic of Congo and animated by an unshakeable will...to answer to a patriotic requirement to save the Congo" that it had resolved the following:

> As to the dawn of the independence, the approaching date of June 30 is a period that will determine our [nation's] history. The time has come for a thorough political change. Following the example of all those countries that have produced colored revolutions, the Democratic Republic of Congo, our country, must also undergo a revolution. We have no apology to spoil this big appointment with history....June 30 must mark the end of the system 1+4 and the departure of the strength of all its coordinators...The juridical framework will be the institutional order coming from the CNS, with some adjustments holding account of the evolution of politics...A shift directing of less than 30 persons driven by a political leadership agreed by the population, must be put in place for the organization of the election in a delay of six months that will follow June 30, 2005.[394]

---

394. Declaration of the Congolese Living Abroad, May 13-16, 2005.

THE FEDERALIST DEBATE AND THE NEW CONSTITUTION

At the same time, people in prominent positions were trying to address the threats of secession. A group of university professors, led by Professor P. Ngoma Binda, Professor Nsuka zi Kabwiku and Professor Luyinduladio N'zinga, published a thorough and thoughtful study of what a new federal government versus a unitary government would mean to the whole of the country. They argue in support of federalism on the basis of their belief that it would achieve a government oriented on the basis of efficiency and would empower people at the local levels to act in their own interests. Their study indicates that the current unitary system is, in fact, likely to promote dictatorship more than democracy and good governance. It contributes to corruption and the poverty of the populace. Given the sheer size of the Congo, they argue that the government must decentralize in order to address the needs of the people.

Thus, the old argument that had separated President Kasavubu and Prime Minister Lumumba during the 1960s about which type of government is best suited for the Congo has now reemerged.

On May 13, 2005, however, the Democratic Republic of Congo endorsed a draft constitution that did not provide for a federal system. The draft, which is to be put to a national referendum later, gives President Joseph Kabila the right to appoint and remove from office the prime minister of the country, to dissolve the national assembly, and to legislate by decree. To accommodate those who maintain that the Congo's system of government should be a federal system, it appears that there will be a large degree of decentralization. Instead of the present 11 provinces, the DRC will be split into 26 provinces, thus multiplying the people who will participate in governance. The minimum age for a presidential candidate was set at 30, and the president is to be elected by universal suffrage to serve for a five-year term that is only once renewable.

The draft constitution reads most poignantly as a proclamation of emancipation from the troubles of the past. It faces head on the corruption, waste, and mismanagement of the earlier governments, and places resounding emphasis on providing the Congolese with their most basic needs (jobs, shelter, rights of citizenship, food security, and, in particular, human rights).

Highlights of the Draft Constitution

The Preamble of the Constitution openly declares that it is injustice with impunity, nepotism, regionalism, clannism, and vote-chasing which are at the heart of a general inversion of values and the ruin of the country. It proposes to correct these matters through the right of free peoples to organize and to elect their leaders, who will solemnly accept the task of correcting the wrongs of the past.

Unlike the Transitional Constitution, the new draft responds to the federalist debate by further decentralizing the country's administration. The Democratic Republic of Congo now consists of the capital city of Kinshasa and 25, as opposed to 10, provinces. The provinces are now divided into Bas-Uele, Equator, Haut-Lomami, Haut-Katanga, Haut-Uele, Ituri, Kasai, Kasai Oriental, Kongo Exchange, Kwango, Kwilu, Lomami, Lualaba, Lulua, Mai-Ndombe, Maniema, Mongala, Nord-Kivu, Nord-Ubangi, Sankuru, South Kivu, South Ubangi, Tanganyika, Tshopo, and Tshuapa.

For administrative purposes, each province is then further broken down into the city, the municipality (commune), the sector, and the chieftainship.

In follow-up to the Transitional Constitution, the new draft concretely establishes the division of powers between the central government and the provinces, allocating those powers which are specific to the central government as follows:

- Foreign affairs including diplomatic relations as well treaties and international trade agreements;
- Foreign trade;
- Matters of nationality, including the status and policing of foreigners;
- Extradition, immigration, emigration, passports, and visas;
- External security;
- National defense;
- The national police force;
- The national public service;
- The national economy;
- Income taxes, including corporate and personal taxes;
- The national debt;
- Foreign loans for the State or the provinces;
- Internal loans for the State;
- The national currency, including its issuance and power of exchange;
- National weights and measures;
- Customs and duties of imports and exports;
- Rules concerning banks, and bank and stock-exchange transactions;

- Currency regulation;
- Laws concerning patents and literary, artistic, and industrial property;
- The postal system and telecommunications;
- Navigation of waterways, airways, railroads, roads, and other fixtures which are in the national interest;
- Universities and other technical or professional establishments which are subsidized by the State or are in the national interest;
- Applicable standards of national education;
- Procuring the needs of the State;
- Agricultural, forestry, and energy programs;
- Laws on hunting, fishing, natural preservation, and catching or breeding foods of animal origin, and the veterinary arts;
- Protection from radiation and elimination of radioactive substances;
- Prevention of economic abuse;
- Historic and public buildings, and parks;
- Meteorology, geodesics, cartography, and hydrography;
- Appointment of provincial inspectors for primary, secondary, professional, and special education;
- Statistics and the national census;
- National planning;
- Scientific and technological research;
- Ports, airports, and stations;
- Assistance to war veterans and war-handicapped persons;
- The following legislation:
- Commercial law;
- The penal code and the penal regime;
- The code of judicial organization and competence;
- Legislation concerning liberal occupations;
- Employment legislation, including the laws governing relations between employers and employees, the safety of the workers, Social Security, and involuntary unemployment;
- Legislation on the arts and professions;
- Medical legislation, including preventive medicine, hygiene, public health, mother and child care, the pharmaceutical industry, bilateral and international sanitary regulations, the technical coordination of medical laboratories, and the distribution of doctors;
- Electoral law;
- Legislation on manufacturing, including the import, export, and the sale of alcoholic and non alcoholic drinks;
- Legislation on manufacturing, including the import, export, and transit of war materials;
- Legislation on human artificial insemination, manipulation of genetic information, and the transplantation of organs and human tissues;

- Legislation on refugees, including expelled and displaced persons;
- Legislation on admission into the medical professions and in other occupations.

As evidence that there is some overlap between Government and provincial functions, thus attesting to decentralization, however, the following are areas where the Government and the provinces share responsibility:

The implementation of mechanisms to protect human rights and fundamental liberties declared in the Constitution;

The civil and customary laws;

Statistics and the censuses;

Internal Security;

Administration of courts, and prisons for punishment or correction;

Culture and sports;

The establishment of taxes, including excise and consumption taxes;

The national public service;

The economy of the Republic;

The establishment of income taxes, including corporate and personal taxes;

The national debt of the Republic;

Foreign loans for the Republic or the provinces;

The internal loans for the needs of the Republic;

The currency, with respect to its issuance and power of exchange;

The national weights and measures;

Customs and duties of import and export;

The rules concerning banks, and bank and stock-exchange transactions;

The currency regulation;

Environmental protection;

Energy, agriculture, and forestry, including rules on the breeding of foods;

The creation of the primary, secondary, and university establishments;

The road traffic and the maintenance of roads of national interest, including the collection of tolls;

Medical and philanthropic institutions;

Initiative for projects, and programs for international economic, cultural, scientific, and social cooperation;

The production, transport, use, and exploitation of energy;

The protection of vulnerable groups.

Finally, the following are prescribed in the draft constitution as being the sole responsibility of the provinces:

Plans for installations;

Provincial cooperation;

Provincial and local public service;

Application of the standards governing the family;

Provincial economics;

Provincial national debt;

Internal loans for the needs of the provinces;

Preservation of real estate titles;

Organization of small business;

Organization and functioning of public utilities, provincial establishments, and public companies;

The works and procurement contracts of provincial and local interest;

Procurement for the provinces;

Maternal, primary, secondary, professional, and special education, as well as the elimination of illiteracy in the citizens;

Fines or imprisonment to ensure respect for edicts;

Internal communications;

Provincial and local taxes, including the land tax, the tax on rental income, and the tax on automobiles;

The establishment of minimum provincial salaries;

The appointment of medical staff, the elaboration of programs to fight epidemic diseases, the organization of hygiene and provincial disease prevention, the application of national medical and pharmaceutical legislation, the organization of remedial medicine, and the organization of philanthropic services and missionaries.

The elaboration of mining, mineralogical, and industrial programs, and their execution according to the national schedule;

The elaboration of programs in agriculture and forestry, and their execution according to the national schedule;

Appointment of veterinary staff, and the elaboration of programs to promote animal health;

Organization of vaccination drives against diseases, and the organization of laboratories, private hospitals, and advice centers;

Tourism, historic and public buildings, and parks of provincial and local interest;

The urban and rural environment, including the public road network and community faculties;

Provincial culture and sports;

Exploitation of non nuclear energy and the production of water for the province;

Execution of the laws of residence and laws for foreigners;

The execution of the common law;

Provincial planning.

Of course, the draft Constitution remains dedicated to the vote by universal suffrage, and the establishment of political associations is encouraged. It remains an offense of high treason for any individual or group to attempt to form a "unique" party that will assume the role of a dictator.

The right to Congolese nationality is, again, conferred upon those who formed the body of the State upon independence in 1960.

Instead of "significant" representation in political institutions, women now have the right to parity representation. The State assumes the responsibility to fight discrimination against women for any reason, and to ensure the woman's safety. The latter extends to both public and private life. Any violence against a person whose object is to destabilize the family is a crime against humanity. No one can be forced into slavery or set to compulsory labor.

No one can be pursued, arrested, detained, or condemned unless it is by virtue of a law and in accordance with those measures which the law prescribes. Every person is presumed innocent until s/he receives his sentence. A person can not be held accountable for the offense of another person. Upon arrest or detainment, a person has the right to know the charge. S/he has the right to immediate counsel or contact with family members, and must be brought before a court of competent jurisdiction within 48 hours. Every prisoner has the right to benefit from a treatment which protects his "life, his physical and mental health, and his dignity."

The courts remain public, unless the prospect of open doors raises some form of threat to the State. But all sentences are openly pronounced in public. And each person sentenced has the right to a formal appeal.

Under Article 24, the media and the freedom of information by radio, television, the print media, and other forms of communication are guaranteed, subject to respect for the laws. The State media are public utilities with access free to all. The State guarantees objectivity, impartiality, and a plurality of opinions in its treatment and distribution of information.

Again, all people have the right to peaceful demonstrations, but can not be coerced into participation. They have the right to submit a petition to the legal authorities without fear of discrimination or retribution.

Unique to the draft Constitution, no one has the right to execute an illegal order. Any agent is released from responsibility for the execution of an order that would result in an infringement on the respect for human rights and public liberties. The proof of the illegality of the order falls to the person who refuses to execute it.

Every person has the right to secretive correspondence. This can be challenged only in cases where a person has violated statutory law.

Through the draft Constitution, the DRC continues to uphold the rights of refugees. It allows for asylum in cases where foreign nationals have been pursued or persecuted for reason of their opinion, faith, racial, tribal, ethnic, or linguistic affiliation, or their actions in favor of democracy and the defense of human rights. Persons seeking asylum with the DRC are forbidden to engage in any subversive activities. They also can not be expelled or repulsed to their state of origin.

The right to private property is enshrined in Article 34. No one, foreign or national, can be deprived of his personal property without it being in the national interest and without proper compensation. Foreigners enjoy equal rights with the Congolese, excepting only those which are political.

Also new to the draft Constitution is Article 51 regarding the protection of all ethnic groups. The State now declares that it has a duty to ensure the peaceful and harmonious coexistence of all the ethnic groups in the country. It also ensures the protection and promotion of all vulnerable groups and minorities.

Under Article 56, any act, agreement, or arrangement which has the consequence of depriving the nation and its people of any or all of their livelihood is an act of plunder punished by law. If such act, agreement, or arrangement, is attributed to a public official, then the crime is one of high treason. All Congolese have the right to enjoy the national wealth. The State assumes the duty to redistribute it fairly and to guarantee laws for its development.

Even during a national state of emergency, there are certain rights of which the public may not be deprived. These concern the right to life; the ban on torture and cruel or inhumane treatment; the ban on slavery and servitude; the laws for infractions and punishments; the rights of defense and the right of appeal; the ban on detention for debts; and the freedom of thought, consciousness, and religion.

Again, it is the obligation of all Congolese to defend the national territory.

The formal institutions of the Republic are: the President, the Parliament, the Government, and the Courts. The President is the symbol of national unity, and he upholds the Constitution. He acts as an arbiter of the authorities and institutions; and it is his duty to ensure national independence, integrity of the territory, national sovereignty, and respect for treaties and international agreements. Elected by direct universal suffrage, the President serves for a five-year term that is renewable only once. He is subject to the laws, and punished by them accordingly.

If the President is not successfully chosen by the first round of the ballot, there will be a second round. The second round will apply to those two candidates who garnered the highest number of votes. No one can be a candidate for President who is not at least 30 years old, obedient to the civil and political laws, and not statutorily barred. The President takes office within ten days of the proclamation of the ballot results. In cases his office becomes vacant due to death or resignation or for any other cause, the functions of the President are temporarily exercised by the President of the Senate. When vacancy has been declared by the Constitutional Court, the election of the new President takes place upon the summons of the national electoral committee within sixty to ninety days. In the case of force majeure, this period can be extended to 120 days.

The President appoints the Prime Minister of the State within a parliamentary majority. If such a majority does not exist, he can form a coalition within thirty days.

The President convenes and chairs his Cabinet. However, he may delegate this power to the Prime Minister.

The President invests the Governors and the elected Deputy Governors of the provinces, and also appoints the foreign ambassadors. He further appoints the superior and general officers of the armed forces and national police, the superior council of defense, the general mayor, the chiefs of staff, the commanders of the armed forces, the high-ranking servants of public administration, and the deputies of the State to companies and public bodies (except the auditors). He may appoint or revoke magistrates and members of the public prosecutor's office upon recommendation by the Council for the Judiciary.

The President is the Supreme Commander of the armed forces. He may declare a state of emergency after dialogue with the Prime Minister and the Presidents of the National Assembly and the Senate for a period of thirty days. The National Assembly and the Senate can approve a continuation of the state of emergency for periods of fourteen days. The National Assembly and the Senate may cancel the state of emergency at any time.

The President may declare war after consultation with the superior council of the defense and the authorization of the National Assembly and the Senate.

The members of the National Assembly carry the title of national representative. They are directly elected by universal suffrage, along with two replacements. The candidates for the general election are presented by political parties, or can appear as independents. The number of national representatives is fixed by the electoral law. No one can be a candidate for general elections if he is not at least 25 years old, obedient to the civil and political laws, and statutorily excluded. A national representative is elected for a period of five years. He is eligible for re-election (but there is no stipulation as to how many times in the draft Constitution).

The Senators represent their provinces, but their mandates are national. The candidates are presented by political parties, or can appear as independents. Every Senator is elected with two replacements, and elections in the second degree are performed by the provincial Assemblies. The former presidents of the Republic are Senators for life by law. A Senator is elected for a period of five years. He is eligible for re-election (but, again, there is no stipulation as to how many times). No one can be a Senator who is not Congolese, at least 30 years old, obedient to the civil and political laws, and statutorily excluded.

No member of parliament can be pursued, arrested, detained, or judged because of his votes or opinions. During the course of sessions, no member can be pursued or arrested, save in the case of flagrante delicto and with the authorization of the National Assembly or the Senate. The detention or pursuit of a parliament member is suspended if the Chamber of which he is a member requires him, however, the suspension can not exceed the length of the session.

The national representatives and senators have the right to enter and exit the national territory. They are also entitled to a fair reparation which assures their independence and dignity. Each of the Chambers sits validly only when the absolute majority of its members are present.

The Judiciary is independent from the legislative and executive power.

The provincial government consists of a Governor, a Deputy Governor and provincial Ministers. The Governor and the Deputy Governor are elected for a period of five years once renewable. They are invested by the President of the Republic. The provincial Ministers are appointed by the Governors. The number of provincial ministers can not exceed ten. The members of the provincial government can be collectively or individually removed by a vote of censure or mistrust within the provincial Assembly.

Two or more provinces can, unanimously, create a frame of harmonization and coordination of their respective policies and manage in common certain services.

This concludes our section on highlights of the draft Constitution.

INTERNATIONAL INPUT

On the UN front, there have been more developments that are consistent with the Secretary-General's efforts to serve the country. At a Budget Committee meeting of May 10, 2005, Catherine Pollard, Director of Peacekeeping Financing Division, said that "MONUC's budget for the period of 1 July 2005 to 20 June 2006 would be submitted at the main part of the Assembly's sixtieth session. Meanwhile immediate cash and additional human resources were required to support additional military personnel and to enable the Mission to reach its operational requirements. The request for commitment authority included 307 additional posts and 52 volunteer positions to support the Missions expansion."[395]

According to Congressman Chris Smith, the United States has thus far been "the world's largest donor to the peacekeeping mission in the Congo, and has contributed three-quarters of a billion dollars since 2000. This year alone, the US is expected to spend $249 million there. The US also contributes over a quarter of the entire peacekeeping budget of the United Nations annually. And that's not counting airlift and other logistical donations that cost US taxpayers not millions, but billions of dollars. The Administration has asked the Congress for an additional $780 million for peacekeeping operations in the supplemental budget request."[396]

---

395. M2 Presswire, "Budget Committee takes up financing for Haiti, Democratic Republic of Congo peacekeeping missions, *M2 Presswire*, May 10, 2005.

Thus, it is clear that the US remains as committed as other countries to the presence and progress of MONUC. But in the same hearing, Congressman Smith noted that despite the UN's zero-tolerance policy with regard to the sexual abuse of women and girls in the Congo, it still "occurred with sickening frequency." "However, to date, there has not been one successful prosecution of UN civilian or military personnel, either in the Congo or elsewhere."[397]

Congressman Smith therefore introduced legislation to address these specific offenses. The Trafficking Victims Protection Reauthorization Act of 2005, HR 972, would "require the State Department to certify to Congress, before it contributes US logistical or personnel support to a peacekeeping mission, that the international organization has taken appropriate measures to prevent the organization's employees, contractors, and peacekeeping forces from engaging in trafficking in persons or committing acts of illegal sexual exploitation."[398] This legislation is in addition to two prior laws that the Congressman introduced, including the Trafficking Victims Protection Act of 2000 and the Trafficking Victims Protection Reauthorization Act of 2003.

The UN reacted strongly to the idea of conditionalities regarding its missions as the prerequisite for US funding. But whether these will act as a bar to more new missions or as more of a stimulus for the UN to meet those conditions is up to the UN.

At the Senate level, the Committee on Foreign Relations met on May 17, 2005 to discuss the problems concerning Africa and a comprehensive response to them. Among the problems that were considered were the spread of HIV/AIDS, joblessness among university graduates, and lack of infrastructure. Giving testimony before the Senate, Nancy Birdsall, President of the Center for Global Development, reported that the Commission recommended, among other things, one hundred percent debt relief for poor African countries and an increase in the amount of support offered to them through a very large endowment. Her report cited a need for another $15 billion in annual aid transfers. Even so, the report noted that "The Commission's proposed increases in aid are trivial in terms of the rich world's wealth, and are well below amounts other countries received at

---

396. Congressman Christopher H. Smith, Committee on International Relations Subcommittee on Africa, Global Human Rights and International Operations, "United Nations Organization Mission in the Democratic Republic of Congo: A Case for Peacekeeping Reform," March 1, 2005.
397. Ibid.
398. Ibid.

critical moments in their development. South Korea received nearly $100 per person...in annual aid between 1955 and 1972. Botswana, the world's single fastest growing country between 1965 and 1995, received annual aid flows averaging $127 per person...By contrast, annual assistance to sub-Saharan Africa today averages about $28 per person — not nearly enough to build a foundation for sustained growth and development."[399]

The proposal of the Commission is to "increase aid flows by $25 billion annually between now and 2010, and then assuming reasonable results, to add another $25 billion annually. This would eventually triple total annual aid inflows to sub-Saharan Africa from the current level of about $25 billion from all sources."[400]

With reference to the DRC specifically, it was noted that the very basic lack of infrastructure should be combated through public works that are funded in cooperation with the government, so as to accommodate commercial traffic while providing gainful employment for those who want to lay down their weapons. And this coincides with the UN's own plans to induce the rebels in the DRC to finally disarm and reintegrate.

What Is To Be Done?

But these plans must take effect now if they are to introduce any meaningful solutions to the war that still ravages the east. People continue to die by the hundreds, and recent pictures show that atrocities are still taking place that are just too horrible to recount. Images that were being passed around by e-mail in mid-2005 show tiny babies lined up in death, their poor, stiff forms completely bereft of clothes. Another shows a soldier in the process of mutilating his victim by sawing off a leg with a knife. These pictures, I am told, were forwarded to US Secretary of State Condoleezza Rice. And shortly after their release, Secretary of State Rice issued a statement that emphasized the role that the United States is trying to play in removing the soldiers of Rwanda and Uganda from the area. According to a further report, the US has officially blacklisted the FDLR, placing it among the top twenty terrorist groups.

---

399. Nancy Birdsall, Testimony before the Senate Foreign Relations Committee, 17 May 2005.
400. Ibid.

Popular outrage over the continuance of atrocities and the slow, steady death toll which continues to plague the east, combined with the fear that, if elections do not take place as originally promised by June 30, 2005, they may be postponed indefinitely — were seen as contributing factors in the riots that recently occurred in the diamond town of Mbuji Mayi. Just after the draft constitution was made public, followers of the UDPS went on the rampage in Mbuji Mayi and burned down three buildings belonging to the political opposition. Two people are said to have been killed and a curfew was imposed.

Hopes, and tempers, were running high as the critical date approached. My correspondence with a young man from Kinshasa, whom I met through an Internet group that is concerned with affairs in the Congo, is reproduced below to help to illumine events of the past and the present. With what Reuters called a potentially "explosive" situation facing the Congo on June 30, 2005, concerned individuals were calling upon the US Congress and the Senate to take this into account and to recommend measures that would help to ensure that it did not become a day of terror. And to some extent they succeeded. President Joseph Kabila continued to maintain a dialogue with the people, assuring them that with the adoption of the draft Constitution the shift toward democracy was unstoppable. Thus, thousands rather than tens of thousands of people turned out for the day of June 30. Viewing the protestors as "insubordinate," the Government reacted with plastic bullets and tear gas. Some were rounded up for imprisonment, but on the whole, the day did not turn out to be as bad as people had feared. Eye witnesses in Kinshasa say that many people had fasted and prayed the whole night before. They wanted peace then and still hope for it now. But the government has, thus far, only announced that the elections will be delayed for one six-month period. Sources at the Canadian organization Peace and Democracy, which works closely with the Kinshasa government, have reported that it was, in fact, already agreed that the elections would not take place until June, 2006. If this is true, then people are still being kept in the dark and it is quite possible that further protests may emerge. The people are war-weary and tired, tired of promises that have not been kept, and their fear is understandable.

APPENDIX I. LETTERS FROM KINSHASA

5 May 2005

Hello Jeanne:

I am a young man of 30 years old. I am graduated from the University of Kinshasa but have not yet found a job. I am not married, nor children. I like music so much. I love American music, series, and movies. I like watching TV, reading.

It is hard living in Kinshasa if you don't have a job, but people are kind here. I struggle for life. I don't have enough for me, so I have to struggle to have something, but there are no jobs here for young graduates. Most of my friends suffer to earn something, but I am still living with my parents.

We are also living in fear of 30 June. People plan to make disorder. Politics are boring. We don't know who is the good leader for us. But I worry about only one thing, find a job that I am still waiting for.

What I want Americans to know about our country is that we are pacific, and we need only one thing, a Good and Conscientious president, someone that people will choose. We seem to be a very wealthy country but people are suffering. We are tired of rebels, dictator, we want to live in peace in our country. If people can be well paid and work, things will be alright.

Life has not changed, but Joseph Kabila has brought peace in our country.

In Kinhasa we have peace but in Ituri people are suffering because of tribal conflicts. Yes, there were riots, but people in Kinshasa avoid such destruction because most of the people have lost jobs because of two big riots that took place in 1991 with Mobutu. Since then we have not yet rebuilt destroyed societies and people are at home. People just went on the road to express their hunger against the government. My life has not been affected by the riots of 2004.

The problem is that due to the lack of a job, that people don't have enough money to take care of children so girls are looking for money in all ways. UN soldiers seem to be best well paid so girls think that it is a way for them by letting themselves be loved by this soldier to earn money. Some soldiers use their influence to get a wife. All this is due to the misery in which we are living; anyone is playing with us.

The UN's presence in Congo is very important. Since they are here we are living in peace. They are doing something even though there are some mistakes.

If American troops come it will be better because people have enough consideration for them. Marines would better secure the country. You know when the French were in Ituri people were happy.

Now in Kivu there are soldiers of FDLR HUTU called RASTA who are killing people; who will stop them?

For details, I am available any time.

Best regards,

A.

5 May 2005

Hello A:

Thank you for answering my letter. I am delighted to have a friend in the Congo.

You mentioned the 30th of June in your letter as being a date that makes you fearful. Is this a date for elections? I had read in the newspapers that the elections had been postponed until the end of the year, but there has been a change? Will this be for the presidential elections? Many people in America had feared that the postponement meant that there would be more stalling and eventually no elections. We want to see democracy come to your country as the means to bring peace and prosperity to you.

If June 30th is a date for elections, why do you think that people will cause destruction? Are they afraid that the elections won't be fair, or are they protesting the state of the country? I am sorry to hear that there is so much hunger in the Congo that the people are marching against it, but it is good that they gather together to protest their state of life. It is the only way to make politicians pay attention. I will pray for you, and continue to write to my Congressmen and Senators to try to get them to help you. That, incidentally, is what my book on the Congo is about. I pray for an American presence that will bring peace to Ituri and the Kivus, and for aid from the United States that would help to fight deprivation.

I know that you find politics boring, but it would be nice to know more about who is running for office against President Kabila. Is there anyone that you feel would be strong and trustworthy in office? Or would you prefer to see President Kabila remain in office? How do you feel about Etienne Tshiskedi? I know that Dr. Tshiskedi suffered much under President Mobut; that he was beaten and placed under house arrest, as were other members of his party.

I had read that the security services were very oppressive; that they imprisoned many people and that these people were also tortured. Have things very much improved under President Kabila?

Is there good security in Kinshasa? You describe your neighbors in Kinshasa as being very kind, and I am happy that they help you.

I thank you for all of the time that you have spent with me, and look forward to hearing from you again.

Sincerely,

Jeanne

6 May 2005

Hello Jeanne Haskin:

I am also delighted to have a friend in the USA. Someone who is interested in my country.

In Sun City during negotiations, politicians signed for a transition period of 2 years, and the main goal of this transition was the organization of the election. People have the impression that the government is doing nothing special to reach this goal, they took all of their time. So people think that on 30th June they will be on the street and do anything possible to get rid of this government. They want to last the longer possible.

The opposition promised to do things that will put an end to this government. The government promises election for next year, and people want it to be this year before 30th June. If they don't organize it there will be riots everywhere in the country. This is the general opinion, not mine. I am a pacific man.

If Americans can do something for us, we would appreciate it.

People, most of them think that Tshisekedi is the most qualified to rule this country. But I have not yet found a good one for me. Tshisekedi has suffered much under Mobutu's reign and also under Kabila the father's reign.

What I don't like in Kabila'a reign is the tribalism that it taking place in the country. Swahili are privileged, all people from East have advantages.

There was security in Kinshasa at the beginning of the transition, but now the situation is not so good. There is no security at this time. People are being killed everywhere and it is not safe to walk at night.

My parents are Christians, I live with them, they are kind too. They are proud of me really, because I speak English and am graduated from the University.

Thank you for being there.

I look forward to hearing from you soon.

A.

9 May 2005

Hello Haskin:

How are you doing?

Here I am again.

Let me tell you once more about my country. Our country DR Congo is a very wealthy one. We have all kinds of minerals.

I am from the region of lower Congo, this region is occupied by people called Kongos, we are from the powerful Kingdom Kongo. Kongos are pacific. The first president was a Kongo, his name was Kasavubu. He was elected and is till now the best president we have ever got in Congo. In '65 Mobutu took the control of the country that he ruled in a dictatorial way. In 1965, Mobutu seized control of the government, suppressed all rival group and opposition, and imposed upon the people a government patterned on his own political ideas. He dominated the country for around 30 years and firmly established it in power. Mobutu carried out a reign of terror and oppression. All a group of people belonging to his party could live easily while the rest of the people lived in poverty.

At the arrival of Kabila the father with the movement AFDL, we thought that the storm was over, but the situation got worse. They have brought to us many years of war and destabilization with about 7,000,000 death.

Mzee Kabila the father was a nationalist, we loved him so much, but he was not appreciated by occidentals (according to general opinion). Occident supported Rwanda and Uganda against us. There is no democracy in Rwanda nor in Uganda, but they are everytime supported by Americans, so called democratic countries. Because of the war caused by Rwanda and Uganda, 7,000,000 Congolese have lost their life. 15 mothers have been buried alive in 1999, villages have been burnt, misery...

We'll never forget what Rwanda and Uganda have done in Congo. It is like a wound in our hearts. The future will tell. Let God forgive them!

Occidentals are doing things that are against justice. They are living in peace in their country but are causing death in Africa. People of America and Europe must know that their leader have blood on their hands, all wars in Africa are supported by occidents.

For the specific case of Congo, they have used Tutsi and Banyamulenge to kill Congolese, so for every Congolese today, a Tutsi is an enemy.

I remember one day we were in church and Ruberwa one of vice president member of RCD came, when he got in people took up shouting against him, saying that he is a murderer. I know that Ruberway is an evangelist but his troops have killed too many people in the east of the Congo.

We have stayed about a month and a half without electricity because of rebels of RCD, they took control of hydroelectric barrier of Inga, many people died in hospital from lack of electricity.

The presidential space is full of murder.

We are pacific, but since AFDL has brought in Congo warriors from the east, Tutsi and Hutu and other nilotic violence, murder has settled in our country.

Today there are many homeless people. We have nothing but God, time will tell!

Our dear Mzee Kabila was killed in his office, we were very sad on that day, there were tears everywhere, we will never forget our President Mzee Kabila. Our hero, he had the courage of saying no to the occident. The problem with Mzee Kabila is that he was not diplomatic. He could say everything that pass by his mind, he is comparable to Lumumba, too much talkative.

Now his son is our president, Joseph Kabila. He is very calm and diplomatic. I personally appreciate him so much. He has brought peace in our country with the support of the international community. But there is some controversy about his past. Too much gossip about his past.

We don't like the system of 1+4, we want one president and someone that will be chosen by people.

There is one negative thing that I don't appreciate in the reign of Kabila, which is tribalism. Swahili are privileged too much. In most office people speak Swahili while we have many ethnic groups and languages in Congo. They must do their best to correct this aspect. If this situation last too long, the country will be divided in many parts.

Yesterday, there was a risk of secession in Katanga again.

I have spent 8 years in the university instead of 5 because of war, rebellion. I know many friends who have lost their life since AFDL is there, they joined the army, they were not well paid, some of them have been killed.

During Mobutu's reign, we suffered too much, there were pillage, rebellion. Imagine that someone working in public function is paid les than $10 a month. Now the situation has not changed at all. People working at OCPT have stayed 52 months without salary.

People are not well paid, how can they live while high ranked politician are living in luxury, they are buying houses everywhere. Member of PPRD the presidential party are living like kings. Many so called advisor to the president are living like kings. This country seems to hold only one political class.

Many internationals NGOs supports the action of this government saying that they have succeeded. I am sorry for that way of seeing things. We are sacrificed people, we do not know what will be our future. Why are they supporting leaders who are subjects of controversy?

I have read part of your book, you're right in most of the things you say inside. I have experienced many things in this country. I have so many things to say that I think it will be better that you ask me many questions and I will be answering you with details.

Thank you for giving us the opportunity of expressing ourselves.

I look forward to hearing from you,

A.

9 May 2005

Hello A:

I thank you for reading my book and explaining more to me about your country.

I have read in many places that when Laurent Kabila was assassinated that people in the Congo who compared him to Patrice Lumumba feared that the Americans or the Belgians were somehow involved in his death. Do you think this yourself?

Although many tears were shed when President Laurent Kabila was killed, he had claimed that the people had to be re-educated before there could be elections. This meant that it would take many years before the country could vote. Did you think that this was wise, and how did you feel about it?

Like President Mobutu, President Laurent Kabila outlawed the oppositional parties. He did not leave them room to speak or to congregate freely. This effectively nullified the Sovereign National Conference and all of the work that it had done to try to set up a transitional government and arrange for new elections. Do you think that President Laurent Kabila did this because he felt that they were a threat during time of war? Was it necessary, in your opinion, for the safety of the country?

You say that the Tutsi are the enemy of the Congolese for having fought on the side of Rwanda and Uganda, but is it not true that President Mobutu oppressed the Banyamulenge and wanted to expel them from the Congo before the fighting began? Since President Mobutu denied them citizenship rights, do you think that they should have just moved to Rwanda or Uganda to avoid being killed by the Hutu genocidaires that Mobutu let into the country instead of fighting to remain? Or do you think that the UN should have moved in quickly to protect the Banyamulenge so that they would have had no cause to fight in the country?

There was originally an offer of American troops to police and return the Hutu genocidaires to Rwanda, but after the RPA and the Banyamulenge broke up the refugee camps, many of the Hutu returned to Rwanda on their own and the American offer was withdrawn. Do you think that American troops should have come anyway to prevent the RPA and the Tutsi from fighting further in the country?

When President Joseph Kabila agreed to pardon the rebel leaders for acts of war so that they could participate in the government (the 1+4 arrangement), his pardon did not extend to crimes against humanity and acts of genocide. If the UN Security Council decides to establish a Congolese war crimes tribunal in order to punish those who are guilty of terrible crimes, do you think that the Congolese people will feel free to cooperate and testify at the tribunal without fear of being killed?

Hoping that you are safe and well,

Jeanne

10 May 2005

Dear Jeanne Haskin:

Yeah, people in Congo think in general that Americans know something on Mzee Kabila's death. People think that Americans and Belgians are involved in that sad event. I remember that day when Mzee Kabila was shot, we didn't know that he died, we expected that it was just a slight wound, but on TV5 (a French channel) Louis Michel was the first to announce Mzee Kabila's death. We found it curious, he seemed to be well informed about that event the same day, while in Congo the news was announced only 2 days after. The condition of Kabila's death is still dark. I know that he was disliked by Americans as he used to say himself. One day I remember that during an interview he said that he had a phone call from Madeleine Albright, and he refused to answer her, he said that he had no lesson to receive from Albright...I can't say that Americans were involved because I have no proofs, but...

When Mzee Kabila said that people had to be re-educated before elections, he was not wrong. Congolese are sometimes strange. A leader can be known as a murderer, stealer, corrupted, but when he give people a T-shirt and $1, people forgive him and forget whatever he's done. We can't vote for a leader just because of a T-shirt and $1. People must really be re-educated but this re-education must be progressive before and after elections. And this re-education must not be a condition before organization of elections.

When Kabila was still a rebel, he told opposition to join him, but we all know that Etienne Tshisekedi is a pacific, he doesn't like the use of military force. As they didn't join him, he qualified them all as Mobutist, that's why when he came he didn't trust in them.

The sovereign national conference was good but Mzee Kabila didn't find his part in that conference. He had Rwanda, Uganda behind him. They spent too much money to get rid of Mobutu, they couldn't let opposition take the control of the country instead do them they had to reorganize the army and the country. The situation of the country changed much. Mobutu was gone, for the safety of the country, Kabila had to organize things first. Mzee Kabila was like our father for Congolese. I think that he really loved the country. He had ruled the country in very difficult condition, he was alone against all, he received no assistance from occident. Mzee was good but we didn't understand him. Ask Congolese they will tell you, politicians opinion is different from that of people.

The former Rwandan president Abyarimana was killed by Tutsi rebel. That's why Hutu considered them as threats and started that sad genocide. Tutsi went in Congo to avoid being killed by Hutu but some days after they (Tutsi) take the control of Rwanda and Hutu run away in Congo. There were then a conflict between these two ethnic groups. As Tutsi took the control of Rwanda, Hutu living in Congo were considered as rebel then the new force in presence in Rwanda wanted to arrest them. That's why they did their best to support Mzee Kabila to get rid of Mobutu because Mobutu was considered as Hutu supporter. This was normal as Abyarimana was Mobutu's friend.

Today Hutu living in Congo are everytime reasons for Kagame to invade our country. The situation in the east is confused, Banyamulenge are Congolese as they say but they seem to be more close to Rwanda than to Congo. When Mbuza Mabe get rid of general Kunda and Mutebusi in the east, Banyamulenge went to Rwanda and Burundi and before going they destroyed shops and put markets in fire. And they wrote in the wall of one shop "in memory of us." Why all this?

I am really sad that in my country people are living with such violence. I think that American troops presence in Congo is required, necessary and helpful for peace in the east and great lake countries.

Congolese can cooperate and testify at any war crime tribunal, provide that their security can be guaranteed. But there will always be act of vengeance.

For June 30th people just want to express themselves. News on some papers and TV tell us about people that have bought some tools that they will use on that day to defend themselves...There are many risk of riots...

Since the creation of the so called department of reconstruction, for this transition, we have not seen something real be done.

Money officially earned, unfortunately built other countries. Congolese live less than South African under apartheid. This is due to the fact that all belong to stranger (occidental and African) who lead everything from far away, they decide everything at our place. Many not Congolese are representing Congo, and taking decision at our place. Predators of Congo don't want to organize election at the deadline in order to finish their building in construction in foreign countries. Sorry for our Congo. Time will tell...

About 9 UN soldiers killed in Ituri, we are very sorry that such a thing has happened. Nevertheless, they are victims of a dark politic of MONUC. This event we think will wake them up.

At many times, the chiefs of war as they are called had many advantages. They were given rooms in luxury hotels in Kinshasa, most of them with those who have sold the country and facilitated the pillage, control of the country by stranger were given many advantages and got army title of general. I hope that their arrestation would promote peace in the region of Ituri and the east of Congo.

There is a force that I respect too much, the patriots MAI MAI. They have struggled to defend the land of the DRC and are still doing it. They have saved the union of the country. In spite of this they are despised, while the killer and murderer of Kasika, Ituri, Makobola live in luxury. Mai Mai deserve to be considered. Because they are real patriots for us...they are defending our country more than anyone else.

Joseph Kabila is a Congolese. Politicians want to discredit him by saying that he is not a Congolese; they are wrong. I think that Joseph Kabila is really a Congolese, he is good and has been able to bring peace back in Congo. He is a good diplomat. But he must pay attention. He is surrounded by too many predators. He must do his best to punish those who use public money for their own needs. He must also do his best to reduce tribalism that is taking place in the country.

One thing that I also regret is the fact that the international community are not condemning the fact that Congolese are being killed in the East because of Tutsi. Tutsi are too much protected and cherished as if they had more rights than Congolese as human being. More than 6,000,000 Congolese have died according to statistic, because of Kagame's multi-invasion of Congo...When Congolese women are buried alive in east of Congo, nobody open his mouth to condemn...There is not justice in this world...

Another dark fact is head of companies, society, enterprise in Congo are stealing money, they are not controlled. The corruption have reached a very high level...If you want to find a job, you must have a parent who's politically high ranked. Today the country belongs to PPRD, MLC, RCD and strangers...If you want to find a job you must belong to one of these groups. Only they are ruling the country, they have money, everything and army...We people of Congo, we have nothing, politicians are getting richer while population are in poverty.

Today there is not security in Kinshasa, we live in scare situation. It is not safe to walk in night. Armed group are causing insecurity at night, if you meet with them they take everything you have...or kill you...

People working are not paid, there is no salary at all. We live here as in a jungle, as if there were not government. Government is there just to earn money for their pockets and ain't doing anything to secure people, to give job to people, to bring country to the development. They have failed. So in Congo we say 1+4=0. Some say 1+4+CIAT=0. We need one president elected no matter if it is Joseph Kabila, Tshisekedi, Ruberwa or anyone else

Why nothing is done to punish Kagame? He is the cause of death, war, pillage in the DRC. He pretend to look for Interahamwe, he is killing Congolese. The Interahamwe that Kagame is looking for in the east of Congo is COLTAN, Golden, copper... brief minerals. Rwandan troops have occupied the east of Congo for 5 years and have never got rid of Interahamwe. All Hutu living in Congo is not genocidaire. International community must control Kagame's act, if not there will be a risk of a war and genocide again in the Great Lake region.

I want to add this: Congolese will never vote for those who have killed Congolese in Kasika, Makobola, Kabinda....Congolese will never vote for those who have put the country in darkness by taking the control of a civil objective that is the hydroelectric barrier of Inga, we have stayed more than a month without electricity and many days without water. And some of them are today in government. International community is strange, you place our murderer and killer in sin city to rule us again... Congolese will never vote for those known as defending Rwandan interest in Congo instead of Congolese one. There are many forces in presence in Congo that must be considered. In lower Congo, land of Nekongo, there is a religious and politic movement called Bundu dia Kongo with their leader Ne Muana Nsemi... Most famous leaders are Joseph Kabila, Etienne Tshisekedi, Diomi Ndongala, Ruberwa, Ne Muanda Nsemi, Antoine Gizenga, Jean Pierre Bemba...

What is the nature of this life of ours? Let's face it: our lives are miserable, we're jobless, we lack even the minimum that every human being should have. We don't know the meaning of happiness or leisure. The life of a Congolese is misery; that's the plain truth. But is this simply part of the order of nature? Is it because this land of ours is poor that it cannot afford a decent life to those who dwell upon it. No, a thousand of times no! The soil of Congo is rich and fertile, its climate is good. Why then do we continue in this miserable condition? Because nearly the whole of the wealth, produce of our soil, money, mineral are stolen from us by stranger and a group of politician and murderer...There is the answer to all our problems, it is summed up in a word: bad government! Bad, corrupted politicians are real enemies that we have. We, people of Congo, need good leader, we want to vote. We need someone we will choose, no more rebellion, no more military chiefs.

Our resolutions will never falter, no argument can lead us to astray. We will not listen what politician will tell us, they are liars. They serve the interest of Rwanda, South Africa and occidental despising Congolese.

Americans, French and other foreign countries by supporting the war and rebellion and dictator in Africa they are indirectly causing death in Africa.

African doesn't have the right to live in freedom? We are not human being? Who will stop this? We are Christian, in my country we go to church very often and our hope is in God. We have nothing but God...One day, time will tell, let's wait and see. I thank nevertheless Joseph Kabila once more for his effort to bring peace in Congo. I also have much esteem for Etienne Tshisekedi, for Ruberwa...

I want to add this: Tutsi are not my enemies. I have many friends among them. They are so much supported, protected and cherished by international community that some of them think that they are almighty. They have caused too many death in Congo. What I expect today is peace. I hope that Americans will help to settle peace in Congo. Congolese, Rwandan, Uganda, we are brothers, sons of Africa, why are we killing each other? No matter the situation we're living in today, I hope that one day we will forget all these death and pillage and forgive each other. I hope that one day Congolese, Tutsi and Hutu will be friends again, this is possible. French and Germans are friends today in spite of what happened during the Second World War.

Peace and love!

Your friend,

A.

12 May 2005

Hello Jeanne:

Very happy to have read you again.

It is told that people are buying machetes; as I told you there is risk of bloody riots on 30th June; if people are buying machetes as it is told on newspapers, we cannot expect a peaceful 30th June.

I wish you all the best things.

As I also told you, I most worry for my job, it is so hard living in such a situation. I do not know where would come the solution. God knows...

Best regards.

Thank you for what you are doing for my country.

You know most people are afraid to talk about the country as I am doing now with you. They are afraid.

See you next,

A.

13 May 2005

Dear A:

You mentioned in one of your earlier emails that there was recently a threat of secession in Katanga. I am reading now that there appears to be a threat of secession in Katanga, Kasai, and the Kivus. Someone wrote that arms are being supplied to the regions and that they are preparing themselves to fight. Is this true, to your knowledge?

I am also in the process of translating a statement prepared by a group of Congolese professors who are calling for a non-unitary sate based on several grounds. They claim that the Congolese state should be decentralized because it oppresses different cultures and stifles economic growth in its present centralized form. They also say that it contributes to conditions of dictatorship if the provinces cannot rule themselves. They say that Yugoslavia, the former USSR, Liberia, and the Ivory Coast are all examples of how states fall apart and cannot be maintained artificially where there is no social cohesion without a dictatorship. So, with the shift toward democracy, they are arguing for a federal arrangement rather than a unitary state. This was much what your first and only elected president Joseph Kasavubu had originally had in mind. He wanted a more decentralized government and this had placed him at odds with Prime Minister Lumumba.

Do you think that they will revise your constitution and that it will be a federal government? Or do you think that the transitional government will resist this, as it would mean a loss of power? Do you think that the provinces will go to war if they can not have autonomy?

What is the general feeling of the people regarding the threats of secession?

I thank you for your time, and, as always, I hope you are well.

Sincerely,

Jeanne

13 May 2005

Hello Jeanne:

How are you doing?

Secession is not good for Congo, we are all hearing these news from TV and papers. There is a risk of dislocation of our country, because people do not trust in this government. I have also received this report of professors about federalism, people want federalism, it is for us the best system that we expect. We want autonomy of regions.

We do not have a constitution in Congo. We people of Congo have never voted for a constitution neither for anyone. We want federalism. Regarding these wave of secession, people are not astonished, it is normal. Many person from Bas Congo have enough of the way leaders from the east are ruling the country.

The system 1+4+CIAT has failed and = 0.

Thank you for whatever you are doing for me and for my country.

Thank you for your comment about my picture, it made me laugh, ah ah ah.

I have only one girlfriend and I love her so much.

Best regards,

A.

APPENDIX II. MEMBERS OF THE US SENATE FOREIGN RELATIONS COMMITTEE

Senator Joseph R. Biden, Jr.
Senate Foreign Relations Committee
201 Russell Senate Office Building
Washington, DC 20510
(202) 224-5042 Phone
(202) 224-0139 Fax

Senator George Allen
Senate Foreign Relations Committee
Russell Senate Office Building, Rm 204
Washington, DC 20510
(202) 224-4024 Phone
(202) 224-5432 Fax

Senator Chuck Hagel
Senate Foreign Relations Committee
248 Russell Senate Office Building
Washington, DC 20510
(202) 224-4224 Phone
(202) 224-5213 Fax

Senator Norm Coleman
Senate Foreign Relations Committee
320 Hart Senate Office Building
Washington, DC 20510
(202) 224-5641 Phone
(202) 224-1152 Fax

Senator Lincoln Chafee
Senate Foreign Relations Committee
141A Russell Senate Office Building
(202) 224-2921 Phone
(202) 228-2853 Fax

Senator George V. Voinovich
Senate Foreign Relations Committee
524 Hart Senate Office Building
(202) 224-3353 Phone
(202) 228-1382 Fax

Senator Lamar Alexander
Senate Foreign Relations Committee
302 Hart Senate Office Building
(202) 224-4944 Phone
(202) 228-3398 Fax

Senator John E. Sununu
Senate Foreign Relations Committee
111 Russell Senate Office Building
(202) 224-2841 Phone
(202) 228-4131 Fax

Senator Lisa Murkowski
Senate Foreign Relations Committee
709 Hart Senate Office Building
Washington, DC 20510
(202) 224-6665 Phone
(202) 224-5301 Fax

Senator Mel Martinez
Senate Foreign Relations Committee
317 Hart Senate Office Building
Washington, DC 20510
(202) 224-3041 Phone
(202) 228-5171 Fax

Senator Paul S. Sarbanes
Senate Foreign Relations Committee
309 Hart Senate Office Building
Washington, DC 20510
(202) 224-4524 Phone
(202) 224-1651 Fax

Senator John F. Kerry
Senate Foreign Relations Committee
304 Russell Senate Office Bldg., 3rd Fl.
Washington, DC 20510
(202) 224-2742 Phone
(202) 224-8525 Fax

Senator Barbara Boxer
Senate Foreign Relations Committee
112 Hart Senate Office Building
Washington, DC 20510
(202) 224-3553 Phone
(415) 956-6701 Fax

Senator Barack Obama
Senate Foreign Relations Committee
713 Hart Senate Office Building
Washington, DC 20510
(202) 224-2854 Phone
(202) 228-4260 Fax

Senator Chris Dodd
Senate Foreign Relations Committee
SR-448 Russell Senate Office Building
Washington, DC 20510
(202) 224-2823 Phone
(202) 228-1683 Fax

Senator Russell D. Feingold
Senate Foreign Relations Committee
506 Hart Senate Office Building
Washington, DC 20510
(202) 224-5323 Phone
(202) 224-2725 Fax

Senator Bill Nelson
Senate Foreign Relations Committee
Hart Senate Office Building, Rm 716
Washington, DC 20510
(202) 224-5274 Phone
(202) 228-2183 Fax

APPENDIX III. MEMBERS OF THE CONGRESSIONAL SUBCOMMITTEE FOR AFRICA, GLOBAL HUMAN RIGHTS AND INTERNATIONAL OPERATIONS

Congressman John Boozeman
1519 Longworth HOB
Washington, DC 20515
(202) 225-4301 Phone
(202) 225-5713 Fax

Congressman Christopher H. Smith, Chair
2373 Rayburn HOB
Washington, DC 20515-3004
(202) 225-3765 Phone
(202) 225-7768 Fax

Congressman Thomas G. Tancredo
1130 Longworth HOB
Washington, DC 20515-0606
(202) 225-7882 Phone
(202) 226-4623 Fax

Congressman Jeff Fortenberry
1517 Longworth HOB
Washington, DC 20515
(202) 225-4806 Phone
(202) 225-5686 Fax

Congressman Donald M. Payne
2209 Rayburn HOB
Washington, DC 20515
(202) 225-3436 Phone
(202) 225-4160 Fax

Congresswoman Betty McCollum
1029 Longworth HOB
Washington, DC 20515
(202) 225-6631 Phone
(202) 225-1968 Fax

Congressman Brad Sherman
1030 Longworth HOB
Washington, DC 20515-0524
(202) 225-5911 Phone
(202) 225-5879 Fax

Congressman Gregory W. Meeks
1710 Longworth HOB
Washington, DC 20515
(202) 225-3461 Phone
(202) 226-4169 Fax

Congressman Jeff Flake
424 Cannon HOB
Washington, DC 20515-0301
(202) 225-2635 Phone
(202) 226-4386 Fax

Congresswoman Diane E. Watson
125 Cannon HOB
Washington, DC 20515-0533
(202) 225-7084 Phone
(202) 225-2422 Fax

Congressman Mark Green
1314 Longworth HOB
Washington, DC 20515

Congresswoman Barbara Lee
1724 Longworth HOB
Washington, DC 20515

(202) 225-5665 Phone   (202) 225-2661 Phone
(202) 225-5729 Fax   (202) 225-9817 Fax

Congressman Edward R. Royce, Vice Chairman
2202 Rayburn HOB
Washington, DC 20515
(202) 225-4111 Phone
(202) 226-0335 Fax

APPENDIX IV. CURRENT VOTING MEMBERS OF THE UNITED NATIONS SECURITY COUNCIL

Permanent Mission of Argentina
to the United Nations
One United Nations Plaza, 25th Fl.
New York, NY 10017
(212) 688-6300 Phone
(212) 980-8395 Fax

Permanent Mission of Benin
to the United Nations
125 East 38th Street
New York, NY 10016
(212) 684-1339 Phone
(212) 684-2058 Fax

Permanent Mission of Brazil
to the United Nations
747 Third Ave., 9th Fl.
New York, NY 10017-2803
(212) 372-2600 Phone
(212) 371-5716 Fax
(212) 308-3384 Fax

Permanent Mission of Denmark
to the United Nations
One Dag Hammarskjöld Plaza
885 Second Ave.
New York, NY 10017-2201
(212) 308-7009 Phone

Permanent Mission of France
to the United Nations
245 East 47th St.
New York, NY 10017
(212) 308-5700 Phone
(212) 355-2763 Fax

Permanent Mission of Greece
to the United Nations
866 Second Ave., 13th Fl.
New York, NY 10017
(212) 888-6900 Phone
(212) 888-4440 Fax

Permanent Mission of the Republic
of the Philippines to the UN
556 5th Ave.
New York, NY 10036
(212) 764-1300 Phone
(212) 840-8602 Fax

Permanent Mission of Romania
to the United Nations
573-577 3rd Ave.
New York, NY 10016
(212) 682-3273 Phone
(212) 682-9746 Fax

Permanent Mission of the UK
One Dag Hammarskjöld Plaza
885 Second Ave.
New York, NY 10017
(212) 745-9200 Phone

Permanent Mission of the US
140 East 45th St.
New York, NY 10017
(212) 415-4050 Phone
(212) 415-4053 Fax

Permanent Mission of Algeria
 to the United Nations
326 E. 48th St.
New York, NY 10017-1747
(212) 750-1960 Phone
(212) 759-5274 Fax

Permanent Mission of China
to the United Nations

Permanent Mission of the Russian
Federation to the United Nations

BIBLIOGRAPHY

Abubakar, A., *Africa and the Challenge of Development: Acquiescence and Dependency Versus Freedom and Development*, Westport, CT: Praeger, 1989.

Africa News Service, "In Kabila's Congo, the Press is Under Siege," *Africa News Service*, January 10, 2000.

———. "Congo Rebels Agree to Merge," *Africa News Service*, January 16, 2001.

———. "Congo Conducting Mass Executions," *Africa News Service*, February 10, 2000.

———. "7,000 Massacred in UPDF-Held DR Congo," *Africa News Service*, February 3, 2000.

———. "Why Congo Dropped ICJ Case Against Rwanda," *Africa News Service*, February 8, 2001.

———. "The Systematic Looting of Congo," *Africa News Service*, April 19, 2001.

———. "France, Libya 'Backing' Kabila," *Africa News Service*, January 9, 1999.

Agence France Presse English, "DR Congo war crimes hearing starts at world criminal court," *Agence France Presse English*, March 15, 2005.

———. "Over 100 killed, 200 women raped in east DR Congo province: UN," *Agence France Presse English*, February 23, 2005.

All Things Considered, "Three Million Could Starve in Zaire," *All Things Considered (NPR)*, December 20, 1993.

———. "Riots and Death in Zaire Over Worthless Currency," *All Things Considered (NPR)*, February 2, 1993.

———. "Zaire's President Pressured by West to Step Down," *All Things Considered (NPR)*, February 4, 1993.

———. "Mobutu's Rise to Power Examined," *All Things Considered (NPR)*, March 12, 1993.

———. "More Rwandans Flee Into Zaire," *All Things Considered (NPR)*, August 21, 1994.

Amnesty International, "Democratic Republic of the Congo: Our Brothers Who Help Kill Us – Economic Exploitation and Human Rights Abuses in the East," New York: Amnesty International, April 2003.

Annan, K., "Report of the Secretary-General on the United Nations Preliminary Deployment in the Democratic Republic of the Congo," New York: UN Documents, July 15, 1999.

———. "Second Report of the Secretary-General on the United Nations Organization Mission in the Democratic Republic of the Congo," New York: UN Documents, April 18, 2000.

———. "Third Report of the Secretary-General on the United Nations Organization

211

Mission in the Democratic Republic of the Congo," New York: UN Documents, June, 12, 2000.

———. "Fourth Report of the Secretary-General on the United Nations Organization Mission in the Democratic Republic of the Congo," New York: UN Documents, September 21, 2000.

———. "Fifth Report of the Secretary-General on the United Nations Organization Mission in the Democratic Republic of the Congo," New York: UN Documents, December 6, 2000.

———. "Ninth Report of the Secretary-General on the United Nations Organization Mission in the Democratic Republic of the Congo," New York: UN Documents, October 16, 2001.

———. "Tenth Report of the Secretary-General on the United Nations Organization Mission in the Democratic Republic of the Congo," New York: UN Documents, February 15, 2002.

———. "Twelfth Report of the Secretary-General on the United Nations Organization Mission in the Democratic Republic of the Congo," New York: UN Documents, October 18, 2002.

———. "Thirteenth Report of the Secretary-General on the United Nations Organization Mission in the Democratic Republic of the Congo," New York: UN Documents, February 21, 2003.

———. "Second Special Report of the Secretary-General on the United Nations Organization Mission in the Democratic Republic of the Congo," New York: UN Documents, May 27, 2003.

———. "Fourteenth Report of the Secretary-General on the United Nations Organization Mission in the Democratic Republic of the Congo," New York: UN Documents, November 17, 2003.

———. "Third Special Report of the Secretary-General on the United Nations Organization Mission in the Democratic Republic of the Congo," New York: UN Documents, August 16, 2004.

———. "Sixteenth Report of the Secretary-General on the United Nations Organization Mission in the Democratic Republic of the Congo," New York: UN Documents, December 31, 2004.

AP Online, "Congo Accused of Executing Soldiers," *AP Online*, February 15, 2000.

AP Worldstream, "Congo Security Forces Deploy in Capital to Quell Protestors Angry Over Election Delay," *AP Worldstream*, January 11, 2005.

Aronson, D., "America's myopic Africa policy: CONGO GAMES," *The New Republic*, January 5, 1998.

Ascherson, N., *The King Incorporated: Leopold II in the Age of Trusts*, London: Allen & Unwin Ltd, 1963.

Askin, S., "Economic Strain Could Help Topple Mobutu: World Diplomats Plot to Oust Zaire Dictator," *National Catholic Reporter*, March 19, 1993.

Balint-Kurti, D., "UN: Some 100,000 have fled a week of fighting in eastern Congo," *AP Worldstream*, December 19, 2004.

——. "Gunfire as Congo's government puts down coup attempt in capital," *AP Worldstream*, June 12, 2004.

——. "UN: Peacekeepers creating buffer zone between warring army factions in east Congo," *AP Worldstream*, December 21, 2004.

Bartlett, V., *Struggle for Africa*, New York: Frederick A. Praeger, 1953.

Berkley, B., *The Graves are Not Yet Full: Race, Tribe, and Power in the Heart of Africa*, New York: Perseus Books, 2001.

Bienen, H., *Armies and Parties in Africa*, New York: Africana Publishing Co., 1978.

Blackman, K., "Zaire-Politics: Kabila Takes Power as Kinshasa Falls Quietly," *Inter Press Service English News Wire*, May 17, 1997.

Blomfield, A., "Tribal slave raids bring new wave of terror to Congo," *Daily Telegraph*, March 9, 2005.

Bloomfield, L., Bowman, E., Morgenthau, H., Dicks, H., Nicholas, H., Fanning, J.,

Schelling, T., Hoffman, S., Urquhart, B., *International Military Forces: The Question of Peacekeeping in an Armed and Disarming World*, Boston: Little, Brown, 1964.

Bolton, J., "United States Policy on United Nations Peacekeeping," *World Affairs*, January 1, 2001.

Braeckman, C., "The looting of the Congo: The Democratic Republic of Congo has

perhaps the richest concentration of precious metals and minerals on earth. Colette Braeckman describes how their exploitation by warring factions has fueled the worst conflict anywhere since the Second World War," *New Internationalist*, May 1, 2004.

Bruasch, G. *Belgian Administration in the Congo*, London: Oxford University Press, 1961.

Burns, A. and Heathcote, N., *Peace-Keeping by UN Forces, From Suez to the Congo*, New York: Praeger, 1963.

Capdevila, G., "Zaire: UN Agencies Hit Kabila's Rebels on Rights Violations," *Inter Press Service English News Wire*, May 7, 1997.

Callaghy, T., *The State-Society Struggle: Zaire in Comparative Perspective*, New York: Columbia University Press, 1984.

Carayannis, T., "Reconstructing the Congo," *Journal of International Affairs*, September 22, 2004.

——. "The complex wars of the Congo: towards a new analytical approach," *Journal of Asian and African Studies*, August 1, 2003.

Christian Science Monitor, "As Congo Collapses, France steps in," *Christian Science Monitor*, June 9, 2003.

Cincinnati Post, "U.S. Troops Head for a Shaky Zaire," *The Cincinnati Post*, March 22, 1997.

——. "Zaire Ponders U.S. Aid Peacekeeper Force Disputed," *The Cincinnati Post*, November 7, 1996.

Collins, C., "Zaire's Democracy Struggle Tests Church, Clinton," *National Catholic Reporter*, February 12, 1993.

——. "The Cold War Comes to Africa: Cordier and the 1960 Congo Crisis," *Journal of International Affairs*, 47.1, 1993.

Conrad, J., *Heart of Darkness*, New York: Dover Publications, Inc., 1990.

Current Events, "Tragedy in Africa (a massive exodus of Rwandan Hutu refugees into eastern Zaire could lead to death by starvation, violence, and disease for up to one million)" *Current Events*, November 18, 1996.

Daily News, "U.S. Supports Canadian Proposal for Zaire Airdrop," *Daily News*, November 28, 1996.

——. "Rwanda-Zaire Refugees Pay High Price," *Daily News*, October 31, 1996.

——. "U.S. Near to Role in Zaire: Clinton Tentatively Commits to Aid Effort," *Daily News*, November 14, 1996.

Dearaujo, E., "Chaotic Congo," *Harvard International Review*, 23.3, 2001.

Deen, T., "UN: Annan Says "Name and Shame" Violators of Arms Embargoes," *Inter Press Service English News Wire*, February 18, 2005.

Dees, L., "Committee on International Relations, Subcommittee on Africa: The Democratic Republic of Congo Peace Accords: One Year Later, Learned Dees, Senior Program Officer for Africa, National Endowment for Democracy," Washington, DC: Committee on International Relations, July 22, 2004.

Diamond Intelligence Briefs, "DRC inquiry does not support UN findings," *Diamond Intelligence Briefs*, March 28, 2003.

——. "Probe launched into sexual abuse allegations against UN Mission staff in DRC," *Diamond Intelligence Briefs*, May 20, 2004.

——. "UN officials warn of impending crisis in DRC," *Diamond Intelligence Briefs*, April 25, 2004.

——. "DRC granted US$10 billion in debt relief," *Diamond Intelligence Briefs*, August 17, 2003.

——. "65 bodies discovered in DRC's Ituri region," *Diamond Intelligence Briefs*, October 13, 2003.

——. "International Criminal Court pays first official visit to the Democratic Republic of the Congo," *Diamond Intelligence Briefs*, August 12, 2004.

Dobert, M., "Zaire: Chapter 2B. Political Participation and National Priorities," In *Countries of the World*, January 1, 1991.

———. "Zaire: Chapter 2A. Government and Politics," In *Countries of the World*, January 1, 1991.

Donovan, G., "Cannibalism shows depths of war's evil, bishop says," *National Catholic Reporter*, February 14, 2003.

Duffy, J. and Manners, R., *Africa Speaks*, Princeton, NJ: D. Van Nostrand Company, 1961.

Edgerton, R., *The Troubled Heart of Africa: A History of the Congo*, New York: St. Martin's Press, 2002.

Ferreira, A., "Mobutu Asks West to 'forget past'," *Weekly Journal*, October 14, 1993.

Fishel, J., *The Savage Wars of Peace: Toward a New Paradigm of Peace Operations*, Boulder, CO: Westview Press, 1998.

Fleitz Jr., F., *Peacekeeping Fiascoes of the 1960s: Causes, Solutions, and U.S. Interests*, Westport, CT: Praeger, 2002.

Gould, P., *Africa, Continent of Change*, Belmont, CA: Wadsworth Publishing Company, 1961.

Gran, P., *Beyond Eurocentrism: A New View of Modern World History*, Syracuse, NY: Syracuse University Press, 1996.

Grignon, F., "Testimony of Dr. Francois Grignon, Central Africa Project Director, International Crisis Group, Before a Hearing of the House of Representatives Committee on Foreign Relations – Africa Subcommittee," Washington, DC: Committee on International Relations, April 3, 2002.

Hamada, T., "African Nations Request Security Council Seat," *Arab American News*, July 2, 1993.

Haq, F., "Zaire: UN Warns Kivu Crisis is Spinning Out of Control," *Inter Press Service English News Wire*, October 29, 1996.

———. "Zaire-UN: Suspicion of France Marks Security Council Debate," *Inter Press Service English News Wire*, November 11, 1996.

———. "Zaire-Arms: Profit Motive Brings Outside Weapons to Conflict," *Inter Press Service English News Wire*, April 30, 1997.

Harbeson, J. and Rothchild, D., *Africa in World Politics: Post-Cold War Challenges*, Boulder, CO: Westview Press, 1995.

Hargreaves, J., *Decolonization in Africa*, New York: Houghton Mifflin Company, 1914.

Hartung, W. and Moix, B., "Deadly Legacy: U.S. Arms to Africa and the Congo War," New York: Arms Trade Resource Center, January 2000.

Hatch, J., *Africa Today—And Tomorrow: An Outline of Basic Facts and Major Problems*, Westport, CT: Praeger, 1960.

Heller, H. "Out of the Heart of Darkness: Rebellion in Zaire," *Canadian Dimension*, May 1, 1997.

Hempstone, S., *Africa, Angry Young Giant*, Westport, CT: Praeger, 1961.

Hennessey, M., *Congo: A Brief History and Appraisal*, London: Pall Mall Press, 1961.

Hochschild, A., *King Leopold's Ghost*, New York: Houghton Mifflin Company, 1998.

Hodgkin, T., *Nationalism in Colonial Africa*, London: Frederick Muller Ltd, 1956.

Hovet, T., *Africa in the United Nations*, Evanston, IL: Northwestern University Press, 1963.

Howlett, D., "Report: Rebels Seize Key Zaire City," *USA Today*, November 5, 1996.

Hranjski, H., "Congo Rebels Claim Fresh Gains," *AP Online*, January 6, 2000.

——. "Congo War Continues Despite Deal," *AP Online*, June 9, 2000.

Huband, M. *The Skull Beneath the Skin: Africa After the Cold War*, Boulder, CO: Westview Press, 2001.

Human Rights Watch, "Democratic Republic of Congo: Eastern Congo Ravaged Killing Civilians and Silencing Protest," Human Rights Watch, Vol. 12, No. 3(A), May 2000.

Ingham, K. "Year in Review 2000: world-affairs Congo, Democratic Republic of the (the former Zaire)," Encyclopaedia Britannica, www.britannica.com.

——. "Year in Review 2003: world-affairs Congo, Democratic Republic of the," Encyclopaedia Britannica, www.britannica.com.

——. "Year in Review 2002: world-affairs Congo, Democratic Republic of the," Encyclopaedia Britannica, www.britannica.com.

——. "Year in Review 2001: world-affairs Congo, Democratic Republic of the," Encyclopaedia Britannica, www.britannica.com.

Inter Press Service English News Wire, "Zaire-Rwanda: United Nations Warns Against Expulsions," *Inter Press Service English News Wire*, August 23, 1995.

——. "Zaire: UN Seeks Cease-Fire as Forces Battle in Goma," *Inter Press Service English News Wire*, November 2, 1996.

——. "Zaire: Still Outside World Bank Books," *Inter Press Service English News Wire*, February 27, 1996.

——. "DR Congo: Kabila's Decision to Ban Existing Parties Criticized," *Inter Press Service English News Wire*, February 5, 1999.

——. "Zaire-UN: Boutros-Ghali Seeks Conference as Tutsis Seize Uvira," *Inter Press Service English News Wire*, October 24, 1996.

International Crisis Group, "Congo at War: A Briefing on the Internal and External Players in the Central African Conflict," International Crisis Group, November 17, 1998.

Isango, E., "10,000 Said Driven From Congo Diamond Zone," *AP Online*, January 30, 2004.

——. "Congo and UN Troops deploy in East," *AP Online*, November 11, 2004.

——. "Congo government forces quash apparent coup attempt," *AP Worldstream*, March 28, 2004.

ITAR-TASS, "Rwanda to Block Passage of International Peacekeepers to Zaire," *ITAR-TASS*, November 26, 1996.

Kayigamba, J., "Rwanda/Zaire-Politics: Daggers Drawn, Refugees the Victims," *Inter Press Service English News Wire*, November 18, 1995.

Keefe, E., "Zaire: Chapter 5C. The Police System," In *Countries of the World*, January 1, 1991.

Knight Ridder/Tribune News Service, "U.S. Must Support Zaire's Fight for Press Freedom and Other Civil Liberties," *Knight Ridder/Tribune News Service*, April 8, 1994.

Lash, J. *Dag Hammarskjold, Custodian of the Brushfire Peace*, 1st ed., Garden City, NY: Doubleday, 1961.

Lawyers Committee for Human Rights, *Zaire: Repression as Policy: A Human Rights Report*, New York: Lawyers Committee for Human Rights, 1990.

Lea, D., *A Political Chronology of Africa*, London: Europa Publications, 2001.

Lefever, E., *Crisis in the Congo: A United Nations Force in Action*, Washington, DC: Brookings Institution, 1965.

——. *Army, Police, and Politics in Tropical Africa*, Washington, DC: Brookings Institution, 1970.

Legum, C., *Congo Disaster*, Harmondsworth, England: Penguin Books, 1961.

Leslie, W., *Zaire: Continuity and Political Change in an Oppressive State*, Boulder, CO: Westview Press, 1993.

Lief, L. and Pasternak, D., "Payback Time: Our Man in Kinshasa," *U.S. News and World Report*, August 2, 1993.

Lippman, T., *Madeleine Albright and the New American Diplomacy*, Boulder, CO: Westview Press, 2000.

Lovgren, S. and Whitelaw, K. "Mobutuism without Mobutu," *U.S. News and World Report*, November 24, 1997>

Lumumba, P., *Congo, My Country*, London: Pall Mall Press, 1962.

Lumumba-Kasongo, T., *The Dynamics of Economic and Political Relations Between Africa and Foreign Powers: A Study in International Relations*, Westport, CT: Praeger, 1999.

M2 Presswire, "Aid activities resume as an uneasy calm returns to Ituri, Democratic Republic of Congo," *M2 Presswire*, March 10, 2005.

——. "Security Council condemns murder of nine UN peacekeepers in Democratic Republic of Congo; In presidential statement, Council calls on Government to bring attackers to justice; welcomes UN Mission's 'continued robust action' in pursuit of its mandate," *M2 Presswire*, March 4, 2005.

——. "Tripartite peace talks on the African Great Lakes," *M2 Presswire*, February 3, 2005.

——. "Security Council expands mission in Democratic Republic of Congo, unanimously adopting resolution 1291 (2000); Extends mandate until 31 August, authorizes 5,537 troops to help implement Lusaka ceasefire agreement," *M2 Presswire*, February 25, 2000.

——. "Democratic Republic of Congo requests World Court to indicate urgent provisional measures in case concerning Uganda," *M2 Presswire*, June 21, 2000.

——. "Security Council extends Democratic Republic of Congo mission until 30 July 2004, raises troop level to 10,800; Unanimously adopts Resolution 1493 (2003); Institutes 12-month arms embargo on North and South Kivu, Ituri," *M2 Presswire*, July 29, 2003.

——. "Security Council extends Democratic Republic of Congo Mission until 31 March 2005; Authorizes additional 5,900 troops, police; Unanimously adopts resolution 1565 (2004).

——. "Security Council expands authorized troop level in democratic republic of Congo to 8,700 noting 'encouraging developments' on ground; Resolution 1445 (2002) adopted unanimously; Welcomes troop withdrawals by Rwanda, Uganda, Zimbabwe, Angola," *M2 Presswire*, December 5, 2002.

——. "Women's anti-Discrimination Committee urges Congo to eliminate traditional practices, customary laws unfair to women," *M2 Presswire*, January 28, 2003.

——. "Troops withdrawals and impending dialogue mean improvements in Democratic Republic of Congo, Security Council told; But concerns remain over fighting in east and human rights violations," *M2 Presswire*, August 31, 2001.

Makhulu, W., "Hoping Against Hope?" *The Ecumenical Review*, 49.4, 1997.

Matthee, H., "State Collapse or New Politics? The Conflict in Zaire 1996-1997 (Statistical Data Included), *Strategic Review for Southern Africa*, June 1, 1999.

Mealer, B., "UN Peacekeepers Kill 60 Militia in Congo," *AP Online*, March 3, 2005.

——. "Tens of Thousands Said Raped in East Congo," *AP Online*, March 7, 2005.

——. "UN: Thousands flee homes after weeks of attacks in eastern Congo," *AP Worldstream*, January 31, 2005.

——. "Congo Security Forces Deploy in Capital," *AP Online*, January 10, 2005.

Meditz, S. and Merrill, T., *Zaire: a Country Study*, Washington, DC: Federal Research Division, 1994.

Melvern, L., *Conspiracy to Murder: The Rwandan Genocide*, New York: Verso, 2004.

Menaker, D., "Amid the haunted history of Congo, a dozen forces compete," *Knight Ridder/ Tribune News Service*, October 11, 2000.

Mengisteab, K. and Daddieh, C., *State Building and Democratization in Africa: Faith, Hope and Realities*, Westport, CT: Praeger, 1999.

Merriam, A., *Congo: Background of a Conflict*, USA: Northwestern University Press, 1961.

Misser, F., "Zaire: The Currency is New, But the Habits Are Old," *African Business*, January 1, 1994.

Mockaitis, T. *Peace Operations and Intrastate Conflict: The Sword or the Olive Branch?* Westport, CT: Praeger, 1999.

Mokoli, M., *State Against Development: The Experience of Post-1965 Zaire*, Westport, CT: Greenwood Press, 1992.

Morning Edition, "Zaire Pressures Rwandan Refugees to Return to Rwanda," *Morning Edition (NPR)*, February 14, 1996.

———. "Human Rights Group Releases Annual Report," *Morning Edition (NPR)*, December 10, 1993.

———. "One Million Rwandan Refugees to Reach Zaire by Weekend," *Morning Edition (NPR)*, July 15, 1994.

Morrison, D., Mitchell, R., Paden, J., *Understanding Black Africa: Data and Analysis of Social Change and Nation Building*, New York: Paragon House, 1989.

Morrison, J., "Zaire Mines on Verge of Collapse," *Weekly Journal*, February 25, 1993.

Mutume, G. and Jayasekera, A., "Zaire: Pragmatic Multinationals Weigh Negotiations With Rebels," *Inter Press Service English News Wire*, April 15, 1997.

———. "Zaire-Politics: Governments Rule Out Military Intervention," *Inter Press Service English News Wire*, January 29, 1997.

Mwanasali, M., "5 Civil Conflicts and Conflict Management in the Great Lakes Region of Africa," In *Zones of Conflict in Africa: Theories and Cases*, eds. Kieh and Mukenge, Westport, CT: Praeger, 2002.

The Nation, "Where Mobutu's Millions Go," *The Nation*, May 19, 1984.

Nduru, M., "Rights: Uganda and Congo in Sights of Global Criminal Court," *Inter Press Service English News Wire*, January 31, 2005.

———. "Politics-Congo: The Challenge of Putting Together a "Failed State,"" *Inter Press Service English News Wire*, March 14, 2005.

———. "Uganda-Zaire: New Border Conflict Flares Up," *Inter Press Service English News Wire*, November 19, 1996.

Neuffer, E., *The Key to My Neighbor's House: Seeking Justice in Bosnia and Rwanda*, New York: Picador, 2002.

News & Record, "Mobutu's Return Won't Fix Zaire; The Country Has Had One of the Worst Human-Rights Records Anywhere," *The News & Record*, December 28, 1996.

News and World Report, "In Zaire, a Big Man Still Rules the Roost," *U.S. News and World Report*, August 10, 1992.

Ngangoue, N., "Zaire-Politics: Between the Devil and Mobutu," *Inter Press Service English News Wire*, December 19, 1996.

Ngemi, Y., *Genocide in the Congo (Zaire): In the Name of Bill Clinton, and of the Paris Club, and of the Mining Conglomerates, So It Is!* New York: Writers Club Press, 2000.

Ngongo, A. "Zaire-Politics: Clutching at an Electoral Straw," *Inter Press Service English News Wire*, October 20, 1995.

Ngowi, R., "Last rebel holdouts in eastern Congo agree to join transitional government," *AP Worldstream*, November 4, 2003.

———. "Renegades battle government forces in eastern Condo, UN evacuates some staff," *AP Worldstream*, June 7, 2004.

———. "Congo Renegade Troops Battle Government," *AP Online*, June 7, 2004.

Niyoyita, A., "Child soldiers: 40 percent of Congo's troops are boys, private groups say," *AP Worldstream*, November 17, 2004.

Nzongola-Ntalaja, G. *From Zaire to the Democratic Republic of the Congo*, Nordiska Afrikainstituet, 1998.

———. *The Congo: From Leopold to Kabila, A People's History*, New York: Zed Books, 2003.

Orogun, P., "Blood diamonds" and Africa's armed conflicts in the post-cold war era," *World Affairs*, January 1, 2004.

———. "Crisis of government, ethnic schisms, civil war, and regional destabilization of the Democratic Republic of Congo," *World Affairs*, June 22, 2002.

Oxfam, "A Forgotten War – A Forgotten Emergency: The Democratic Republic of the Congo," Oxfam.

Oyog, A., "Zaire: No Repeat of 1994 French Intervention in Rwanda," *Inter Press Service English News Wire*, November 5, 1996.

Passin, H. and Jones-Quartey, K., *Africa: The Dynamic of a Change*, Ibadan, Nigeria: Ibadan University Press, 1963.

Philadelphia Tribune, "Mass Media Holding Back on the Reality in Zaire," *Philadephia Tribune*, June 27,1997.

Pitman, T., "Now serving 5 million people: With single courthouse, Congo tries to restore rule of law in lawless east," *AP Worldstream*, June 4, 2004.

Powers, E., "France Seeks Backing for Zaire Plan," *USA Today*, November 6, 1996.

Raghavan, S., "In wake of massacre, UN peacekeepers to step up efforts in Congo," *Knight Ridder/Tribune News Service*, October 15, 2003.

Rocky Mountain News, "Rebels in Zaire Capture Kisangani," *Rocky Mountain News*, March 16, 1997.

Rieff, D. "Realpolitik in Congo: should Zaire's fate have been subordinate to the fate of Rwandan refugees? *The Nation*, July 7, 1997.

———. *A Bed for the Night: Humanitarianism in Crisis*, New York: Simon & Schuster, 2002.

Roddy, M., "Mobutu Rejects Outside Support," Weekly Journal, July 8, 1993.

Rusamira, Dr. Etienne, "The problem of the disarmament of the negative forces in the Democratic Republic of Congo: A critical analysis of possible options," *Strategic Review for Southern Africa*, November 1, 2002.

Sahnoun, M. and Nyerere, J., "From Zaire to the Congo: (change of leadership in Zaire)," *New Perspectives Quarterly*, June 22, 1997.

Saideman, S., *The Ties That Divide: Ethnic Politics, Foreign Policy and International Conflict*, New York: Columbia University Press, 2001.

Salmon, K., "Politics-Eastern Congo: Upsurge in Fighting Worsens Food Situation," *Inter Press Service English News Wire*, October 19, 2002.

Samboma, L., "Zaire: Britain Urged to Press for Human Rights in Zaire," *Inter Press Service English News Wire*, October 23, 1996.

Schatzberg, M., *The Dialectics of Oppression in Zaire*, Indianapolis, IN: Indiana University Press, 1988.

Scherrer, C., *Genocide and Crisis in Central Africa: Conflict Roots, Mass Violence, and Regional War*, Westport, CT: Praeger, 2002.

Seattle Post-Intelligencer, "Zaire's Rebels Reject a Call For Monitors," *Seattle Post - Intelligencer*, March 7, 1997.

———. "The Chaos Spreads in Zaire City," *Seattle Post-Intelligencer*, October 29, 1996.

———. "U.S. Scales Back Military Relief Plan for Zaire," *Seattle Post-Intelligencer*, November 20, 1996.

———. "Zaire Uses Airstrikes on Civilians in City Held by Rebels,"*Seattle Post-Intelligencer*, February 18, 1997.

———. "Zaire Rebel Fears U.S. Presence Troops 'Don't Recognize Sovereignty,' Leader Says," *Seattle Post-Intelligencer*, April 7, 1997.

———. "Massacre of 500 People Reported in East Congo," *Seattle Post-Intelligencer*, January 6, 1999.

Segal, R., Hoskyns, C., Ainslie, R., *Political Africa: A Who's Who of Personalities and Parties*, New York: Frederick A. Praeger, 1961.

Shawcross, W., *Deliver Us From Evil: Peacekeepers, Warlords and a World of Endless Conflict*, New York: Simon & Schuster, 2000.

Simpson, C., "DR Congo: First Within the Rebel Movement Appear to be Widening," *Inter Press Service English News Wire*, February 1, 1999.

Singleton-Gates, P. and Girodias, M., *The Black Diaries: An Account of Roger Casement's Life and Times with a Collection of His Diaries and Public Writings*, New York: Grove Press, 1959.

Sizemore, B., "Political Questions Entangle Robertson's Links to Zaire," *The Virginian Pilot*, January 26, 1997.

Slade, R., *King Leopold's Congo: Aspects of the Development of Race Relations in the Congo Independent State*, London: Oxford University Press, 1962.

Slade, R. and Taylor, M. *The Belgian Congo*, 2nd ed., London: Oxford University Press, 1961.

Smyth, F. "A New Game the Clinton Administration on Africa," *World Policy Journal*, 15.2, 1998.

St. Louis Post-Dispatch, "Rebels in Zaire May Have Hit Strong Resistance From Army," *St. Louis Post-Dispatch*, March 16, 1997.

——. "Rescue Zaire From President Mobutu," *St. Louis Post-Dispatch*, February 10, 1993.

——. "Zaire Stands Firm on Refugees It Wants Tutsis Out, Hutus in Camps to Go Back Home to Rwanda," *St. Louis Post-Dispatch*, November 8, 1996.

Stassen, W., "UN: Women and children among militia terrorizing northeastern Congo," *AP Worldstream*, March 6, 2005.

Stoessinger, J., *The Might of Nations: World Politics in Our Time*, New York: Random House, 1962.

Stoppard, A., "Politics: Congo's Belligerents to Sign Power-Sharing Accord," *Inter Press Service English News Wire*, November 1, 2002.

Susman, T., "Zaire in No Hurry to Hold Elections Announcement is Due Today on Composition of New Government," *Denver Rocky Mountain News*, May 20, 1997.

Syracuse Post Standard, "Administration Seeks Aid for Zaire," *Syracuse Post Standard*, August 5, 1983.

Taylor, C., *Sacrifice as Terror: The Rwandan Genocide of 1994*, New York: Berg, 1999.

Tayler, J., *Facing the Congo: A Modern-day Journey Into the Heart of Darkness*, New York: Three Rivers Press, 2000.

Theobald, R., *The UN and its Future*, New York: H.W. Wilson Company, 1963.

Tremblay, "The Transition in the Democratic Republic of Congo: A Historic Opportunity," Montreal, Quebec: Droits et Democratie, April 2004.

Tri-State Defender, "CONGO: Cabinet reshuffle in Congo," *Tri-State Defender*, January 12, 2005.

——. "CONGO: Thousands flee hotspot," *Tri-State Defender*, December 22, 2004.

Turner, T., "War in the Congo," *Foreign Policy in Focus*, April 5, 2000.

Umoren, R., "Zaire-U.S.: U.S. Visit Ends Mobutu's Isolation," *Inter Press Service English News Wire*, May 23, 1996.

UN Security Council, "Peacekeeping in the DRC: Causes of Conflict and Key Protagonists," New York: UN Documents, Monograph No. 66, October 2001.

——. "Peacekeeping in the DRC: The Lusaka Ceasefire Agreement," New York: UN Documents, Monograph No. 66, October 2001.

——. "Peacekeeping in the DRC: MONUC Phase I," New York: UN Documents, Monograph No. 66, October 2001.

——. "Peacekeeping in the DRC: MONUC Phase II," New York: UN Documents, Monograph No. 66, October 2001.

——. "Peacekeeping in the DRC: MONUC Phase II: Progress and Revised Concept," New York: UN Documents, Monograph No. 66, October 2001.

——. "Peacekeeping in the DRC: MONUC and the Road to Peace: The Situation in the Kivus," UN Documents, Monograph No. 66, October 2001.

——. "Peacekeeping in the DRC: MONUC and the Road to Peace: Facing the D3 Challenge," New York: UN Documents, Monograph No. 66, October 2001.

——. "Peacekeeping in the DRC: MONUC and the Road to Peace: The Inter-Congolese Dialogue," New York: UN Documents, Monograph No. 66, October 2001.

U.S. Department of State Dispatch, "Zaire: Troika Demarche to Political Leadership (Protests From the U.S., France and Belgium on the Slowness of Political Reform in Zaire," *U.S. Department of State Dispatch*, May 8, 1995.

US Newswire, "IRC Study Reveals 31,000 Die Monthly in Congo Conflict, 3.8 Million Died in Past Six Years, When Will the World Pay Attention? Asks IRC," *US Newswire*, December 9, 2004.

USA Today, "U.S. Troops Won't Intervene in Zaire, State Dept. says," *USA Today*, April 8, 1997.

University Wire, "Editorial: UN officials' behavior horrific, intolerable," *University Wire*, February 16, 2005.

Usborne, D., "UN to tackle claims of Congo sex abuse," *The Independent*, March 2, 2005.

Virginia Pilot, "Clinton Approves Narrowly Defined Mission Troops for Zaire," *The Virginian Pilot*, November 15, 1996.

——. "New Regime Puts Off Elections Leaders of the Former Zaire Say Citizens Must be "Re-educated" Before They Can Vote," *The Virginian Pilot*, May 20, 1997. The Voice, "Election in Congo Gets Euro Boost," *The Voice*, January 9, 2005.

Wack, H., *The Story of the Congo Free State: Social, Political, and Economic Aspects of the Belgian System of Government in Central Africa*, New York: G.P. Putnam's Sons, 1905.

Weekly Journal, "Zaire—an inter-African battlefield?" *Weekly Journal*, February 18, 1997.

Weinstein, J., "Africa's "Scramble for Africa," Lessons of a Continental War," *World Policy Journal*, June 22, 2000.

Wesseling, H., *Imperialism and Colonialism: Essays on the History of European Expansion*, Westport, CT: Greenwood Press, 1997.

Wesseling, H. and Pomerans, A., *Divide and Rule: The Partition of Africa*, Westport, CT: Praeger, 1996.

Willsher, K., "Aid worker admits sex with under-age girls in Congo," *Sunday Telegraph*, February 13, 2005.

World Bank, *The World Bank in Africa: A Summary of Activities*, Washington, DC: World Bank, 1961.

Wrong, M., *Living on the Brink of Disaster in Mobutu's Congo: In the Footsteps of Mr. Kurtz*, New York: Perennial, 2002.

Xinhua News Agency, "Rwanda wants all Congo-based rebels disarmed in 2005," *Xinhua News Agency*, January 26, 2005.

———. "Over 5,000 Congolese refugees return home from Uganda," *Xinhua News Agency*, February 1, 2005.

———. "Annan urges reinforcements of UN peacekeeping forces in DRC," *Xinhua News Agency*, March 4, 2005.

Zagorin, A., "Leaving Fire in His Wake (Zaire's Mobutu Sese Seko," *Time*, February 22, 1993.

INDEX

A

ABAKO cultural association, 14–19, 21
Adoula, Cyrille, 5, 16, 19, 31, 33–36
Africa War I, 7
African Association of Defense of Human Rights representing Katanga (ASADHO/Katanga), 174–175
Albright, Madeleine, 76, 198, 217
Alexander, Senator Lamar, 205
Allen, Senator George, 205
Allied Democratic Forces (ADF), 86, 93–94, 106, 128
Amnesty International, 57, 60, 64, 114, 164, 211
Angola, 7, 41, 49, 78–80, 86, 88–89, 92–94, 100, 116, 122, 126–127, 148, 218
Annan, Kofi, 110, 113, 117–118, 120–121, 123–124, 127, 131, 159–162, 164–168, 211, 214, 224

B

Baluba, 26, 30, 33
Bandung Treaty, 24
Banyamulenge, 82, 87, 89, 91, 118, 127, 152, 159, 162, 196, 198–199
Baudouin, King (of Belgium), 18, 20–21, 68
Belgian Congo, 2–3, 6, 11, 16, 221
Belgium, 1–2, 4, 6, 9, 12, 14–15, 18–19, 23, 28, 34, 36–37, 41, 45, 66, 68, 74–75, 85, 148, 160, 223
Bemba, Jean-Pierre, 91, 95, 130, 161
Biden, Senator Joseph R. Jr., 205
Blumenthal, Erwin, 51
Boozeman, Congressman John, 207
Boutros-Ghali, Boutros, 77, 216
Bowles, Chester, 11
Boxer, Senator Barbara, 206
Brussels Round Table Conference, 20
Bugera, Deogratias, 78, 90
Bukavu, 17, 40, 78, 87, 114, 123, 153, 162
Bululu, Lunda, 64, 90
Burns, Arthur Lee, 26, 31–32, 34

Burrows, Captain, 10
Burundi, 7, 74, 77, 87, 91–93, 114–115, 126, 151, 168, 199

C

CADER, 55–56
cannibalism, 23, 88, 159
Casement, Roger, 10, 12
Catholic Church, 3, 42, 88
Central Intelligence Agency (CIA), 5, 26–27, 48
Chad, 7, 88, 94, 126
child soldiers (kadogos), 80, 97, 123
CIAT, 148, 176, 200, 203
Clinton, President William J., 76–77, 214, 219, 221, 223
Coleman, Senator Norm, 205
coltan (Columbite-tantalite), 113–115
Conciliation Commission, 30–31
Congo Advisory Committee, 30
Congo Free State, 1–2, 9, 223
Congo Reform Association, 10
Congolese Charter for Human Rights, 125
constitution, 20, 28, 42, 65–68, 125, 135–140, 142, 150–152, 154–155, 180, 184, 192, 203
copper, 45, 49, 51–52, 61, 113, 201
Coquilhatville, 31
coup d'état, 162
Court of Military Order, 84, 149

D

Decree Law 171, 84
Democratic and Social Christian Party (PD-SC), 63, 65–66, 84, 125
Democratic Forces for the Liberation of the Congo (FODELICO), 59
Dodd, Senator Chris, 205

225